The Peninsula Campaign

of 1862

Yorktown to the Seven Days

Volume One

The Peninsula Campaign of 1862

Yorktown to the Seven Days

Volume One

Essays on
the American Civil War

series editor
William J. Miller

SAVAS WOODBURY PUBLISHERS
1475 S. Bascom Avenue, Suite 204
Campbell, California 95008

Series Editor
William J. Miller

The Peninsula Campaign of 1862:
Yorktown to the Seven Days, Volume One

Copyright 1995 by Savas Woodbury Publishers
1475 S. Bascom Avenue, Suite 204,
Campbell, California 95008 (408) 879-9073

Maps copyright by Savas Woodbury Publishers

Includes bibliographic references and index

Printing Number
10 9 8 7 6 5 4 3 2

ISBN 1-882810-75-9
(Second Edition)

This book is printed on sixty-pound
Glatfelter acid-free paper

The paper in this book meets or exceeds the guidelines for permanence
and durability of the Committee on Production Guidelines for Book
Longevity of the Council on Library Resources

This volume is dedicated
to the memory of the forgotten casualties of the Peninsula Campaign: the
families of the killed, maimed, missing and diseased.

Gen. George B. McClellan

To Edwin M. Stanton   (TELEGRAM)

Camp Lincoln June 27 8 p.m. 1862

Have had a terrible contest–attacked by greatly superior numbers in all directions. On this side we still hold our own, though a very heavy fire is still kept up.

On the left bank of Chickahominy the odds have been immense. We hold our own very nearly. I may be forced to give up my position during the night, but will not if it is possible to avoid it. Had I (20,000) twenty thousand fresh & good troops we would be sure of a splendid victory tomorrow. My men have fought magnificently.

G B McClellan
Maj Genl

Gen. Robert E. Lee

Headquarters
June 27, 1862

Mr. President:

Profoundly grateful to Almighty God for the signal victory granted to us, it is my pleasing task to announce to you the success achieved by this army today. The enemy was this morning driven from his strong position behind Beaver Dam Creek and pursued to that behind Powhite Creek, and finally, after a severe contest of five hours, entirely repulsed from the field. Night put an end to the contest. I grieve to state that our loss in officers and men is great. We sleep on the field, and shall renew the contest in the morning.

I have the honor to be, very respectfully
R. E. Lee
General

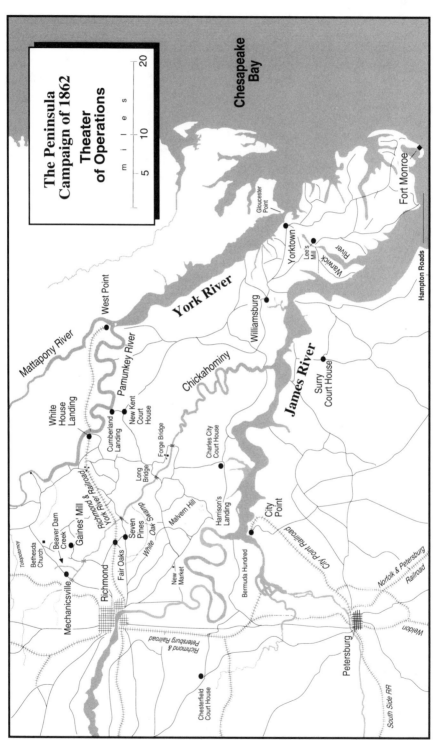

The Peninsula Campaign of 1862
Theater of Operations

miles
5   10   20

Chesapeake Bay

Fort Monroe

Hampton Roads

Gloucester Point

Yorktown

Lee's Mill

Warwick River

Williamsburg

York River

West Point

Mattapony River

Pamunkey River

Chickahominy

James River

Surry Court House

White House Landing

New Kent Court House

Cumberland Landing

Forge Bridge

Charles City Court House

Long Bridge

Richmond & York River Railroad

Gaines' Mill

Beaver Dam Creek

Totopotomoy

Bethesda Church

Seven Pines

White Oak Swamp

Malvern Hill

Harrison's Landing

City Point

Mechanicsville

Fair Oaks

Richmond

New Market

Bermuda Hundred

City Point Railroad

Norfolk & Petersburg Railroad

Richmond & Petersburg Railroad

Weldon

Chesterfield Court House

Petersburg

South Side RR

David A. Woodbury

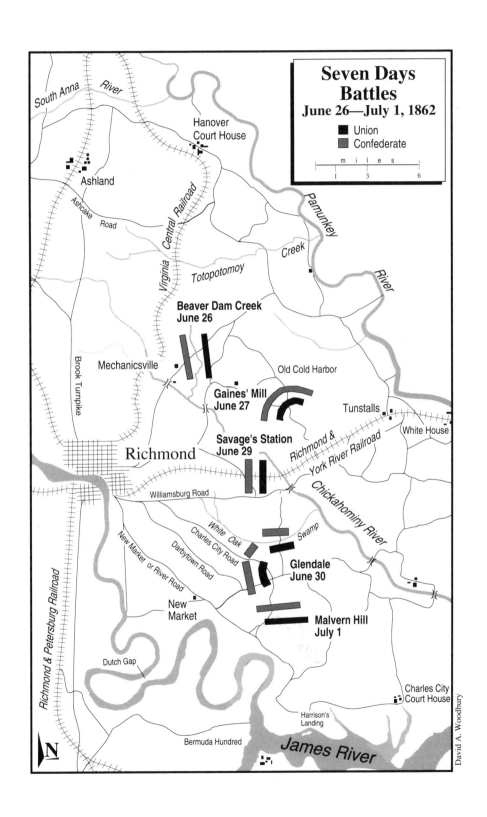

Seven Days Battles June 26—July 1, 1862

David A. Woodbury

CONTENTS

List of Maps

List of Illustrations

William J. Miller

The series editor of *The Peninsula Campaign of 1862: Yorktown to the Seven Days* holds a B.A. degree in English from Villanova University and an M.A. in English from the University of Delaware.

He has published articles on various Civil War topics in numerous periodicals, including *Civil War Regiments: A Journal of the American Civil War* and *America's Civil War*. Mr. Miller is the author of three books dealing with Civil War subjects: *The Training of an Army: Camp Curtin and the North's Civil War* (White Mane, 1990), *The Men of Fort Ward* (Friends of Fort Ward, 1990), and the forthcoming *Mapping for Stonewall: The Civil War Service of Jed Hotchkiss* (Elliott & Clark, 1993).

In addition to serving as the editor of this series, Mr. Miller also serves as the editor for the American Blue & Gray Association.

Introduction

Not long ago, while browsing among the groaning shelves of the Civil War section in a local bookstore, I overheard two businessmen, apparently killing time on their lunch hour. Both fortyish and well dressed, they showed no interest in the history books, but for a passing remark. In a tone of disbelief, one said to the other, "Look at all the Civil War books!" The other man replied, "I saw a Civil War book on Gettysburg. It was huge, about 500 pages or more." Then he chuckled as he got to what he clearly thought was the incredible payoff line, "And it was only on the *second day* of the battle!" They smiled, shook their heads, and went their way.

Most of us who study the war have encountered similar reactions from friends, spouses and acquaintances who just do not understand how we can devote so much time and energy to a war that ended more than a century and a quarter ago. Most of these good people, like the gentlemen in the bookstore, clearly think that society has learned all that the Civil War can teach us. It was, after all, a war, and wars are bad. Why must we, they ask, spend our time studying the hatred and suffering and death of that terrible conflict? The answer, of course, or part of it, is quite simply to try to understand hatred and suffering and death. These evils exist today just as they did in the 1860's and just as they will 130 years from now and as long as man chooses to perpetrate them. So for that reason alone, study of the war and its effects is relevant and ultimately a worthy undertaking.

In truth, though, we are not so much studying the evil aspects of war as we are studying the human reaction to them. This brings us the understanding that war is composed of much more than suffering and death. It contains courage and sacrifice and even love. It is a human enterprise and therefore contains all that is humanity. Military history, then, like all other branches of history, is really anthropology, the study of mankind. Despite all our interest in weapons and tactics and other minutia of the conflict, I think it is essentially the humanness of the military endeavor that keeps us interested and thirsting to learn more.

Americans have a fascination with the Civil War because it remains so close to us. Our ancestors fought it; participants came from our own hometowns and some of us live on former battlegrounds or campsites. The warfare ran the gamut from the frigid, snowy fields of Fort Donelson and Fredericksburg to the bayous of Louisiana, to the beaches of the Carolinas, and the swamps of the Peninsula. This was our war. Everyone in the nation was involved in it somehow, and it touches us still. Those of us who study it have often thought how it must have been to have our peaceful towns and counties convulsed by the destruction of marching armies—our homes and property ruined, our communities devastated by the loss of sons and neighbors and nephews. And the men and women who persevered through that most terrible time were ours as well. Their blood still runs in our veins. In our quest for understanding them and their time, we read their letters and diaries and study narratives of battles and campaigns, including Harry Pfanz's 601-page book on the second day at Gettysburg. Scholars and historians continue to mine libraries and archives for new information because, surprising as it may be to our acquaintances, spouses and gentlemen in bookstores, we know very little about some of the major events of the war. One of the campaigns we know little about is the Peninsula Campaign of 1862.

It was one of the monumental campaigns of the war. From the Federal perspective, the Peninsula Campaign was the most complex and ambitious operation of the war to that point, as well as the most expensive. It was also a thoroughly modern campaign in that it required close cooperation between army and navy, called for amphibious landings, the logistical and even tactical use of railroads, demanded siege trains and the widespread use of engineer troops. It was so large and so expensive and conducted on such an enormous scale, that nothing in the American military experience could compare to it. Probably only a man with the colossal ego of George B. McClellan could have envisioned and proposed such an enormous movement of men and matériel under his own direction.

For the Confederacy, the Peninsula Campaign was the greatest crisis the young government would face in the first three years of the war.

Despite all his logistical problems, his procrastination and his feuding with Washington, McClellan could have taken Richmond in that second summer of the war. Jefferson Davis and his advisor Robert E. Lee were very concerned indeed about the fate of their capital, for they knew they might not be able to counterbalance the huge Federal advantages in matériel, the eventual dominance in the James River of the U.S. Navy, and, perhaps most worrisome, the siege guns that McClellan hoped to push up to the very outskirts of the city. It seems certain that Richmond could not have survived a siege, and Lee determined that only bold, aggressive action could prevent McClellan from bringing the city under his guns. As Lee would do so many times in the future when he found himself at a disadvantage, he attacked. Joseph E. Johnston might have done the same in late June 1862, but we can never know. The patient and meticulous Johnston might have been the man to save Richmond, the audacious Lee unquestionably was.

Despite the enormous scope, high stakes and compelling drama of the campaign, historians have devoted remarkably little time to its study. This is undoubtedly due in part to its daunting size, in part to its political complexity and in part to the anonymity of many of its principals. Who were these men whose names are just vaguely familiar to most Civil War buffs? Heintzelman, Keyes, Morell, McCall, Holmes, Magruder and Huger all played significant roles in the campaign; their names appear in narratives and reports, yet soon after the campaign ended they disappeared from center stage and remained out of the spotlight for the rest of the war. Few students of the war can put faces to these men, and fewer still know what became of them and why.

The complexity of the operation discourages investigation as well. Few campaigns included as many distinct combats. According to the U.S. war department tally, McClellan's extended foray on the Peninsula included 48 skirmishes, seven battles, nine engagements, six actions, one demonstration, 27 reconnaissances, four expeditions and one scout between April 4 and August 6. Moreover, the fighting occurred in scores of places unfamiliar to even the best geography students among us. From Dam Number One and Slash Church to Meadow Bridge and Malvern Cliff, few students of the war can gain an understanding of what happened in the campaign and where without very good maps, which are rare. But even with a first rate chart, the multiplicity of names given to places frustrates our sense of place. Indeed, this same fact confused the combatants, and topographical confusion played a significant role in the climactic battles in late June. The crossroads of Glendale, for example, was known by no fewer than three other names, and participants in the battle there had at least six names for the engagement.

Despite the imposing obstacles, there have been several noteworthy efforts to record the history or interpret the meaning of the campaign. In 1881, Gen. Alexander S. Webb wrote his 219-page study of the campaign as part memoir, part analysis and part critique. As a young staff officer serving under the Army of the Potomac's chief of artillery on the Peninsula, the West Point-trained Webb was an intelligent observer of events and personalities at the upper reaches of that army. When he sat down almost 20 years later to write the first volume devoted entirely to the campaign, he brought a rare perspective to his task. Though far from comprehensive, Webb's *The Peninsula* (New York, 1881, rpt. Broadfoot 1989) belongs on every student's reading list.

The Peninsula Campaign (Harrisburg, PA: 1973), by Joseph P. Cullen, is a very short (185 pages), very general look at the campaign. Using material that is mostly "well known to students" and offering no citations, Cullen presents a balanced but inadequate overview, accenting McClellan's failure rather than Lee's triumph. Mr. Cullen was an employee of the National Park Service in Richmond and also wrote the Park Service guidebook to the park (*Richmond National Battlefield Park*, NPS Historical Handbook Series No. 33 (Washington, D.C., 1961)), in which he presents a concise, 27-page campaign outline (the booklet also covers the 1864-1865 campaigns around Richmond). Though this modest pamphlet has merit, by far the better concise overview is Dr. Emory Thomas' magazine format *Richmond*. Dr. Thomas published a series of articles on the Peninsula Campaign in *Civil War Times Illustrated* in 1979, from which this 48-page, illustrated volume was compiled. Dr. Thomas' insightful, though infrequent, analysis of events makes this publication worthwhile.

The ubiquitous Richard Wheeler fleetingly turned his attention to the campaign in *Sword Over Richmond: An Eyewitness History of McClellan's Peninsula Campaign* (New York, 1986). Mr. Wheeler's volume, one in his series of "Eyewitness History" books on the Civil War, attempts to present "in a chronological running narrative a representative selection of experiences and descriptions from writings of scores of Union and Confederate politicians, officers, soldiers from all ranks, chaplains, medical personnel, newsmen, and women of Richmond whose letters, diaries, reports, and memoirs have been discovered by the author" (from the dust jacket). Unfortunately, Mr. Wheeler seems to have relied very heavily on well-known published sources, especially *Battles and Leaders of the Civil War*, which, while a valuable source, is very familiar to students. Most disappointing is Mr. Wheeler's decision not to offer citations.

In *The Seven Days: The Emergence of Lee* (Boston, 1964), Clifford Dowdey looks at Lee's role in the Peninsula Campaign, but focuses on the events of June and July during Lee's first weeks in command of the Army of Northern Virginia. Dowdey deals little with McClellan and the whole Federal tableau of hesitation, paranoia, frustration and excessive caution that had Washington and "Little Mac" at loggerheads. The focus is squarely on Lee and his lieutenants, especially Jackson. The author devotes considerable space discussing "Old Jack's" performance in The Seven Days, finally concluding that the general suffered from stress, a conclusion far more courageous and controversial in 1964 than it would be today.

The Seven Days has great value because of Dowdey's analysis of Lee's decisions, but the book concentrates on only one side of the story, and its usefulness as a resource is limited by the absence of citations.

Mr. Dowdey's important book is bettered in terms of presenting the Confederate perspective by several chapters in Dr. Douglas Southall Freeman's *R. E. . Lee: A Biography* (New York, 1934). Dr. Freeman, who lived in Richmond for much of his life, knew the Confederate *dramatis personae* better than has any other historian of the campaign. Though the narrative centers on Lee and scarcely treats the Army of the Potomac at all, Freeman's trenchant analysis and fluid, logical presentation should give this book a very high place on the reading list of any student wishing to gain a better understanding of the campaign, particularly The Seven Days.

Certainly the best history of the campaign is Stephen W. Sears' *To the Gates of Richmond: The Peninsula Campaign* (New York, 1992). Though not definitive, this study succeeds better than any other in presenting a broad picture of the campaign and addressing the problems and personalities that make the operation so interesting. Mr. Sears covers the issues and event from both the Federal and Confederate perspectives, but not always with the desired depth and objectivity. Sears' dislike of McClellan is no secret to readers of his previous books, and one does not have to be an admirer of McClellan to see the author's treatment of the general in *To the Gates of Richmond* as rough to the point of unfairness. Despite its shortcomings, however, Mr. Sears' book may be the best place to begin a study of the campaign.

There are many other worthy books, articles, special studies, biographies and standard primary sources that relate to various aspects of the campaign, and readers of this and future issues of this series will undoubtedly be introduced to them through the citations of the articles herein.

Our hope with this project is to further the general understanding of this long-neglected campaign by providing the place and the opportunity for historians to:

1. Examine in depth major controversies of the campaign—e.g. the overall performance in the campaign of Jackson, McClellan, Johnston, Magruder and others, Longstreet at Seven Pines, Huger at Glendale, Lee vs. Magruder, Johnston vs. Davis, etc.

2. Study specific operations—movements and engagements—in greater detail than ever before possible.

3. Focus more attention on the people involved—from the commanding generals to the privates.

Future articles already in development for subsequent volumes of this series will present original research on such subjects as the relative strengths of the armies, the conduct of specific battles and engagements, biographies of units and commanders, logistical support for the armies, topography and engineering in the campaign, naval participation and new, unpublished first-hand accounts. The result, we hope, will be a portrait of the campaign that, while perhaps not comprehensive, will be rich in detail and analysis. Whatever it may eventually lack in breadth it will compensate for in depth.

When all the articles in this series of volumes have been read and digested, we hope we will have brought students closer to an under-standing, not just of the actual conduct of the campaign from the strate-gic and tactical standpoints and the cost of the campaign in spent dollars, abandoned matériel and lost soldiers, but in more human terms. We hope the work of the scholars and historians on these pages will permit a deeper, fuller knowledge of what it was like to serve between the rivers east of Richmond that spring and summer and of how those who were there responded to the suffering and death that surrounded them on the Peninsula.

William J. Miller, Manassas, Virginia

ACKNOWLEDGEMENTS: I would like to thank Mr. Michael Andrus, Supervisory Historian at Richmond National Battlefield Park, for his general support and his assistance in identifying authoritative maps, and Dr. Richard J. Sommers, Archivist/Historian at The U.S. Army Military History Institute at Carlisle Barracks, for his assistance in identifying and obtaining photographs.

Cover photo: Battery Number 4 before Yorktown (LC). Battery Number 4 consisted of ten 13-inch sea-service mortars (1861) and was manned by Batter-ies F and G of the 1st Connecticut Heavy Artillery. Situated on a branch of Wormley's Creek and just 400 yards from the York River, Battery Number 4 sat 2,500 yards—just over 1.4 miles—from the main Confederate works southeast of Yorktown. Each one of the mortars weighed 17,120 pounds and, according to Maj. Alexander Doull, ordnance officer of General McClellan's siege train, exceeded in weight ". . .By 50 per cent. any guns that have ever before been placed in siege batteries."[1] None of these mortars fired a shot at Yorktown.

[1]U.S. War Department, *The War of the Rebellion: The Official Records of the Union and Confederate Armies,* 128 vols. (Washington, D.C., 1890-1901), series I, vol. 11, pt. 1, pp. 354-358.

Steven E. Woodworth

Steven Woodworth has published widely on the Civil War and is the author of the highly acclaimed *Jefferson Davis and his Generals: The Failure of Confederate Command in the West* (University Press of Kansas, 1990), which won the Fletcher Pratt Award. He is series editor for a new *Campaign Chronicles* project entitled *Leadership and Command in the Civil War*. Dr. Woodworth teaches history at Toccoa Falls College in Toccoa Falls, Georgia.

"I give you the material to be used at your discretion":

Jefferson Davis and Robert E. Lee
in The Seven Days

Darkness was settling over the landscape of eastern Virginia as two riders urged their horses along the muddy roads leading to Richmond. Ahead of them, the spires of the young Confederacy's capital rose in silhouette against the fading light of the last day of May, 1862. The two men had just witnessed the unraveling of a promising plan in the bungled Battle of Seven Pines. In an appalling finale, they had seen the commander of their army, General Joseph E. Johnston—from whom much had been hoped but little gained—carried to the rear gravely wounded. The military outlook was dismal, and if it was to be brightened these two riders, Confederate president Jefferson Davis and his senior military advisor General Robert E. Lee, would have to make the crucial decisions. Most of what passed between them on that ride is unknown, but one thing is certain. At some point Davis informed his companion that he was appointing him to take over the bloodied Confederate army defending Richmond.[1]

Thus began what would become one of the more successful civilian-military partnerships in the history of warfare. Rarely has the chief executive of a republic at war worked as closely and effectively with his top general as Davis did with Lee. Rarely has a commanding general shown the wisdom and tact in dealing with his civilian superiors that Lee did with Davis. And rarely has such a team had the successes that Davis and Lee enjoyed. Yet, in the end, after almost four years of working

---

[1] Jefferson Davis, *The Rise and Fall of the Confederate Government*, 2 vols. (New York, 1959), vol. 2, p. 130.

together, they failed, and defeat tested and measured their skills as no triumph ever could. The mistakes of Davis and Lee loom larger for the consequences that followed them. The patterns of cooperation between these two men were hammered out during the first five tension-filled weeks of Lee's command of the Army of Northern Virginia, and particularly during the climactic fifth week, The Seven Days.

Lee had not been Jefferson Davis' favorite general at the outset of hostilities. That honor had belonged to the president's old friend, Albert Sidney Johnston, who had at one time been Lee's commanding officer in the 2nd U.S. Cavalry of the Old Army.[2] Davis also seems to have had great respect for the abilities of Joseph E. Johnston and Pierre G. T. Beauregard, giving them important posts in the new Confederate army. Lee, on the other hand, seems to have enjoyed the president's respect, but more as a staff officer than as a field commander. Lee had been a favorite of Gen. Winfield Scott during the Mexican War, and Davis and Scott were inveterate enemies.[3] The Confederate president probably did not hold this against Lee, but it was a fact that would have made previous familiarity between them less likely. In addition, Lee was an engineer officer, and Davis, whose low grades at West Point had precluded his entry into that branch of the service, seems to have considered engineers bookish, timid, and of little value as practical soldiers.[4]

During the first 13 months of the war, Lee had held high rank but had not held the positions of key responsibility within the Confederacy's system of defense. The enormously important trans-Appalachian command had gone to Sidney Johnston, the Shenandoah Valley to Joseph Johnston, and Richmond's direct overland approaches to Beauregard. Of the Confederacy's original five full generals, only Lee and the decrepit old Samuel Cooper—for whom field service was out of the question— did not receive important field commands. In the fall of 1861 Lee was dispatched to the mountains of what was to become West Virginia to command a handful of troops and their fractious officers in a forlorn

---

[2] Davis, *Rise and Fall*, 2, p. 38.

[3] William C. Davis, *Jefferson Davis: The Man and His Hour* (New York, 1991), p. 228-245.

[4] Davis, *Rise and Fall*, 2, p. 132.

Jefferson Davis, circa 1862

(Photo courtesy of the National Archives, Washington, D.C.)

attempt to hold the area for the Confederacy. He spent the early months of 1862 directing the defense of the Georgian and South Carolinian coasts. Relegated to these secondary commands, Lee had served quietly while others had held the more important posts.

By June 1862, however, the situation had changed considerably. Albert Sidney Johnston was dead, killed at Shiloh. Beauregard was discredited in Davis' eyes, both by the unruly temperament that had led to his transfer to the west and by his actions since succeeding Albert Sidney Johnston in command there. Joseph Johnston, while still retaining a fair amount of the president's confidence as a commander, had been wounded at Seven Pines (May 31, 1862) and would be out of action for some months.[5] Major General Gustavus W. Smith, Johnston's successor at Seven Pines, did not inspire confidence and could not be considered for permanent command in Johnston's absence. That left Lee, and Davis—perhaps with some reservations—gave him command of the South's largest and most important army. Davis stressed that the appointment was temporary.[6] Lee was still to be the president's military advisor—in theory, commanding general of all the Confederate armies—and his appointment to command of a particular army was merely a stop-gap measure not unlike his brief assignments in the mountains of western Virginia and on the southern coast. Nor was Lee particularly popular with the army or the public. "Officers of the line," loyal Johnston supporter James Longstreet later wrote, "are not apt to look to the staff in choosing leaders of soldiers, either in tactics or strategy. There were, therefore, some misgivings as to the power and skill for field service of the new commander."[7]

---

[5] Letter from Jefferson Davis to Varina Davis dated June 23, 1862, Museum of the Confederacy, Richmond, Virginia.

[6] Letter from Davis to Lee dated June 1, 1862, in U.S. War Department, *The War of Rebellion: The Official Records of the Union and Confederate Armies,* 128 vols. (Washington, D.C., 1890-1901), series I, vol. 11, pt. 3, pp. 568-569. Hereinafter cited as *OR.* All references are to Series I unless otherwise noted.

[7] James Longstreet, *From Manassas to Appomattox* (Bloomington, 1960), p. 112.

The Richmond press was less gentle. "Evacuating Lee," sneered *The Examiner,* "who has never yet risked a single battle with the invader."[8] Others dubbed him"the king of spade" for his insistence that the troops entrench, while still others called him simply "Granny Lee." His opponent, Federal Maj. Gen. George B. McClellan, expressed satisfaction that he would now be opposing Lee rather than Johnston, since Lee, as McClellan observed, was "cautious and weak under grave responsibility. . . .wanting in moral firmness when pressed by heavy responsibility, and is likely to be timid and irresolute in action."[9]

Whence, then, came Davis' confidence, limited as it appears to have been, in this untried general? It may have come at least in part from one of the president's own military aides. Colonel Joseph C. Ives had been a member of the West Point class of 1852. Though a New Yorker, Ives had married a Southerner and had remained in the Confederacy when war came. About two weeks after Lee's assumption of command, Ives rode along the Confederate lines with artillery officer E. P. Alexander. The two men fell to discussing the recent newspaper criticisms of Lee. "Ives, tell me this," Alexander said at last. "We are here fortifying our lines, but apparently leaving the enemy all the time he needs to accumulate his superior forces, and then to move on us in the way he thinks best. Has General Lee the audacity that is going to be required for our inferior force to meet the enemy's superior force—to take the aggressive, and to run risks and stand chances?"

Ives drew up his horse in the middle of the road and, looking his fellow officer in the eye, replied: "Alexander, if there is one man in either army, Confederate or Federal, head and shoulders above every other in audacity, it is General Lee! His name might be Audacity. He will take more desperate chances and take them quicker than any other general in this country, North or South; and you will live to see it, too."[10] Where Ives had gained his insight into Lee's character is unclear, but it was manifestly correct. Whether Ives impressed his insight on the presi-

[8] Hudson Strode, *Jefferson Davis, Confederate President* (New York, 1959), p. 220.

[9] *Shelby Foote*, The Civil War, 3 vols. (New York, 1986), vol. 1, p. 465.

[10] E. Porter Alexander, *Military Memoirs of a Confederate* (New York, 1912), pp. 110-111.

dent or gained it from him, it is clear that Lee's qualities were recognized by Davis' staff.

Whatever the degree of confidence Davis might have placed in Lee during those early days, there can be no question that he liked the courtly Virginian. The two had worked together closely in Richmond since March, and Lee had shown marked skill in getting along with the proud and opinionated president. This alone meant that relations between head-quarters and capital would be vastly better than they had been during the tenure of Joseph E. Johnston, whose pride, resentment of authority, and fear of responsibility had continually taxed Davis' patience. When Lee was appointed to command, Davis immediately showed his eagerness to keep relations with Lee strong and cordial. Davis met the general's request for the appointment of new officers to replace the losses of Seven Pines with less delay and more generosity than Johnston had encountered in similar situations. The president also showed his confidence in Lee's administrative ability by giving him complete discretion in the assignment of the newly promoted generals. "You will know best how to dispose of these officers," he wrote. "I give you the material to be used at your discretion."[11] Johnston might have had that sort of relationship with his commander-in-chief had he more of Lee's tact and humility.

Davis' kindness to his new army commander extended even to something as minor as the general's horse. Lee's favorite mount, Traveler, had a jolting gait that would have exhausted a less accomplished rider than the general. Davis had apparently noticed the animal's difficult habits during rides with Lee. Now, with Lee in command of the army and required to spend much time in the saddle, Davis thoughtfully offered to lend him his own horse. Lee was flattered but gracefully declined.[12]

No sooner had Lee taken command than he began to show both his skill in handling the president and his military aggressiveness. The day after formally assigning Lee to command the army before Richmond,

[11] Letter from Davis to Lee dated June 2, 1862, *OR* 11, pt. 3, pp. 569-570.

[12] Letter from Lee to Davis dated June 3, 1863 in Douglas Southall Freeman, ed., *Lee's Dispatches* (New York, 1957), pp. 3-5.

Davis rode out to check on things at the front. Seeing a number of horses, including Lee's, hitched in front of a house, Davis dismounted and went inside. Lee was in the midst of a council of war with his senior officers. The tone of the conversation at that moment was not at all to Davis' liking. Lee's subordinates were speaking despondently of the inevitability of McClellan's victory by the slow but sure methods of siege. Showing no reticence as a visitor, Davis waded into the discussion, expressing "in marked terms," as he later described it, his "disappointment at hearing such views." Lee spoke up and said he had been saying the same thing before the president came in.

Not long afterward Davis left the meeting and rode on to the front, where Lee joined him a short time later. The general respectfully asked the president "what, under the circumstances, [he] felt it most advisable to do." Davis replied that he still believed in the plan they had worked out together with Johnston before the Battle of Seven Pines and that Johnston had failed to carry out, that is, by flank and frontal attack to destroy one wing of the enemy's army as it lay straddled across the Chickahominy River. However, Davis believed it would be necessary to modify the original plan. Because Johnston's botched movement had alerted the Federals and presumably allowed them to improve their preparations, it would now be necessary that the flanking force be larger and more powerful, and that could only be accomplished by bringing in Maj. Gen. Thomas J. "Stonewall" Jackson's army from the Shenandoah Valley.[13] Lee concurred.

And so with Lee and Davis of much the same mind, the general began laying plans for his offensive. Lee knew of the bad feelings that arose from Johnston's failure to confide in his civilian superior, so he kept Davis fully informed of his preparations. The president remained in complete agreement with the general's views.[14] Meanwhile, Davis sought to find what reinforcements he could for Lee in other parts of the Confederacy. The president's attitude remained ambivalent. "I have

---

[13] Davis, *Rise and Fall*, 2, pp. 130-131.

[14] Letters from Lee to Davis dated June 5 and 10, 1862, letter from Jackson to Lee dated June 13, 1862, with endorsements by Lee and Davis, in Clifford Dowdey and Louis H. Manarin, eds., *The Wartime Papers of R. E. Lee* (New York, 1961), pp. 183-184, 188, 193.

much confidence," he wrote with some exaggeration, "in our ability to give [the enemy] a complete defeat."[15] But he went on to add, "The issues of campaigns can never be safely foretold." In a letter to his wife about the same time Davis again expressed his misgivings but also revealed the degree to which he considered the plan for the campaign his own. "We must find if possible the means to get at him without putting the breasts of our men in antagonism to his heaps of earth," the president wrote. "I will endeavor by movements which are not without great hazard to countervail the enemy's policy" by forcing McClellan into the open for a stand-up fight. Several days later, he wrote his wife that the time for the climactic battle was drawing near. "I am hopeful of success," he said, but confided that "the stake is too high to permit the pulse to keep its even beat."[16]

His worry came in part, no doubt, from his knowledge of just how much audacity Lee was already planning to display in the coming battle. By June 16, Lee had finalized his plans for the coming attack on McClellan, deciding to strengthen his blow against the Federal right by weakening the defenses of his own right, the section of his line immediately covering Richmond.[17] Not long thereafter Lee presented the plan to Davis, and the president would have been a cool man indeed if his pulse kept an even beat upon contemplation of the risk Lee was taking. The president pointed out to Lee that the Confederate right, that part of the line south of the Chickahominy, was too weak to stand up for long against a determined assault. Davis believed McClellan would not let such an opportunity pass. The president had a high opinion of the Federal commander. As secretary of war in the 1850's, Davis had honored the young McClellan by putting him up for promotion and assignment to one of two new cavalry regiments. He had also assigned McClellan to the highly responsible role of military observer for the Crimean War. If McClellan was the man he had taken him for back then, Davis warned Lee, "as soon as he found that the bulk of our army was on the north side

---

[15] Letter from Davis to John C. Pemberton dated June 4, 1862, *OR* 11, pt. 3, p. 572.

[16] Davis, *Jefferson Davis,* pp. 430-431.

[17] Douglas Southall Freeman, *R. E. Lee,* 4 vols. (New York, 1936), 2, pp. 104-106.

of the Chickahominy, he would not stop to try conclusions with it there, but would immediately move upon his objective point, the city of Richmond."

Davis was not the risk taker that Lee was, and the plan troubled him. Still, perhaps to avoid offending the ever-courteous Lee, he conceded, "If, on the other hand, [McClellan] should behave like an engineer officer, and deem it his first duty to protect his line of communication," the plan would be excellent. If the intent was to avoid offending Lee, the words were ill chosen. Lee had been an engineer officer. As Davis later wrote, "Something of his old esprit de corps manifested itself" in his first response. He was not aware, he told the president, that engineers were any more given to such mistakes than other officers. Then, his self control reasserting itself, Lee got to the main point: "If you will hold him as long as you can at the entrenchment, and then fall back on the detached works around the city," he told Davis, "I will be upon the enemy's heels before he gets there."[18] Lee's statement appeased Davis, and also indicated a measure of the mental dominance the general was already gaining over the president.

Yet Davis remained uneasy out of Lee's presence. On June 23, he wrote his wife, "Genl. J. E. Johnston is steadily and rapidly improving. I wish he was able to take the field. . . . He is a good soldier . . . and could at this time render most valuable service."[19] This was not quite the opinion Davis would have expressed a month earlier, and it would seem that Lee's heady risks were already making Davis wistful for the timid caution of Joe Johnston.

Davis was a man much given to nervousness, to the great detriment of his health. He always handled his nerves better when he could take some action connected with the source of his worries, so it was natural that he rode often out to see the army defending the capital. He rode out on June 24, but missed seeing Lee, who had ridden to another part of the line to check on some skirmishing there. Lee's attack two days later brought the president a new opportunity for activity and also ended the

[18] Davis, *Rise and Fall*, 2, p. 132.

[19] Letter from Jefferson Davis to Varina Davis dated June 23, 1862, Museum of the Confederacy, Richmond, Virginia.

long period of suspense. Davis felt so relieved from the affects of his nervous illness that he told his wife that he felt "almost well again."[20]

Besides a nervous desire to do something, Davis was also driven by his perception of his role as commander-in-chief. He took his responsibility in this capacity very seriously. Throughout the first year and a half of the war, he showed a desire to lead his armies in person when they went into action. He had hurried to the field of Manassas but arrived too late to take part. He had frequently visited Johnston's headquarters near Richmond in hopes of being present for the crucial battle. The president had actually arrived in time for Seven Pines (much to the annoyance of Johnston) and had come under fire and issued orders. He saw no reason to alter his battlefield activity now that the army was under Lee. What role, if any, a commander-in-chief had on the battlefield was one of the issues Davis and Lee would address in the coming days.

Lee began his offensive by sending a copy of the day's general order to the president, as well as a notice that his headquarters would that day be on the Mechanicsville Turnpike.[21] Later in the day, when the assault was delayed due to Jackson's failure to get his command into position, Lee took the time to send Davis a note explaining the situation.[22] Lee probably did not intend his revelation of the location of his headquarters as a request for a visit, but the dispatch was all the invitation the president needed. By about 2 p.m., Davis had joined Lee on the Mechanicsville Turnpike on the south side of the Chickahominy a little over a mile west of the Federal-held hamlet that gave the road its name. With the president had come the secretary of war and a number of other men.[23] One observer, at least, thought Davis gave the impression of one who had come not to watch but to take part.[24]

---

[20] Letter from Lee to Davis dated June 24, 1862, Freeman, *Lee's Dispatches*, pp. 12-13; Quotation in Davis, *Jefferson Davis*, p. 434.

[21] Letter from R. H. Chilton to Davis dated June 26, 1862, Freeman, *Lee's Dispatches*, p. 17; letter from Lee to George W. Randolph dated June 26, 1862, *OR* 11, pt. 3, p. 617.

[22] Letter from Lee to Davis dated June 26, 1862, Freeman, *Lee's Dispatches*, pp. 15-17.

[23] Freeman, *R. E. Lee*, 2, p. 129.

[24] Alexander, *Memoirs*, p. 118.

Late in the afternoon Confederate forces opened the battle with a headlong and ill-coordinated assault on the Federal positions north of the river. As Southern forces surged across the Chickahominy, Davis, still followed by his excited cavalcade of staff officers, cabinet members and other politicians, galloped across the rickety bridges spanning the river's two channels. So closely was Davis following the front lines that he got across just behind the infantry of the leading Confederate brigade, and before that unit's artillery could go over.[25] Confederate infantry quickly drove the opposition out of Mechanicsville but found the Federal main line of resistance behind Beaver Dam Creek, a small watercourse beyond Mechanicsville. The position was a strong one, and waves of Confederate troops surged against it only to break and roll back again. From the shell-swept open ground around Mechanicsville, Lee watched in frustration as his plan went awry. Intent on achieving success, he was oblivious to the heavy and accurate fire of the Union artillery batteries on the other side of the creek. He soon became aware, however, of the presence of someone else. Not far off, and under the same hot fire, Davis and his entourage sat their horses, anxiously watching the progress of the battle.

Whether moved by fear of Davis being killed or wounded, by apprehension for the muddling of the command structure created by the commander-in-chief's presence on the field, or by frustration at having the president see the less-than-perfect progress of this battle, Lee reacted quickly. Riding over to Davis he saluted stiffly and, before the president could get a word out, said sternly, "Mr. President, who is all this army and what is it doing here?" This was not the way Davis was accustomed to being spoken to by an equal, much less a subordinate. By this time, Davis was not quite thinking of Lee as a subordinate or even an equal. During the lifetime of Jefferson Davis there were a few men to whom he looked as father figures. To them and them alone he inwardly deferred. In his youth it had been his brother Joseph, 23 years his senior. Later, Albert Sidney Johnston, now almost three months in his grave, had held

---

[25] Daniel H. Hill, "Lee's Attacks North of the Chickahominy," in Robert U. Johnson and Clarence C. Buel, eds., *Battles and Leaders of the Civil War*, 4 vols. (New York, 1956), vol. 2, p. 352.

that place in Davis' esteem. Lee would never quite exert Johnston's power over the Confederate president, but he was beginning to come close. Despite the doubts Davis had entertained about Lee and his daring plans, he seems to have been increasingly prone to respond to the Virginian with an almost instinctive deferential respect.

Receiving this shocking rebuke from the normally mild-spoken Lee, Davis seemed uncomfortable. "It is not my army, General," he replied. The other civilians had come of their own volition, and Davis hoped Lee would not blame him for their presence. He was not to be let off so easily. "It is certainly not my army, Mr. President," Lee continued sternly, "and this is no place for it."

"Well, General," the president replied meekly, "if I withdraw, perhaps they will follow me." With that he tipped his hat to his imperious subordinate, turned his horse and rode down the hill away from the enemy. His entourage, some of them no doubt relieved to be able to do so without losing face, followed. Once out of sight of Lee, however, the president turned and stole back onto the battlefield. Again he came under artillery fire, and a Confederate soldier was killed by an exploding shell within a few feet of him.[26]

As the Battle of Mechanicsville neared its climax, the confused system of command that had to result from having an active commander-in-chief on the battlefield became apparent. Davis could not resist becoming directly involved in the conduct of the battle. Seeing the assaulting columns of A. P. Hill falter in their efforts to breach the Beaver Dam Creek line, Davis decided that D. H. Hill must send over a brigade in support, and, accordingly, the president wrote out the order and sent it off in the hands of a courier to Brig. Gen. Roswell S. Ripley of D. H. Hill's division. If an infantry assault was to be made, Davis' order for the advance of Ripley's brigade made excellent sense. In fact, it was precisely the move that Lee himself, unbeknownst to Davis, had ordered a few minutes before. In ordering it, however, Davis had bypassed two links in the chain of command, including that of army commander. If the president had a legitimate role on the battlefield, this was

[26] Freeman, *R. E. Lee,* 2, pp. 131-132.

not it. The confusion caused by Davis' duplication of Lee's order did not help matters during the closing hours of the already muddled Battle of Mechanicsville.[27]

As the week-long struggle continued, Davis could not stay away. He may have been on the field with Lee on June 27 as Confederate troops went into action at the Battle of Gaines' Mill.[28] The following evening he inspected the lines of Gens. Benjamin Huger, Lafayette McLaws and John B. Magruder on the south side of the Chickahominy. Lee had, in some of his communications, implied for Davis a more direct supervisory role in this sector, almost suggesting that he considered the president—or that the president considered himself—a sort of informal commander for the three divisions holding the line south of the river.[29] As Davis visited these commands that night he gave the officers there his opinion "that the enemy would commence a retreat before morning" and "gave special instructions as to the precautions necessary in order certainly to hear when the movement commenced." If the enemy could be attacked while withdrawing, the Confederates would gain a large advantage. Satisfied, Davis returned to Richmond, but during the night the Federals did indeed make good their retreat undetected by the Confederates opposite them.[30]

Lee faithfully informed Davis of the army's progress throughout the week, and the president carried on his more conventional role of forwarding reinforcements to the front.[31] At Frayser's Farm, however, the president was back in the thick of the action. Coming into a forest clearing about 2:30 p.m. on that last day of June, Lee discovered Davis in conversation with Maj. Gen. James Longstreet, a senior division commander. The president was ready for Lee this time and not about to be

---

[27] Alexander, *Memoirs*, p. 119; Longstreet, *Manassas to Appomattox*, p. 124; Douglas Southall Freeman, *Lee's Lieutenants: A Study in Command*, 3 vols. (New York, 1942), vol. 1, p. 515.

[28] Freeman, *R. E. Lee*, 2, p. 157.

[29] Davis, *Rise and Fall*, 2, p. 132; Letter from Lee to Benjamin Huger dated June 27, 1862, Freeman, *Lee's Dispatches*, pp. 18-19.

[30] Davis, *Rise and Fall*, 2, p. 140.

[31] Letter from Lee to Davis dated June 29, 1862, *Lee's Dispatches*, pp. 19-22; Freeman, *R. E. Lee*, 2, p. 172.

caught off guard as he had been at Mechanicsville. "Why, General," he exclaimed, "what are you doing here? You are in too dangerous a position for the commander of the army."

Lee, who was exasperated almost to the limits of his considerable patience by the failures of his staff and subordinate generals to carry out his plans, replied, "I'm trying to find out something about the movements and plans of those people," meaning the Federals. "But you must excuse me, Mr. President," he continued, "for asking what you are doing here, and for suggesting that this is no proper place for the commander-in-chief." Of course, Davis could have answered that as commander-in-chief he would go wherever he pleased, but this was Lee to whom he spoke, a man to whom he inwardly deferred as his superior morally if not legally. Instead, he was able to dodge Lee's suggestion. "Oh," he answered, "I am here on the same mission that you are." With that Lee could do nothing, and the president stayed. Within minutes, however, the clearing came under heavy bombardment. A courier was wounded and several horses killed. The Confederates, generals, president and all, quickly vacated the area.[32]

Later that same day, when Brig. Gen. Theophilus Holmes' green division broke under the fire of Federal artillery, Davis endeavored to rally the fleeing troops. He had just succeeded in stopping them when, as he described it, "Another shell fell and exploded near us in the top of a wide-spreading tree, giving a shower of metal and limbs, which soon after caused them to resume their flight in a manner that plainly showed no moral power could stop them within the range of those shells." Still within that range, Davis again encountered Lee, who at considerable personal risk was surveying the ground in search of a less exposed position for Holmes' battered division. Again the president remonstrated with his top general for exposing himself to the enemy's fire. It may have been another ploy of the president's to avoid being sent away himself, but it was probably sincere at the same time. Davis had lost Sidney Johnston, killed by enemy fire at Shiloh, and Joe Johnston, wounded at Seven Pines. He could not afford to lose Lee, but, besides,

---

[32] Longstreet, *Manassas to Appomattox,* p. 134; Alexander, *Memoirs,* p. 140; Freeman, *R. E. Lee,* 2, pp. 181-182.

he was also coming to feel a genuine affection for the reserved and respectful Virginian.

This time Lee made no effort to shoo the president off the battlefield. The frustrated general merely explained that going to look the ground over for himself was the only way he could get the information he needed.[33]

The next day—July 1, 1862—saw the disastrous assault on Malvern Hill. Again Davis seems to have been lurking in the area.[34] The morning after the failed attack, the president, accompanied by his nephew, Col. Joseph Davis, paid a call to Lee's headquarters at the Poindexter house. Lee was present along with Jackson and a number of staff officers. Curiously, the general seems to have been surprised to see Davis, perhaps because of the cool temperatures and incessant rain. Dr. Hunter McGuire, Jackson's medical director, noticed that the apparently startled Lee addressed Davis not as "Mr. President," but rather as simply "President."

"President," Lee said, "I am delighted to see you." Davis greeted Lee and his aide, Maj. Walter Taylor, before turning with a questioning look toward the ungainly but obviously high-ranking officer who stood stiffly nearby. Davis and Jackson had never met, and their official relations had not been happy. The president's meddling had driven Jackson to submit his resignation six months before. Jackson had felt his authority had been usurped when a subordinate had convinced Richmond authorities to overrule one of Jackson's orders. The government ultimately reversed itself and supported Jackson, and he had retracted his resignation, but the general's feelings remained bruised. When Davis had come in, McGuire had whispered to Jackson the identity of the visitor and Jackson, ever mindful of his duty to a military superior—even one he disliked—came to attention, as McGuire put it, "as if a corporal on guard, his head erect, his little fingers touching the seams of his pants."

"Why President," Lee interjected, apparently still trying to regain his mental equilibrium, "don't you know General Jackson? This is our

---

[33] Davis, *Rise and Fall*, 2, pp. 143-144.

[34] Freeman, *Lee's Lieutenants*, 1, p. 617.

Stonewall Jackson." Davis bowed. Stonewall saluted. With that unpleasant preliminary out of the way, Davis and Lee got down to the business at hand. Spreading their maps on the dining room table, they began to discuss the tactical situation. Lee explained the previous day's action and the subsequent withdrawal of McClellan's army. As the discussion continued, Dr. McGuire noticed something. "Every now and then," he later wrote, "Davis would make some suggestion; in a polite way, General Lee would receive it and reject it. It was plain to everybody who was there that Lee's was the dominant brain."[35]

As The Seven Days Battles ended, the basic boundaries of the working relationship between Jefferson Davis and Robert E. Lee had been established. Lee had established that he, not Davis, would fill the role of field commander. Davis had made it plain that he would continue to take a close interest in the army and, when possible, would endeavor to view its operations in person. Each had won a large measure of respect from the other. Davis must have impressed Lee with his battlefield courage as well as his often sound tactical and strategic advice, despite the frequency with which the general had to reject his less practical suggestions. The president had come to a level of deference to Lee that he felt for only a handful of other individuals in his life. On such persons he tended to rely with almost childlike trust, and this was no doubt the basis—along with Lee's superior military abilities—for the mental ascendancy the general had gained over the president.

The results of this relationship were both good and bad for the Confederacy. Lee, a general of brilliant abilities on the grand tactical level, was allowed free reign and given full support through the rest of the war in Virginia. No setback could shake Davis' confidence in him, nor could personal problems arise of the sort that had strained civil-military relations and hampered Confederate operations during the commands of Beauregard and Joe Johnston. If Lee failed to conquer a peace, it would not be for any failure by Davis to exert his considerable organizational talents in his support.

---

[35] Jedediah Hotchkiss Papers, Library of Congress Manuscript Division, Washington, D.C., microfilm reel 34, frame 125.

Yet if Lee had a fault as a general it was an excess of the very audacity that made him effective. Left to his own devices, he would gamble too often and for very high stakes. He gambled with soldiers the South could ill afford to lose. Caught up in the events and emotions of campaigning, with final victory beckoning to him—his to be had for one more infantry assault, for one more daring thrust—Lee was often too close to the action to see the fine line that separated daring from madness. A firm and wise hand was needed, a leader removed from the immediate turmoil of battle and able to judge the South's prospects against its dwindling resources. That hand should have been that of Jefferson Davis, but the president was unable to fulfill that role, first because he desired the role of field commander for himself and second because he made his field commander an alter ego. He would, in the end, give Lee everything the president of the Confederacy could have given except the strategic guidance of a wise commander-in-chief.

Richard A. Sauers

A native of Lewisburg, Pennsylvania, Dr. Richard Sauers was graduated from Susquehanna University in 1976. Sauers received both his M.A. and Ph.D degrees in American History from the Pennsylvania State University. He researches and writes widely on the Civil War, and is the author of numerous books on the subject, including A *Caspain Sea of Ink: The Meade-Sickles Controversy* (Butternut and Blue, 1989), *The Gettysburg Campaign, a Comprehensive, Selectively Annotated Bibliography* (Greenwood, 1982), and *Advance the Colors*, a two-volume history of Pennsylvania's Civil War battle flags. His next book will be a study of Gen. Ambrose Burnside's North Carolina Campaign. Dr. Sauers makes his home in Lewisburg.

THE PENNSYLVANIA RESERVES:
General George A. McCall's Division on the Peninsula

Major General George B. McClellan fought the Seven Days Battles with five army corps containing 11 divisions of infantry. The bulk of the fighting, however, fell to the V Corps of Brig. Gen. Fitz John Porter, and, consequently, that corps suffered disproportionately heavy losses. Of the 15,672 men killed, wounded or missing in action in the five corps of the Army of the Potomac in The Seven Days, 49 percent were from the V Corps. Moreover, two divisions in Porter's Corps together sustained 40 percent of the casualties suffered by the entire army. The divisions of Brig. Gen. George W. Morell and Brig. Gen. George A. McCall each lost more men than did any other *corps* in the army.[1]

The performance of McCall's Pennsylvania Reserves division is especially worthy of consideration. The division was heavily engaged in three of the five major engagements during The Seven Days. The fighting in which these Pennsylvanians were involved was intense and often at close quarters. Almost an entire regiment and most of a battalion were captured; one brigade commander was killed, another—a future commander of the Army of the Potomac—was seriously wounded and a third was taken prisoner. General McCall himself became a prisoner at the close of the Reserves' final and most severe engagement on the Peninsula—the Battle of Glendale. Despite its staggering casualty rate, McCall's men would be at the center of controversy before the end of

---

[1] McClellan's "Return of Casualties" in United States War Department, *The War of the Rebellion: The Official Records of the Union and Confederate Armies*, 128 vols. (Washington, D.C., 1880-1901), series I, vol. 11, pt. 2, pp. 24-37. Hereinafter cited as *OR*. All references are to Series I unless otherwise noted. Morell's division suffered 3,132 casualties and McCall's lost 3,067.

the campaign, having to defend themselves against charges of poor fighting and cowardice.

Under the April 1861 call for 75,000 three-month militia to suppress the Rebellion, Pennsylvania supplied 25 infantry regiments. As a result, the state's militia system was seriously weakened. Governor Andrew G. Curtin, anxious to remedy the situation, on May 15 created by act of law the "Reserve Volunteer Corps of the Commonwealth." This bill, commonly called "the Reserve Bill" provided that the commonwealth raise and equip a force of 13 infantry regiments, one of artillery and one of cavalry. The corps would be placed at the disposal of the Federal government if needed.[2]

The Reserve regiments quickly filled with recruits. Many companies formed for service in three-month regiments had been rejected by the governor because the commonwealth's quota had been filled. Now, these extra companies were among the first to be mustered into the Pennsylvania Reserve Corps. They came from Gettysburg, Pittsburgh, Philadelphia, Factoryville, Meadville and scores of small towns from 59 of the commonwealth's 66 counties. The companies sported names such as the Cumberland Guards, Slifer Guards, Irish Infantry, and Bailey's Invincibles. By the time the corps came together at Camp Curtin in Harrisburg, the state capital, it numbered 15,000 men.[3]

Curtin selected George A. McCall to command the Reserves. A native of Philadelphia, McCall (1802-1868) was an 1822 West Point graduate. He served in Louisiana and Florida, then took part in the Mexican War, where he fought at Palo Alto and Resaca de la Palma.

---

[2] Richard A. Sauers, *Advance the Colors! Pennsylvania Civil War Battle Flags*, 2 vols. (Lebanon, 1987-1991), 1, p. 80.

[3] Each Pennsylvania Reserve regiment had two designations—a "line" number and the Reserve Corps number. The infantry regiments were numbered the 30th Pennsylvania (1st Reserves) through 42nd Pennsylvania (13th Reserves), the 43rd regiment was the 1st Pennsylvania Artillery and the 44th regiment was the 1st Pennsylvania Cavalry. All infantry regiments were more popularly known by their Reserves designations. The 13th Reserves was better known as the Bucktails, or the 1st Rifles.

After the war, McCall was promoted to major and commanded the 3rd Infantry prior to assignment as colonel and inspector general of the army in 1850. In 1853, his health impaired, McCall resigned and retired to civilian life on a farm in Chester County near Philadelphia.[4]

On July 22, the day after the First Battle of Bull Run, the Reserves were mustered into Federal service. McCall moved the division to Washington, where it went into camp at Tenallytown, Maryland. While in camp, McCall divided the Reserves into three brigades, placing Brig. Gens. John F. Reynolds, George G. Meade and Edward O. C. Ord in command.[5]

In mid-April 1862, the division marched to Fredericksburg as part of Maj. Gen. Irvin McDowell's I Corps. The Reserves served as occupation troops in the city for almost two months. Several organizational changes altered the composition of the corps, the most significant being the change in command of the Third Brigade. General Ord was promoted and transferred and Brig. Gen. Truman Seymour succeeded.[6]

Farther to the South, Maj. Gen. George B. McClellan's Army of the Potomac lay on the peninsula formed by the York and James Rivers, east of the Confederate capital at Richmond. As McClellan advanced westward toward Richmond, he repeatedly asked Washington to send reinforcements. In response, the Lincoln administration detached McCall's division from McDowell's corps and sent it to the Peninsula. Transports began leaving Fredericksburg on June 9, and by June 14, the entire division had landed at the main Union supply base, White House Landing on the Pamunkey River.

Upon arriving at White House Landing, Reynolds and Meade immediately marched their brigades to Tunstall's Station on the York River Railroad. The Pennsylvanians found the depot in flames. Brigadier General Jeb Stuart's Confederate cavalry was riding a circuit around McClel-

---

[4] George W. Cullum, *Biographical Register of the Officers and Graduates of the U. S. Military Academy, at West Point, N. Y., From Its Establishment, March 16, 1802 to the Army Re-organization of 1866-1867*, 2 vols. (New York, 1868), 1, pp. 233-234; Samuel P. Bates, *Martial Deeds of Pennsylvania* (Philadelphia, 1875), pp. 624-626.

[5] Sauers, *Advance the Colors!*, 1, pp 80-81.

[6] Sauers, *Advance the Colors!*, 1, p. 82; J. R. Sypher, *History of the Pennsylvania Reserve Corps . . .* (Lancaster, 1865), pp. 169-180, 187-189.

Brig. Gen. George A. McCall

lan's army, and the Reserves had just missed the Southern troopers. The opportune landing of Seymour's brigade at White House, however, had prevented Stuart's men from destroying the Federal army's main supply depot.[7]

When the Reserves landed on the Peninsula, their effective fighting strength totaled slightly more than 10,000 officers and men. The division was organized as follows:

Pennsylvania Reserves:
Brig. Gen. George A. McCall

First Brigade
Brig. Gen. John F. Reynolds
1st Reserves, Col. R. Biddle Roberts
2nd Reserves (8 companies), Lt. Col. William McCandless
5th Reserves, Col. Seneca G. Simmons
8th Reserves, Col. George S. Hays
13th Reserves (6 companies), Maj. Roy Stone

Second Brigade
Brig. Gen. George G. Meade
3rd Reserves, Col. Horatio G. Sickel
4th Reserves, Col. Albert L. Magilton
7th Reserves, Col. Elisha B. Harvey
11th Reserves, Col. Thomas F. Gallagher

Third Brigade
Brig. Gen. Truman Seymour
6th Reserves, Col. William Sinclair
9th Reserves, Col. C. Feger Jackson
10th Reserves, Col. James T. Kirk
12th Reserves, Col. John H. Taggart

---

[7] Sypher, *Pennsylvania Reserves*, pp. 192-196; Evan M. Woodward, *History of the Third Pennsylvania Reserves* (Trenton, 1883), pp. 75-78.

Artillery

Battery A, 1st Pennsylvania, Capt. Hezekiah Easton

Battery B, 1st Pennsylvania, Capt. James H. Cooper

Battery G, 1st Pennsylvania, Capt. Mark Kerns

Battery C, 5th United States, Capt. Henry V. De Hart

Cavalry

4th Pennsylvania, Col. James H. Childs

Four companies of the Bucktails, with the 1st Pennsylvania Cavalry, were operating in the Shenandoah Valley, while the other batteries of the 1st Artillery had been scattered to service posts throughout the eastern theater.[8]

The division left its camp near Dispatch Station on the morning of June 17, leaving the 6th Reserves behind with Brig. Gen. Silas Casey's command to protect White House Landing. Marching up the north bank of the Chickahominy River, the troops reached New Bridge the next day. On the 19th, McCall received orders to move the division to Mechanicsville and take position on the extreme right of the Army of the Potomac. McCall's command would form part of Brig. Gen. Fitz John Porter's V Corps.[9]

McCall left Meade's brigade in reserve, commanding New Bridge from a bivouac on the Gaines Farm. Reynolds and Seymour moved their brigades westward to Beaver Dam Creek, taking up a position on the east bank with the creek in their front, Reynolds on the right and Seymour on the left near the Chickahominy. Beaver Dam Creek presented a strong military obstacle to the Confederates. Its western banks were

---

[8] "The Opposing Forces in the Seven Days' Battles," in Robert U. Johnson and Clarence C. Buel, eds., *Battles and Leaders of the Civil War*, 4 vols. (New York, 1884-1889), 2, p. 315; Sypher, *Pennsylvania Reserves*, p. 196. Only eight companies of the 2nd Reserves were present for duty. The elaborate mustering procedure repeatedly administered during the unit's organization in 1861 disgusted many of the men in the regiment and some of them declined to serve. Authorities disbanded four companies and added two more to the regiment prior to the campaign, leaving the 2nd badly understrength. See Evan M. Woodward, *Our Campaigns* (New York, n.d.), pp. 48-50, 59.

[9] Sypher, *Pennsylvania Reserves*, pp. 196-197; *OR* 11, pt. 2, p. 384.

swampy and prevented an easy approach by an attacker. Only two roads—the Cold Harbor Road at Ellerson's Mill on the left and the Old Church Road on the right—crossed the creek. McCall ordered his units to entrench the crossings of both roads.[10]

Once the Beaver Dam Creek line was established, McCall directed Reynolds to post two regiments beyond the creek to picket the approaches to Mechanicsville. These pickets watched the approaches to Meadow and Mechanicsville Bridges three miles west of the Beaver Dam line, while cavalry patrols guarded the roads leading westward and northward from Mechanicsville. The infantry pickets found this duty quiet and even pleasant because they were on good terms with their Confederate counterparts across the river. Once, when Lt. Col. Henry M. McIntire of the 1st Reserves was out inspecting his lines, Southern pickets presented arms to him.[11]

The Confederate leaders were developing plans to attack Porter's corps, the only Union troops north of the Chickahominy. On June 23, General Robert E. Lee and his four highest-ranking commanders—Thomas J. "Stonewall" Jackson, Ambrose P. Hill, Daniel H. Hill and James Longstreet—met in council to devise plans to attack Porter. The plan called for Jackson's troops to come from the Shenandoah Valley and advance on the Federal positions from the northwest. When Jackson came within supporting range, A. P. Hill was to send his Light Division across the Chickahominy, capture Mechanicsville and sweep eastward. This advance would clear more bridges to the south and enable Longstreet and D. H. Hill to cross the river to join the advance. The attack would begin on June 26.[12]

Everything went wrong for the Confederates. Jackson's march was delayed by felled trees across roads and his column was hours behind

---

[10] Sypher, *Pennsylvania Reserves*, pp. 197-198; William H. Powell, *The Fifth Army Corps (Army of the Potomac), A Record of Operations During the Civil War in the United States of America, 1861-1865* (New York, 1896), pp. 75-76; *OR* 11, pt. 2, p. 384.

[11] Sypher, *Pennsylvania Reserves*, p. 199; Howard Thomson and William H. Rauch, *History of the "Bucktails"* (Philadelphia, 1906), pp. 100-101; Woodward, *Our Campaigns*, p. 115.

[12] James I. Robertson, Jr., *General A. P. Hill: The Story of a Confederate Warrior* (New York, 1987), pp. 64-67.

schedule. The impetuous A. P. Hill tired of waiting and, at 3 p.m., decided to move forward, hoping Jackson would soon appear. His brigades
crossed at Meadow Bridge and headed toward Mechanicsville. The pickets before the Reserves' position that day were the Bucktail battalion and
the 5th Reserves. Hill's troops engaged Major Stone's Bucktails at
Meadow Bridge. Forced to retire, the Pennsylvanians put up a fierce
resistance as they fell back. Stone had sent three of his six companies
north to reinforce the cavalry pickets (the 8th Illinois and two companies
of the 4th Pennsylvania), leaving him with just three companies to contest Hill's advance. As these units retreated, Stone had to send word to
the other companies to withdraw as well. Capt. Edward A. Irvin, commanding Company K, failed to act promptly and was cut off by the
enemy advance. Irvin led his men into the swamps along the Chickahominy and tried to reach the Union army. Five days later, surrounded
and having been without food since the morning of June 26, Irvin surrendered his company when discovered by Confederate cavalry.[13]

As the Bucktails fell back, McCall sent Reynolds with the 1st and
2nd Reserves toward Mechanicsville. Reynolds formed line and covered
the withdrawal of the pickets behind Beaver Dam Creek. McCall now
deployed his line of battle to meet the oncoming Southern troops.
Reynolds' brigade formed on the right of the line, with the 2nd and 13th
Reserves north of Old Church Road and 5th, 1st and 8th Reserves south
of the road, some companies manning the rifle pits, others remaining in
reserve. Capt. Cooper's battery (four 10-lb. Parrotts) and a section of
Capt. John R. Smead's Battery K, 5th United States (two Napoleons,
from the Artillery Reserve) commanded the road. De Hart's battery of
six Napoleons unlimbered toward the left of Reynolds' line.[14]

Seymour's brigade guarded the left flank of McCall's line (the 10th,
12th and 9th Reserves, from right to left). One section each of Cooper's
(two 10-lb. Parrotts) and Smead's (two Napoleons) batteries swept the

---

[13] Thomson and Rauch, *Bucktails*, pp. 101-106; Robertson, *A. P. Hill*, pp. 69-70; *OR* 11, pt. 2,
p. 406.

[14] Sypher, *Pennsylvania Reserves*, p. 215; Bates Alexander, "Pennsylvania Reserves,"
Hummelstown Sun, November 3, 1893; Archibald F. Hill, *Our Boys, the Personal Experiences of a
Soldier in the Army of the Potomac* (Philadelphia, 1864), pp. 284-285; Alfred Rupert letter of July
27, 1862, Rupert Letters, Chester County Historical Society; *OR* 51, pt. 1, pp. 109-110.

road at Ellerson's Mill. Seymour's remaining unit, the 11th Reserves, was absent on picket duty along the Chickahominy. Meade's brigade (3rd, 4th and 7th Reserves), together with Easton's (four Napoleons) and Kerns' (six 12-lb. howitzers) batteries, was held in reserve.[15]

The Reserves had not long to wait, for at 6 p.m., Hill sent three brigades—Joseph R. Anderson's, James J. Archer's and Charles W. Field's—charging against the Union right. Hill struck here because he believed that Jackson's advancing corps would soon join his attack. The gallant Southern battle lines advanced past Mechanicsville and across open fields that descended to Beaver Dam Creek. Union artillerists opened a terrific fire that tore gaps in the advancing ranks.[16]

Undaunted, the Confederate lines recoiled, then charged again and again. Some troops actually managed to get across the creek in front of the 2nd Reserves' position. Lieutenant Colonel McCandless had five companies in line, one detached in a dry swamp to connect with the Bucktails and two detached to guard a ford. Southern troops penetrated gaps between the Union detachments but were met by counterattacks personally led by McCandless.[17]

McCall, seeing that his right flank was the target of the main Confederate attack, sent reinforcements. The 1st Reserves moved from its position in support of De Hart's battery to the right rear of the 2nd Reserves. The 3rd Reserves arrived from Meade's brigade, as well as Kerns' battery. Later, Brig. Gen. Charles Griffin's brigade of Morell's division arrived to bolster McCall's right flank.[18]

As twilight approached, Hill refocused his attack on Ellerson's Mill, sending forward Brig. Gen. William D. Pender's Brigade from the Light Division and Brig. Gen. Roswell S. Ripley's from D. H. Hill's Division. The assault was repulsed quickly and bloodily by the accurate rifle and artillery fire from across the creek. Ripley got only one regiment—the

---

[15] Sypher, *Pennsylvania Reserves*, p. 215; *OR* 11, pt. 2, pp. 399, 424, 426.

[16] Robertson, *A. P. Hill*, pp. 71-73.

[17] Woodward, *Our Campaigns*, pp. 119-120; Samuel P. Bates, *History of Pennsylvania Volunteers, 1861-5 . . .*, 5 vols. (Harrisburg, 1869-1871), 1, pp. 579-580.

[18] Sypher, *Pennsylvania Reserves*, pp. 211-212; Powell, *Fifth Corps*, pp. 79-80; *OR* 11, pt. 2, p. 386; *OR* 51, pt. 1, p. 110.

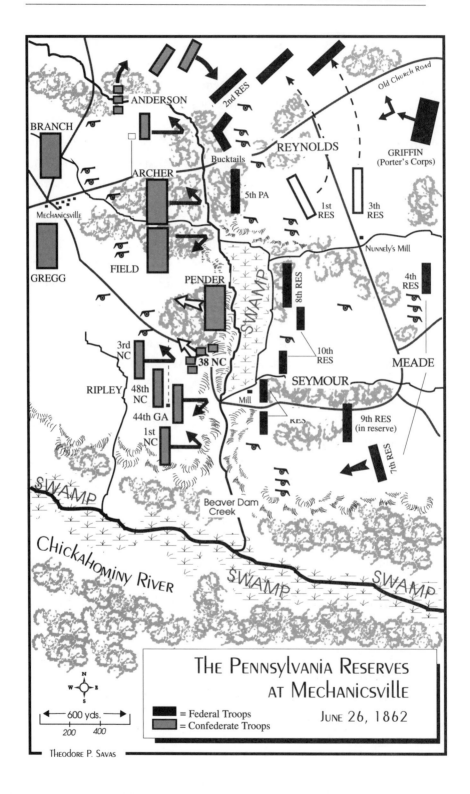

ANDERSON

BRANCH

2nd RES

Old Church Road

REYNOLDS

GRIFFIN
(Porter's Corps)

ARCHER

Bucktails

5th PA

1st
RES

3th
RES

Mechanicsville

Nunnely's Mill

GREGG

FIELD

PENDER

SWAMP

8th RES

4th
RES

3rd
NC

38 NC

10th
RES

MEADE

RIPLEY

48th
NC

44th GA

SEYMOUR

Mill

RES

9th RES
(in reserve)

1st
NC

7th RES

SWAMP

Beaver Dam
Creek

CHICKAHOMINY RIVER

SWAMP

SWAMP

THE PENNSYLVANIA RESERVES
AT MECHANICSVILLE

JUNE 26, 1862

= Federal Troops
= Confederate Troops

600 yds.

200   400

THEODORE P. SAVAS

44th Georgia—into action; it suffered 335 casualties out of 514 engaged.[19]

When this Confederate attack started, McCall buttressed his left by ordering forward the 7th Reserves from Meade's brigade. Easton's battery also followed. Porter sent Batteries L & M, 3rd United States (Capt. John Edwards) to McCall's left near the close of the action, but it was able to fire only a few rounds before darkness fell.[20]

The repulse at Ellerson's Mill ended the infantry assaults for the day. Cannonading continued into the night, but the Pennsylvania Reserves had handed Hill's Division a defeat. Including the troops from other brigades in the V Corps, McCall suffered 361 casualties—49 killed, 207 wounded and 105 missing. The Reserves had inflicted at least 1,400 casualties, and Porter later claimed the enemy suffered a loss of 2,000.[21]

But the Federals could not rest on their laurels; they had to prepare for the Southern attacks likely to come the next day. Porter, having been advised of Jackson's approach on June 24, was kept informed of his advance by cavalry pickets. Based on current intelligence, McClellan, at 3 a.m. on June 27, ordered Porter to withdraw from Mechanicsville and take position east of Gaines' Mill. Here, the V Corps would oppose any further Rebel advance and give McClellan time to carry out his plan to change supply bases from the York to the James Rivers.[22]

McCall received orders to withdraw just before dawn. The distance involved was six miles. The sun had risen by the time McCall passed the information along to his troops. Meade's and Griffin's brigades marched off first, followed by Reynolds' units. Major Stone's Bucktails, supported by Cooper's battery, remained behind to cover the retreat. Seymour's brigade also tarried long enough to oppose a Confederate advance, which began as the last Union soldiers fell back. The Bucktails were flanked by the more numerous Southerners and Company E, Capt. Alanson E. Niles, was surrounded and captured. The men hid the regi-

---

[19]   Robertson, *A. P. Hill*, pp. 73-74.

[20]   *OR* 11, pt. 2, p. 356; Sypher, *Pennsylvania Reserves*, pp. 212-213.

[21]   *OR* 11, pt. 2, pp. 38-39; Robertson, *A. P. Hill*, p. 77.

[22]   Fitz John Porter, "Hanover Court House and Gaines' Mill," *B & L*, 2, pp. 326, 331.

mental colors in a swamp but some enterprising Confederates found the flag and later presented it to President Jefferson Davis.[23]

Near Gaines' Mill, Porter formed his line of battle in the shape of an arc behind Boatswain's Creek. From this position, he covered four bridges across the Chickahominy. Morell's division held the left of the line, while Brig. Gen. George Sykes' division deployed on the right. When McCall's exhausted men reached the field, Porter placed them in reserve, Meade on the left of the division, Reynolds on the right, and Seymour to the rear. The troops were all in position by noon. [24]

In less than an hour, Southern troops advanced to attack. The main assaults began at 2:30 p.m. as Longstreet and A. P. Hill launched a series of charges against the left of Porter's line. Although furious, the attacks failed as massed Federal infantry and artillery mowed down scores of Confederates. The steady pressure all along the line, however, forced Porter to feed his reserves into the battle when ammunition in many regiments began to run dangerously low. McCall received orders to send in a regiment or two at a time. By battle's end, the Reserves had been dispatched to danger points all along the line and the regiments fought individually. The regiments of Reynolds' brigade generally were sent to reinforce the right of Morell's division and left of Sykes'. The 1st Reserves, and later the 8th, relieved Col. Gouverneur K. Warren's small brigade (5th and 10th New York) and held that part of the line against several enemy assaults. The 2nd Reserves went into action on the left of the 1st, in a wooded section originally held by Griffin's brigade. The 5th and 13th Reserves moved into battle farther to the right, where Southern infantry was sheltered in a wood.[25]

Meade's brigade was fragmented as his four units were sent to different points along Morell's line of battle. The 3rd Reserves at first lay in

---

[23] Thomson and Rauch, *Bucktails*, pp. 112-115; Sypher, *Pennsylvania Reserves*, p. 222; "Army Correspondence," *Lawrence Journal*, July 26, 1862; *OR* 11, pt. 2, pp. 415-416. General Ord found the captured Bucktail banner in the abandoned Confederate capitol in 1865.

[24] Sypher, *Pennsylvania Reserves*, pp. 223-224.

[25] Sypher, *Pennsylvania Reserves*, pp. 227-229; *OR* 11, pt. 2, pp. 413, 416-417; *OR* 51, pt. 1, p. 111; Woodward, *Our Campaigns*, pp. 125-126.

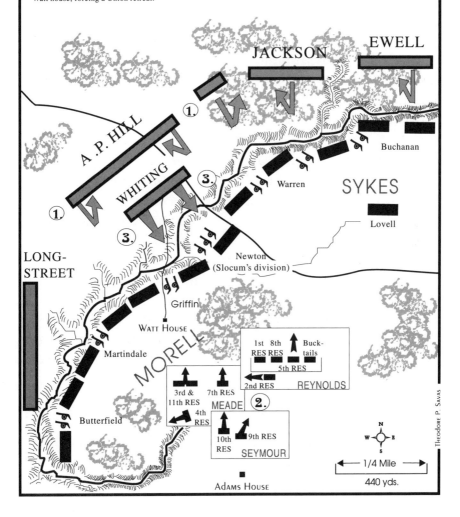

THE PENNSYLVANIA RESERVES AT GAINES' MILL

JUNE 27, 1862

= Federal Troops
= Confederate Troops

1. LEE'S CONFEDERATES attack the Union-controlled heights behind Boatswain Swamp and are repulsed at all points with heavy losses.

2. McCALL'S BRIGADES begin in reserve and are dispersed piecemeal to reinforce portions of the line. Reynolds' brigade divides and the regiments bolster the left of Sykes and the right of Morell; Meade's regiments (3rd, 4th, 7th and 11th Reserves) do likewise, the 3rd relieving the 4th Michigan, and the 4th supporting Warren's Zouves before moving to the left of the line. The 11th fought with the 4th New Jersey and was captured en masse; Seymour left the 12th Reserves in support of artillery on the far right (not pictured), and committed his remaining two units (9th & 10th Reserves) in support of Griffin's brigade.

3. WHITING'S CONFEDERATE DIVISION drives forward at about 7:00 p.m. and pierces Porter's line near the Watt house, forcing a Union retreat.

support of Kerns' battery, then moved forward into the woods along Boatswain's Creek and took position on the right of the 4th Michigan. It remained in this position for more than two hours until its ammunition was exhausted. Then, the 11th Reserves moved up to replace Colonel Sickel's men. The 4th New Jersey also occupied the line next to the 11th. The 4th Reserves at first moved to support Warren's brigade, then shifted to the extreme left of the line. Meade's other regiment, the 7th, was countermarched to and fro, finally halting to support two batteries.[26]

Seymour's brigade was also split up. The 9th Reserves moved up to support the 9th Massachusetts and 62nd Pennsylvania, remaining with those units until the whole line fell back. The 10th Reserves went to Sykes' division to support some of his artillery, while the 12th Reserves lay in support of Griffin's battery and was not heavily engaged.[27]

Porter's troops continued to defy Longstreet and Hill, but by 7:00 p.m., Jackson's Corps had finally reached the field and the entire Southern line advanced to strike the exhausted Federals. Though Brig. Gen. Henry W. Slocum's division of the VI Corps had arrived in support, Porter was still heavily outnumbered and the new Southern attack pierced the line near the center. The relentless pressure finally cracked the Northern line, and regiment after regiment began to retreat.

Heavy smoke prevented the 11th Reserves (9 companies) and 4th New Jersey from seeing other units retiring, and the two regiments continued to maintain their positions in the woods. Discovering enemy troops to their left, the Pennsylvanians tried to retreat and, with the Jerseymen, fought their way to the edge of the woods, only to see that they were surrounded. Rather that fight on and risk destruction, both regiments surrendered. Only stragglers escaped. [28]

General Reynolds was an unwilling witness to the 11th's surrender. Because the fighting along the 11th's front seemed heavy as the enemy broke through farther to the left, Reynolds and two aides rode to the

---

[26] Sypher, *Pennsylvania Reserves*, pp. 225-226; *OR* 11, pt. 2, pp. 420-421; Woodward, *3rd Reserves*, p. 89.

[27] Sypher, *Pennsylvania Reserves*, pp. 226-227; *OR* 11, pt. 2, pp. 422, 424-425, 427-428.

[28] Bates, *Pennsylvania Volunteers* 1, pp. 847-848. Company B of the 11th Reserves had been detached as pioneers earlier in the day and was not present on the field.

11th's sector to survey the situation. The trio was cut off when other regiments retreated. Rather than surrender, Reynolds and his two companions concealed themselves in the woods during the night. The next morning, they attempted to escape but were discovered by a patrol and captured.[29]

The breaking of the Federal line brought the enemy in contact with McCall's four batteries. Southern infantry came out of the woods some 800 yards in front of Easton's battery, which was posted to the left of the Gaines House. Easton's gunners, firing double-shotted canister, defied the enemy for half an hour. Then, Southern troops rushed the battery and drove away the survivors at bayonet point. Easton himself, after declaring that "the enemy shall never take this battery but over my dead body," fell dead as the battery was overrun; all four guns and two caissons fell to the enemy.[30]

Cooper's battery fared better. Throughout the engagement the six guns expended 350 rounds. One batteryman wrote home:

> The destruction was horrible. Our spherical case shot are awful missiles, each of these consisting of clotted musket balls, with a charge of powder in the centre, that is fired by a fuse the same as a shell. The missile first acts as a solid shot, ploughing its way through masses of men, and then exploding hurls forward a shower of balls that mow down heaps. We had the exact range and every shot told with frightful effect.

Battery B remained on the field until its support fell back and the enemy was again moving forward.[31]

Battery G also engaged the enemy at close range. Captain Kerns, wounded at the beginning of the battle, remained on the field until the battery retreated. The guns of the battery were not limbered for withdrawal until Confederate soldiers were within 20 yards. Kerns left two

---

[29] Sypher, *Pennsylvania Reserves*, pp. 232-233.

[30] *OR* 11, pt. 2, p. 408.

[31] *Lawrence Journal*, July 26, 1862.

guns on the field, the horses having been slain and several artillerists disabled. The battery fired 249 rounds.[32]

De Hart's battery suffered heavy losses as well, including De Hart, who was mortally wounded. When the front line retreated, the men of the exposed battery withdrew, leaving three cannon and their caissons on the field.[33]

Including the morning withdrawal from Beaver Dam Creek, the Reserves had suffered 1,651 casualties on June 27: 177 killed, 436 wounded and 1,038 missing and captured (mostly of the 11th and 13th Reserves). Col. Seneca G. Simmons of the 5th Reserves assumed command of the First Brigade in place of the captured General Reynolds. The division artillery suffered severely, losing nine guns. Still, the men had acquitted themselves well under trying circumstances.[34]

The shattered divisions of the V Corps reformed on the Trent Farm south of the Chickahominy. With his army entirely south of the river, McClellan now began his change of base and the army began to withdraw toward Harrison's Landing. The general ordered McCall to have his division escort Col. Henry J. Hunt's Artillery Reserve through the White Oak Swamp to the Quaker (Willis Church) Road south of that quagmire. McCall distributed his regiments among the artillery and trains and moved south. The head of the long column arrived at Savage's Station at 1 a.m. on June 29. After a short halt, the column moved on, crossed the swamp, then took up position to repel an attack from the direction of Richmond. Late in the afternoon, the Reserves were discharged from their escort duty and ordered to follow the rest of the corps toward the James River.[35]

General Porter had orders to move via the Quaker Road. To local residents "the Quaker Road" meant an old abandoned road, which was not shown on military maps. The maps did show another, larger road labeled "Quaker Road" a few miles to the east of the local Quaker Road.

---

[32] *OR* 11, pt. 2, pp. 411-412.

[33] Sypher, *Pennsylvania Reserves*, p. 231; *OR* 11, pt. 2, p. 990; *OR* 51, pt. 1, p. 115.

[34] *OR* 11, pt. 2, p. 40.

[35] Sypher, *Pennsylvania Reserves*, pp. 247-254; *OR* 11, pt. 2, p. 389.

A guide led the troops to the "wrong" Quaker Road, with McCall's division in the lead. By midnight, General Meade was sure they were on the wrong road. He halted and reported his feeling to McCall, who in turn advised Porter of the situation. Porter ordered McCall to bivouac by the road even as the remainder of the corps countermarched and reached the correct route by the morning of June 30.[36]

Unaccountably, Porter failed to issue orders to McCall to follow the rest of the corps. McCall's command lay in a field bordering the New Market (or Long Bridge) Road. This road intersected the Charles City Road less than a mile to the rear of the Reserves' position. Running southward from this intersection, which was known as Glendale, was the Willis Church Road, another name for the "large" Quaker Road, over which the army was withdrawing. If the Confederates seized the crossroads, they might be able to cut the army's retreat.[37]

After a night of false alarms, barking dogs and nervous sentries, McCall gathered his regiments and formed them in a large open field surrounded by pine forests, some dense, some more open. A marshy stream ran through the woods to the west, while a smaller brook flowed through the eastern woods. McClellan ordered McCall to hold his position until the army's trains had passed the crossroads at Glendale. The commanding general of the army then departed the field where his army was to fight a crucial engagement. The battle, which opened that afternoon (known variously as Glendale, Frayser's Farm, Nelson's Farm, New Market Crossroads and Charles City Crossroads), was fought by several Union divisions without overall direction. Brigadier General Phil Kearny's division of the III Corps took position on McCall's right, while Joseph Hooker's division of the same corps was on the left, separated from McCall by about half a mile. Brigadier General Edwin V. Sumner's II Corps was posted to Hooker's rear.[38]

A squadron of the 4th Pennsylvania Cavalry at first provided a picket screen for the Reserves. Generals Meade and Seymour rode for-

---

[36] Sypher, *Pennsylvania Reserves*, pp. 254-255; Woodward, *3rd Reserves*, pp. 99-100.

[37] Sypher, *Pennsylvania Reserves*, pp. 260-262; Martin D. Hardin, *History of the Twelfth Regiment Pennsylvania Reserve Volunteer Corps . . .* (New York, 1890), pp. 53-54.

[38] Ibid., pp. 53-54.

ward past this line and found Confederate soldiers moving toward their position. They reported the facts to McCall, who sent forward the 1st and 3rd Reserves to skirmish with the approaching foe. The remainder of the division formed on the east edge of the open plain, which was some 800 yards long and about 1,000 yards wide.[39]

A row of batteries reinforced the thinned ranks of the Reserve regiments. On the right of the New Market Road was stationed Lt. Alanson M. Randol and Batteries E & G, 1st United States (6 Napoleons), which had taken De Hart's place with the division. South of the road were the four remaining cannon of Kerns' battery, now led by Lt. Frank P. Amsden. Cooper's battery was still farther south, while two "German" batteries (Batteries A and C, 1st Battalion New York Light Artillery, Capts. Otto Diederichs and John Knieriem, of four 20-lb. Parrotts each) were near the division's left flank.[40]

Meade's brigade held the right flank north of the New Market Road. The 7th (to which the remaining men of the 11th were attached) and 4th Reserves supported Randol's battery. Seymour's brigade held the left flank. The 9th Reserves supported Cooper's guns, followed to the left by the 10th and 12th Reserves. Simmons' depleted brigade was held in reserve along the woods at the east edge of the field. The remainder of the 4th Cavalry was deployed behind Seymour, generally in a ravine at the south end of the open plain.[41]

The Confederates advancing against McCall were the divisions of Longstreet and A. P. Hill. Lee had planned to catch McClellan's army as it crossed White Oak Swamp, but when that plan failed, the general attempted to cut the Federal army in two by attacking it before it reached the James. Lee delayed Longstreet's attack until he found that other divisions were not in position as expected. Then, hoping to still break through the Federal line, Lee sent Longstreet's men forward. Field guns

---

[39] Sypher, *Pennsylvania Reserves*, pp. 263-264; James M. Linn, "The Ninth Army Corps. Pennsylvania Reserves," *Lewisburg Chronicle*, July 25, 1896; R. Biddle Roberts, "The Battle of Charles City Cross Roads," *Philadelphia Weekly Press*, March 3, 1886.

[40] Sypher, *Pennsylvania Reserves*, p. 262; Linn, July 25, 1896.

[41] Sypher, *Pennsylvania Reserves*, p. 262; Linn, October 17, 1896.

exchanged artillery fire as the infantry began moving. The time was now after 5 p.m.[42]

The Confederate attack drove the 1st and 3rd Reserves back to the main line. The 1st took position to support Amsden's guns, while the 3rd, fired on from the rear as well, broke up completely. Individuals and squads seem to have rallied and fought with other units. The first assault came on the right, where Brig. Gen. James L. Kemper's Virginians emerged from the woods with a rush and headed straight for the left flank. Here, General Seymour had changed McCall's dispositions by dividing the 12th Reserves. He moved four companies to a small log farmhouse (Whitlock's) ahead of the main line. Two additional companies supported the line here, which erected a small barricade of fence rails. The rest of Colonel Taggart's men supported the two New York batteries.[43]

Kemper's furious attack struck at the Whitlock House and overran the six companies of the 12th Reserves. The two New York batteries fired a few more rounds of ammunition and withdrew, leaving six of their eight cannon on the field. The retreating limbers and horses ran into the remaining companies of the 12th and over some of the men. These companies were carried away in the flight. Some of the 4th Cavalry also were affected, as were the 2nd Reserves, which was moving southward along the edge of the woods. Colonel Taggart finally managed to rally a number of men and reported to Hooker for assignment, while others joined the 2nd Reserves.[44]

The breaking of the 12th Reserves, New York batteries, and some of the 4th Cavalry, influenced General Hooker to write in his report: "Meanwhile, the enemy's attack had grown in force and violence, and after an ineffectual effort to resist it, the whole of McCall's division was completely routed, and many of the fugitives rushed down the road on

---

[42] Douglas S. Freeman, *R. E. Lee: A Biography*, 4 vols. (New York, 1934-1935), 2, pp. 179-185.

[43] Linn, October 17, 1896; *OR* 11, pt. 2, p. 420; Hardin, *12th Reserves*, p. 59; Woodward, *3rd Reserves*, pp. 107-108.

[44] Linn, October 24, November 14, 1896; *OR* 11, pt 2, pp.407, 428; Hardin, *12th Reserves*, pp. 59-61, 73, where Hardin wrote that the 12th remained on the field until Brig. Gen. Cadmus Wilcox's brigade charged later in the fighting.

1. KEMPER'S BRIGADE unleashes a heavy attack to the Whitlock house, that breaks up the 12th Reserves and the adjacent artillery, forcing the 4th Pennsylvania Cavalry and 2nd Reserves to retreat. The Union counterattack (5th, 8th, 9th, and 10th Reserves) drives back Kemper.

2. BRANCH AND JENKINS drive back the Reserves. The Union retrograde movement is halted with the assistance of troops from Sumner and Hooker (whose troops are not shown on map).

3. WILCOX'S ALABAMA REGIMENTS advance north and south of the Long Brigade Road. After a desparate bayonet fight among Randol's guns, the Alabamians are forced to retire. Pryor's and Featherston's brigades arrive on the field piecemeal before nightfall, and meet fresh Union reinforcements from Philip Kearny's division, posted on the right of McCall's Pennsylvanians.

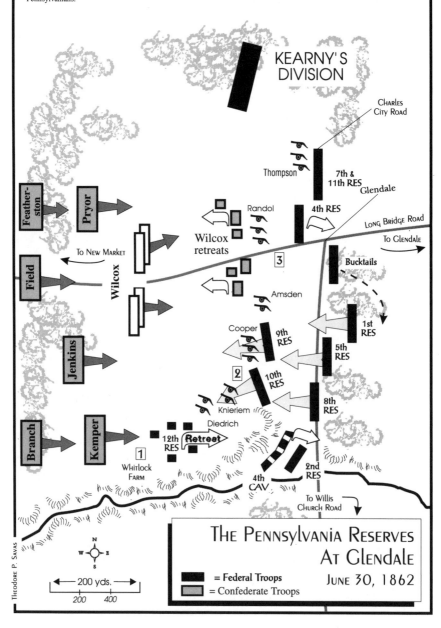

THE PENNSYLVANIA RESERVES
AT GLENDALE
JUNE 30, 1862

which my right was resting, while others took to the cleared fields and broke through my lines from one end of them to the other, and actually fired on and killed some of my men as they passed."[45]

As Kemper's attack drove away the 12th Reserves and captured six cannon, McCall sent Colonel Simmons to counterattack. Simmons took with him the 5th and 8th Reserves and was joined by the 9th and 10th as well. This entire force charged headlong into Kemper's Brigade, driving it back across the open field. Captain Thomas L. Chamberlain of the 5th Reserves recalled the charge:

> Without giving us one substantial volley they soon broke and fled in wild haste towards the heavy timber at the far side of the field. Many were overtaken and captured before reaching the high stake-and-rider fence, but the greater number succeeded in gaining the shelter of the woods, from which they opened a telling fire on our now disordered line. Strange to say, our men scarcely fired a shot, but in their eagerness to take prisoners plunged forward in utter recklessness, bounded over the fence, and urged the pursuit far into the woods.[46]

The Federal charge cleared Kemper's Brigade from the field, with men of the 10th Reserves seizing the 17th Virginia's colors. However, as Kemper's disordered regiments fell back, Brig. Gen. Lawrence O. Branch's North Carolinians of A. P. Hill's Division advanced to the attack. Seymour and Simmons saw Branch's men coming and endeavored to recall the charging Reserves.

The Pennsylvanians managed to deploy a line near the Whitlock House to face the oncoming Carolinians. Simmons had the men lie down. Then, as the Rebels came into range, he ordered the line to rise and open fire. As the men in blue arose, the Carolinians fired a deadly volley, which swept the ranks with fearful accuracy. Simmons received a

---

[45] McCall was incensed at this writing, especially when New York papers printed it. See *OR* 11, pt. 2, pp. 111, 113-114, 393-398, for exchanges of letters between the two generals over this issue. McCall later published the pamphlet, *Pennsylvania Reserves on the Peninsula* (Philadelphia, 1862), to rebut Hooker's statements.

[46] Linn, October 24, November 7, 1896.

death wound, and Seymour's horse was shot, throwing the general to the ground. The Reserves stood and fired back with their smoothbore weapons. After a fierce struggle, the Federals fell back toward the ravine at the south end of the field, where the Bucktails and 2nd Reserves formed to cover the retreat. [47]

The breaking of the Reserves' left flank led Hooker to send troops north to the edge of the plateau overlooking the ravine behind the Reserves' line. Sumner also sent some troops forward. Together, the fresh units drove Branch's Brigade back and punished its supports (Brig. Gen. George Pickett's Brigade, Col. Eppa Hunton commanding). Meanwhile, the tide of battle had shifted to the north end of the Federal line. Brigadier General Micah Jenkins' South Carolina Brigade advanced on Kemper's left. The regiments emerged into the open field and were hammered by Amsden's and Cooper's batteries. The 1st Reserves counterattacked whenever the enemy approached the guns. When Simmons' brigade moved to attack, three companies of the 1st followed, leaving Colonel Roberts with six companies to defend Cooper's guns. [48]

Later in the action, Amsden's cannoneers ran out of ammunition. Gen. Seymour had sent this battery's caissons to the rear and Amsden was unable to locate them. He reported the situation to McCall, who ordered him to limber up his guns and retire out of range. As the 1st Reserves charged one last time, they were met by fresh troops—Brig. Gen. Cadmus M. Wilcox's Alabama Brigade. The 9th and 10th Alabama regiments advanced on the south side of the New Market Road, following the retiring 1st Reserves into Cooper's battery. [49]

The Alabamians fired a deadly volley that cut through the battery. They charged forward and claimed the cannon, driving the 1st Reserves into the woods to the rear. Here, the survivors met the returning 9th Reserves, which had participated in Simmons' attack. Cooper implored the regiment to save his guns. Aided by the remnant of the 1st, the 9th charged into the battery and waged hand-to-hand combat. Corporal Wil-

---

[47] Linn, November 14, 21, 1896; *OR* 11, pt. 2, p. 417; "Army Correspondence," *Bellefonte Central Press*, July 25, 1862.

[48] Linn, November 28, 1896; *OR* 51, pt. 1, p. 111. Co. A of the 1st Reserves was absent.

[49] Linn, November 28, 1896.

liam J. Gallagher of the 9th seized the 10th Alabama's colors as a trophy. Finally, the Pennsylvanians were victorious and the Southerners sullenly fell back, leaving the Union troops in possession of the battery's wreckage.[50]

Meade's brigade also bore heavy Confederate assaults. After Jenkins advanced, two more Confederate brigades (those of Brig. Gens. Roger A. Pryor and Winfield S. Featherston) headed for McCall's and Kearny's lines. The left wing of Wilcox's Brigade (8th and 11th Alabama) charged for Randol's battery. Randol's gunners opened with effectiveness, but so eager was the 7th Reserves for battle, that Colonel Harvey ordered a charge when the Alabamians faltered before the guns. Randol's guns, which were still firing on the enemy, killed some men of the 7th as the infantrymen returned from their pursuit. General Meade was severely wounded not far from Randol's position and was carried from the field.[51]

The Alabamians renewed their attack and again failed. A third attempt brought them into Randol's battery. By this time, most of the 4th Reserves had disintegrated under the pressure. The survivors, aided by Randol's gunners, fought head-to-head with Wilcox's stout men. Gen. McCall rode up and witnessed the fight over the battery. "Bayonet wounds, mortal or slight, were given and received. I saw skulls crushed by the butts of muskets, and every effort made by either party in this life-or-death struggle, proving indeed that here Greek had met Greek." The Federals were victorious and the Alabamians fell back.[52]

The Union success was short-lived, however, for Brig. Gen. Charles W. Field's Brigade of Hill's Division soon appeared, advancing astride the New Market Road. The Virginians moved forward and drove the Reserves away from Randol's and Cooper's wrecked batteries. They advanced into the woods behind the guns but then retired as darkness approached and Union troops continued to fire.[53]

---

[50] Ibid.

[51] Alexander, *Hummelstown Sun*, October 26, November 23, 1894; *OR* 11, pt. 2, p. 255.

[52] *OR* 11, pt. 2, pp. 391, 421; Linn, *Lewisburg Chronicle*, December 5, 1896.

[53] Linn, *Lewisburg Chronicle*, December 5, 1896.

By this time, McCall, after seeing the Alabamians repulsed, rode south to see what had transpired on that part of the field. He located Major Stone and the remnant of Simmons' and Seymour's brigades. Stone had taken command when no one else had volunteered, and he soon was able to get six regimental colors in line to rally any survivors. The major heard the noise of battle still continuing on the right and led his men forward to see if he could be of service. McCall led the troops north until they almost reached the New Market Road. The general then halted the command and rode forward with Stone and an aide to find the 4th Reserves. In the darkness, McCall rode into the 47th Virginia and was captured along with his aide. Stone spurred his horse away and was wounded in the hand as he galloped off.[54]

The whereabouts of Gen. Seymour has grown into a controversy. He made no mention of his own actions in his official report. Three years after the war, Evan M. Woodward wrote that Seymour returned and assumed command about 9 p.m. McCall learned in 1868 from Gen. William B. Franklin that Seymour appeared in that general's command quite agitated about the battle, and was only calmed by brandy. Yet at the beginning of the engagement, Woodward recalled seeing the general calmly sitting on his horse peering at the advancing Southern troops. Woodward concluded that Seymour "was not 'the bravest of the brave,' yet he was no coward."[55]

Darkness finally brought an end to the confused Battle of New Market Crossroads (as it was known to the Reserves). After Meade's brigade was attacked, fighting spilled northward and engulfed Kearny's division, which repulsed some of Longstreet's and Hill's regiments. Both Confederate divisions had fought well and had inflicted many casualties, but they could not cut off McClellan's retreat. McCall's division had blunted their assaults and had suffered dearly in the process. Only Amsden's four cannon had been saved. After dark, even though the abandoned and wrecked batteries lay just in front of the Union lines,

[54] Thomson and Rauch, *Bucktails*, pp. 128-131; Linn, *Lewisburg Chronicle*, December 5, 1896; *OR* 11, pt. 2, pp. 417-418.

[55] Woodward to Samuel P. Bates, February 3, 1868, Bates Papers, Pennsylvania State Archives. Harrisburg, PA.

Gen. Heintzelman decided not to attempt to rescue the cannon for fear of bringing renewed combat.

The Reserves had endured what was probably the most severe fighting they would see in three years of service. Adjutant Robert Taggart of the 9th Reserves echoed the confused struggle in his diary: "It was warm work. My horse killed. Constant fighting. No rest. When will it end. Fortunately was only hit once with a ball not burst. The poor wounded. Their moans. It is terrible. Yet this is war. Heaven interpose."[56]

At 11 p.m., the Reserves, formed 100 yards behind their original position, were withdrawn and marched to Malvern Hill. Here, they were placed in reserve and did not take part in the July 1 fighting. The division reached Harrison's Landing the next day, where it was joined by the 6th Reserves, which had embarked aboard ships at White House Landing when that base was abandoned. The Reserves counted their losses during the preceding days. Casualties were tallied as 318 killed, 1,176 wounded and 1,573 captured and missing, for a total of 3,067. Only Morell's division sustained a higher loss than McCall's. General Seymour now commanded the division, with the First Brigade led by Colonel Hays of the 8th, the Second Brigade by Colonel Magilton of the 4th and the Third by Colonel Jackson of the 9th.[57]

While the army lay at Harrison's Landing, McCall and Reynolds returned after being exchanged on August 13. Although many Reserves welcomed McCall when he came back, some were not happy to see him. A soldier in the 1st Reserves thought that the general had lost status among his men and brother officers because of the confused battle on June 30.[58] McCall, his health impaired by the campaign, procured a furlough and went home, leaving Reynolds in command.

---

[56] Taggart diary, June 30, 1862, Taggart Papers, Pennsylvania State Archives, Harrisburg, PA.

[57] *OR* 11, pt. 2, pp. 32-33; Sypher, *Pennsylvania Reserves*, p. 313. Sypher enumerates the casualties as 310 killed, 1,340 wounded and 1,581 missing, for a total of 3,180.

[58] Alfred Rupert letter of October 22, 1862, Rupert Letters; Woodward, *Our Campaigns*, p. 167; Sypher, *Pennsylvania Reserves*, p. 323.

State color of the 11th PA Reserves captured at Gaines' Mill, June 27, 1862.
The flag was returned to Pennsylvania in 1905 when all other captured
flags held by the government were returned to the states.

Despite the criticism, however, the Pennsylvania Reserves had acquitted themselves well in their first real test of combat.[59] They had fought in three battles in five days and were at the heart of the fighting at Gaines' Mill and Glendale, two of the more bloody and intense engagements of the war. The Reserves had won laurels and respect, both from their comrades in the Army of the Potomac and from their opponents, and, as the war progressed, the Pennsylvanians would build a reputation as a fighting division. They performed consistently and well under a succession of commanders, notably at Second Manassas, South Mountain, Antietam, Fredericksburg and Gettysburg.

[59] Edward Ord's (Seymour's) brigade had fought a small engagement at Dranesville, Virginia, on December 20, 1861.

Kevin Conley Ruffner

Kevin Ruffner holds degrees from The College of William and Mary, The University of Virginia, and a doctorate in American Studies from The George Washington University. His publications include *44th Virginia Infantry*, a title in the Virginia Regimental Series, and *Luftwaffe Field Divisions, 1941-45*, in the Osprey Men-at-Arms Series, in addition to many articles in various journals. Dr. Ruffner is a captain and company commander in the U.S. Army Reserve and lives in Washington, D.C.

BEFORE THE SEVEN DAYS:
The Reorganization of the Confederate Army in the Spring of 1862

In analyzing the results of The Seven Days, Douglas Southall Free-man, Robert E. Lee's biographer, put forward several explanations for the Confederate failure to destroy the Federal Army of the Potomac. The primary reason for the Army of Northern Virginia's failure, according to Freeman, was that Lee lacked topographical information and accurate intelligence due to subpar staff work and ill-used cavalry. Lee himself indicated that "the want of correct and timely information," was a major hindrance, and historians have seized upon this statement as an explanation for the Virginian's mixed success.[1]

However accurate the observations of Freeman and other historians may be, they do not take into account other significant circumstances affecting the performance of Lee's army in The Seven Days and, for that matter, of Gen. Joseph E. Johnston's army during the early part of the Peninsula Campaign. The army Johnston took to the Peninsula in April of 1862 was in the midst of an unprecedented upheaval in personnel, organization and leadership—the most extensive reorganization the Confederate army in Virginia experienced during the war. Scant weeks be-

---

[1] Douglas Southall Freeman, *R. E. Lee,* 4 vols (New York, 1934-1935), 2, p. 241. Freeman wrote: "To summarize, then, the Federal army was not destroyed, as Lee had hoped it would be, for four reasons: (1) The Confederate commander lacked adequate information for operating in a difficult country because his maps were worthless, his staff work inexperienced, and his cavalry absent at the crisis of the campaign; (2) the Confederate artillery was poorly employed; (3) Lee trusted too much to his subordinates, some of whom failed him almost completely; and (4) Lee displayed no tactical genius in combating a fine, well-led Federal army." For Lee's statement, see U.S. War Department, *The War of the Rebellion: The Official Records of the Union and Confederate Armies,* 128 vols. (Washington, D.C., 1890-1901), series I, vol. 11, pt. 2, p. 497, hereinafter cited as *OR*. All references are to Series I unless otherwise noted.

fore the fighting began in earnest east of Richmond, the leaders of the Confederate government feared the Southern army in Virginia was on the verge of disintegration. Dramatic action by the Confederate Congress kept the army intact, but the fabric of the army changed drastically as a result. Throughout the campaign, inexperience and inefficiency in the officer corps and widespread discontent in the ranks limited the effectiveness of the Confederate army as a fighting tool. Any conclusions drawn about the failures of Johnston and Lee must take into account the character of the new and still-cumbersome weapon with which they had to wage war.

The Confederate States of America faced a crisis unprecedented in the annals of American military history during the winter of 1861 and the spring of 1862. Southern volunteers who had so eagerly rushed to join the army immediately after Fort Sumter now approached the end of their one-year enlistment. The Confederate government feared the army would dissolve during April, May and June 1862, just as the Union Army of the Potomac under Maj. Gen. George B. McClellan opened the spring campaign to seize the Confederate capital at Richmond.

President Jefferson Davis, the Confederate Congress, and the Confederate military hierarchy—especially Secretary of War Judah P. Benjamin and General Johnston—spent countless hours discussing means to keep the volunteers in service and preserve the army's fighting strength. As early as November 30, 1861, Benjamin told President Davis that "it is impossible to view without disquiet the approach of the period when many of the twelve-months' volunteers will be mustered out of service." The secretary then went on to state:

> The experience of the past eight months has amply demon-
> strated if, indeed, demonstrations were needed, the radical
> vices of a system of short enlistments and the impossibility of
> conducting effective campaigning with raw levies. . . It is
> impossible to estimate the extent to which our arms will be
> weakened if the twelve months' volunteers, inured to hard-
> ship, recovered from camp diseases, steadied by discipline,
> and inspired by the consciousness of their own improved
> condition and efficiency, shall be replaced by raw recruits in

the approaching spring at the very opening of the season for vigorous operations." [2]

This article will discuss steps the Confederate government took to preserve the Confederate army in Virginia, will examine the morale of Confederate officers and men as it affected reenlistments and unit reorganizations in the spring of 1862 and will assess the impact of conscription on Confederate soldiers and the army as a whole.

The seeds of this crisis were sown the previous year when thousands of volunteers took up the Confederate cause. Most of the Confederate army was organized under the "Act to Provide for the Public Defense," which Congress adopted in March 1861. This act accepted volunteers from the various Southern states "to serve for twelve months after they shall be mustered into service, unless sooner discharged." The act stipulated that the president could accept previously organized companies, battalions, and regiments, "whose officers shall be appointed in the manner prescribed by in the several States to which they shall respectively belong." Once the volunteers and their units had been mustered and inspected, they were received into Confederate States service. [3]

This system would have been sufficient had the South achieved victory in the summer of 1861. The Confederacy's failure to seize Washington after First Manassas condemned the volunteer troops to months of inactivity and boredom in camps throughout Virginia. Halsey Wigfall, a member of the Washington Artillery of New Orleans camped near Centreville, Virginia, and the son of a Confederate general, admitted by mid-December 1861 that "any one who talks of a fight here this winter is laughed at—in fact it has come to be a standing joke." [4]

Camp diseases, such as dysentery, typhoid fever and measles, produced far more casualties than Union bullets during the first months of the war. The 5th Alabama Infantry Regiment at Union Mills in Fairfax County, Virginia, numbered 56 officers and 1,040 enlisted men in Au-

---

[2] *OR* IV, 1, p. 763.

[3] *OR* IV, 1, pp. 126-127.

[4] Halsey Wigfall to mother, December 17, 1861, Wigfall Family Papers, Library of Congress, Washington, D.C. Hereinafter cited as LC.

gust 1861. That same month, the regiment's surgeon reported that some 400 men had been treated for various ailments. The majority of sick cases had to be evacuated from camp and, in many cases, the soldiers were sent home for proper treatment.[5]

The widespread illness fostered disharmony because the army seemed unable to preserve the health of the men in the ranks. The Confederate government received increasing numbers of requests for discharge from soldiers suffering poor health, disabilities or anxiety about hardships faced by their families at home. Sergeant Thomas C. Morgan of the 44th Virginia Infantry Regiment appealed to President Davis for his release in early August from his isolated post in northwestern Virginia:

> I have now been in service about two months & one month of that time been unable owing to my health to perform any duty whatever & am now very feeble and continue to decline in health believing that a camp life does not suit my constitution. . .I have an old mother about 70 years old with 40 or fifty negroes on a plantation with no other white person the overseer having joined the army & my plantation adjoining with some eight or 10 more with nobody but my wife & five little children my overseer having entered the service[.][6]

President Davis and Secretary Benjamin also received hundreds of pleas from desperate families throughout the South for the release of family members from the army. E. E. Morgan, the wife of Sergeant Morgan of the 44th Virginia, submitted a lengthy letter in September to urge the president to discharge her husband:

> If you have a family, I conjure you to picture to you [sic] my *unhappy situation*, so lonely with five children to look up to

---

[5] Report of Sick and Wounded in Records, Muster and Pay Rolls, 5th Alabama Infantry Regiment, Record Group 109, War Department Collection of Confederate Records, National Archives, Washington, D.C. (hereinafter cited as RG 109, NA).

[6] Sergeant Thomas C. Morgan to Secretary of War, August 12, 1861, Letter 5549-1861, Letters Received by the Confederate Secretary of War, RG 109, M437, NA. Hereinafter cited by letter number, date, and LSOW.

> me, so unworthy—the Sheriff has been here for Taxes, & I
> cannot get Money to pay them O! Sir I might fill pages,
> would words suffice I write in confidence to you knowing
> you have the power to grand [sic] my request.[7]

Increasingly, soldiers grew frustrated with military life. In late September, Private Henry M. Price, also a member of the 44th Virginia, protested to the secretary of war about the treatment of soldiers by surgeons at Camp Bartow in northwestern Virginia. He told the secretary that "we object to the sick being keep in Camp & suffered to die & be buried like dogs—when if sent home & permitted to go, where they would be carefully nursed & cared for they would recover—this is indirect murder to say the least of it."[8]

Perhaps the greatest source of discontent among the volunteers centered around relationships between officers and enlisted men. In some cases, there were sympathetic feelings based on mutual affiliations, such as family or home ties. Richard W. Habersham of the Hampton Legion (South Carolina) admitted to his father that "I have gotten into a habit lately of calling Mr. Gaillard, Sam: I know it does not look well for a boy of my age to be so familiar with a man of his age and I am trying to break my self of it. . . .I am trying to call him 'Major' but the 'Sam' will slip out sometimes in spite of all that I can do to prevent it." Habersham added, "you can form an idea of the intimacy that exist [sic] between men, who eight months ago never even had heard of each other."[9]

This intimacy also created resentment. Francis Marion Parker, a second lieutenant in the 1st North Carolina Infantry Regiment (Six Months) at Yorktown, responded to his wife's questions regarding the members of his company. "You wanted to know if Capt. [David B.] Bell is an efficient officer. I must answer candidly that he is not: in the first

---

[7] E. E. Morgan to Secretary of War, September 22, 1861, Letter 5549-1861, LSOW; for further information on the history of this regiment, see Kevin C. Ruffner, *44th Virginia Infantry* (Lynchburg, 1987) and Kevin C. Ruffner, "Civil War Desertion from a Black Belt Regiment: An Examination of the 44th Virginia Infantry," in Edward L. Ayers and John C. Willis, eds., *The Edge of the South: Life in Nineteenth-Century Virginia* (Charlottesville, 1991), pp. 78-108.

[8] Henry M. Price to Secretary of War, September 24, 1861, Letter 5882-1861, LSOW.

[9] Richard W. Habersham to family, February 9, 1862, Habersham Family Papers, LC.

place he is a little indolent, and then he is not very capable: so far as the stand which the company may take under his command, I can not say: Bell has some influence on account of his means: he is tolerably wealthy: this you know will have its influence. I would greatly prefer a man of more intellectual standing for Captain."[10]

Rivalry among officers fomented discontent among common soldiers as Capt. William Harrison discovered in the 23rd Virginia Infantry Regiment. Harrison told his brother that his lieutenant had been "trying to make the impression that they could n[o]t have strict discipline with volunteers & that I was trying to be a king over them which was very well calculated to create dissatisfaction."[11] Harrison was able to quell the turmoil within his company, but he admitted that "I have had a good [deal] of trouble with some of the boys trying to have there [sic] way but they have given it up but I reckon they will give me fits when they write home but I have told them that I had to obey orders & I was carrying out orders of my superior officers & I had to obey & they should obey."[12]

Other officers simply disliked the men they were called upon to command. Major Richard A. Maury was stationed at Union Mills along Bull Run with his regiment, the 24th Virginia Infantry, in the fall of 1861. He relayed his impression of the regiment to his father:

> Cast down here in the midst of a set of illiterate ill-bred whiskey drinking card-playing men with nothing in the world in common between us, no sympathies the same no similarities in taste or disposition, in habits or breeding I live the life of a perfect hermit. . . .The men of whom the 24th is composed are about the same material of which armies are generally composed they are all of the lower classes of society— some—many, from the very lowest and as officers are elected from the ranks they are very little better. I do not believe there is a man in the whole Regiment from the Chaplain

---

[10] Francis Marion Parker to wife, June 26, 1861, Francis Marion Parker Papers, North Carolina State Archives, Raleigh, NC. Hereinafter cited as NCSA.

[11] William F. Harrison to brother, July 26, 1861, William F. Harrison Papers, Duke University, Durham, NC. Hereinafter cited as Harrison Papers.

[12] William F. Harrison to wife, July 4, 1861, Harrison Papers.

down who does not drink Whiskey and play cards—gambling and drinking is the order not only of the day but of the night.[13]

A great many of the enlisted men throughout the army were unhappy as well, and their disgruntlement hindered the development of unit *esprit de corps*. Private John S. Anglin of the 4th North Carolina Infantry Regiment resented his treatment in camp near Richmond in mid-1862. "We have to answer five roll-calls a day, but if our High Officers had to do it there wouldn't be just as much unnecessary duties for the Private to perform. I tell you men in this war (in low rank) as a general thing, are imposed on, treated like negroes, only not as good."[14]

Private Price of the 44th Virginia echoed many of the same complaints in his letter to the secretary of war in the fall of 1861. Price resented "the arbitrary manner in which the officers from General down deal with men—their equals, frequently superior in social position—deal with all by rule & law." Price was particularly incensed that "Officers cursing & swearing at men while we are punished for the like."[15]

The men of the ranks became especially unhappy when it seemed to them that officers received furloughs while enlisted men remained in camp. William King protested that his commander, Capt. H. Grey Latham "seems almost to have deserted this Company—He has not been here more than 20 hours for the last six days—No one can well imagine the loss accruing to the public interest by the management of this Company."[16] Private Anglin of the 4th North Carolina Infantry Regiment complained that two of his officers were at home and "I tell you their presence is needed very much. A good many of the company have fallen out with the Capt. for nothing. They are mad," Anglin explained, "be-

[13] Richard L. Maury to father, November 10, 1861, Matthew F. Maury Papers, LC.

[14] John S. Anglin to family, July 14, 1862, Miscellaneous Manuscripts Collection, LC. Hereinafter cited as MMC, LC.

[15] Price to Secretary of War, September 24, 1861, Letter 5882-1861, LSOW. For other examples of officer indiscipline, see Orders and Circulars Issued by the Army of the Potomac and the Army and Department of Northern Virginia, C.S.A., 1861-1865, M921, RG 109, NA.

[16] William King to "My Dear Little Nannie," January 30, 1862, King Family Collection, University of Virginia, Charlottesville, NC.

cause he is at home sick on furlough but I dont see how they can be when sick people fare so badly here." He went on to say that "I am going to write to Capt Simonton and if he is willing I intend to join another Company or Regt. if I can be transferred if things dont get better very soon."[17]

Private John A. Garnett of the 44th Virginia told his uncle in January 1862 that "we have sevean out of our Company that have gone home without Ferlows and it is thought they will [be] dealt with very swiley [severely] when they return, but what more could be expected when Capt Marshall set the examples left here about 10th of Oct, and have not bin seen since & drawing Capt wages and Wm Gilliam doing Capt business and drawing Lieutenant wages. . .he has bin of but little service to the Southern Confederacy."[18]

During the Romney campaign, Captain Harrison of the 23rd Virginia also noted the high rate of absenteeism among officers, writing to his wife that "we have only two Captains in our Regt. for duty which makes my duty very hard nearly all of our officers left us on this expedition & returned to Winchester which is a disgrace to the Southern Army." Harrison asked, "if officers fail to do their duty what must be expected of privates[?]"[19]

At the end of 1861, General Joseph E. Johnston reported an aggregate present and absent strength of slightly over 98,000 officers and men in the Department of Northern Virginia. This vast region included troops in three districts: the Potomac, Aquia, and Valley districts.[20]

Additional troops were also stationed on the Virginia Peninsula and at Norfolk as well as in northwestern Virginia.[21] Almost all of these

[17] John S. Anglin to family, November 27, 1861, MMC, LC.

[18] John A. Garnett to William Gray, January 19, 1862, William Gray Papers, Virginia Historical Society, Richmond, VA. Hereinafter cited as VHS.

[19] William F. Harrison to wife, January 31, 1862, Harrison Papers.

[20] *OR* 5, p. 1015; the order establishing the department and assigning commanders is found in *OR* 5, pp. 913-914.

[21] For the strengths and locations of other commands in Virginia at the end of 1861, see *OR* IV, 1, p. 822.

troops and their commanders were dissatisfied with their assignments. War Department clerks spent huge amounts of time responding to requests from commanders and soldiers for transfers.[22]

Some of this discontent actually influenced the conduct of military operations and command and control. Colonel William B. Taliaferro of the Army of Northwestern Virginia and 10 regimental and battalion commanders protested to Brig. Gen. W. W. Loring about the conditions their troops faced during the Romney campaign in January 1862. The officers reminded the army's commander that "all must be profoundly impressed with the paramount importance of raising an army for the next summer's campaign" and that the reenlistment of units depended on "if they are yet removed to a position where their spirits could be revived." Loring concurred with the sentiment of his subordinate officers. He commented that "I am most anxious to re-enlist this fine army, equal to any I ever saw, and am satisfied if something is not done to relieve it, it will be found impossible to induce the army to do so, but with some regard for its comfort, a large portion, if not the whole, may be prevailed upon."[23]

At the regimental level, Capt. James S. Greever of the 48th Virginia Infantry Regiment noted at Romney that "volunteering seems to be progressing very slowly. There have been but few reenlistments in this regiment." Greever added, "it seems that the men want to serve out this term before reenlisting and moreover at the expiration of their twelve months to go home and stay a little while."[24]

Congress passed the "Act providing for the granting of bounty and furloughs to privates and non-commissioned officers in the Provisional Army" on December 11, which increased the concern of many officers and soldiers throughout the army. Published as General Orders Number

[22] As an example, see Colonel William C. Scott to assistant secretary of war, November 14, 1861, Letter 7621-1861, LSOW.

[23] *OR* 5, pp. 1046-1047. For a full discussion of the Romney crisis, see Robert G. Tanner, *Stonewall in the Valley: Thomas J. "Stonewall" Jackson's Shenandoah Valley Campaign, Spring 1862* (New York, 1976), pp. 82-88. This letter created a crisis in Confederate chain of command as General Thomas J. Jackson asked to be relieved and reassigned to the Virginia Military Institute because of "such interference in my command." Jackson threatened to resign his commission if he did not receive his reassignment, *OR* 5, p. 1053.

[24] James S. Greever to father, January 31, 1862, Greever Family Papers in private collection of T. C. Greever.

One by the Adjutant and Inspector General's Office on New Year's Day 1862, the Bounty and Furlough Act became the basis for the reorganization of the Confederate army.

The act authorized a bounty of $50 to be paid to all one year volunteers (except officers) from all states in Confederate service who reenlisted for an additional two years. The act also granted bounties to soldiers who had already enlisted for three years service and to new, long-term recruits. Likewise, Congress permitted the army to furlough newly-reenlisted soldiers "at such times and in such numbers as the Secretary of War may deem most compatible with the public interests." The actual duration of the furloughs (a minimum of 30 days and a maximum of 60) depended on the residences of the soldiers while commutation money could be used to pay for soldiers unable to take their furloughs due to the exigencies of the service.

The most critical element of the Bounty and Furlough Act appeared in Section 4, which stated that "all troops revolunteering or re-enlisting shall, at the expiration of their present term of service, have the power to reorganize themselves into companies and elect their company officers, and said companies shall have the power to organize themselves into battalions or regiments and elect their field officers." The Confederate adjutant general provided further guidance that promulgated the administration of the new act in the army.[25]

The December 14 edition of the Richmond *Enquirer* hailed the Bounty and Furlough Act as a wise law that demonstrated the government's trust in Southern volunteerism.[26]

Five days later, another Richmond paper, the *Dispatch*, claimed that an entire Mississippi regiment had reenlisted under the new law.[27]

This enthusiasm for the new act appeared premature. The law did not receive the same reception from the army's high-ranking commanders. General Johnston wrote the secretary of war on January 18 to say that he had not officially received a copy of General Orders Number One

---

[25] *OR* 5, pp. 1016-1017; and *OR* IV, 1, pp. 825-827.

[26] Richmond *Enquirer* (semi-weekly), December 14, 1861.

[27] Richmond *Dispatch,* December 19, 1861.

at his headquarters in Centreville. He had, however, read Gen. Pierre G. T. Beauregard's copy and found it impractical to grant furloughs "within the time specified in such numbers as will induce any considerable re-enlistments among the twelve-months' regiments in this command." Johnston requested guidance from Secretary Benjamin in implementing the new law.[28]

Benjamin responded a week later and admitted that he "could not undertake to determine when and in what numbers the furloughs could be safely granted." He did, however, urge Johnston to take advantage of the poor weather and furlough as many troops as possible. "All I can say," Benjamin commented, "beyond what is contained in the general order is to advise, very urgently, that you go to the extreme verge of prudence in tempting your twelve-months' men by liberal furloughs, and thus secure for yourself a fine body of men for the spring operations."

The secretary of war promised to send raw recruits to northern Virginia to take the place of those men on furlough. Beyond that, Benjamin confided that "the Department can only trust to the skill and prudence of our generals and the indomitable spirit of our people to maintain a struggle in which the disparity of numbers, already fearful, becomes still more threatening from the impossibility of adding to our stock of arms."[29]

These words did not comfort General Johnston and he immediately replied on February 1 by protesting the government's furlough policy. Johnston was particularly disturbed by the War Department's interference with items that normally fell under an army commander's responsibilities, such as furloughs, discharges, and resignations. At the same time, Confederate authorities in Richmond authorized the transfer of infantry companies to the artillery branch without Johnston's knowledge or consent. The general complained that "the discipline of the army cannot be maintained under such circumstances." He considered that his soldiers "disposition is not very good," although Johnston promised to "do what I can to stimulate it into activity. Care must be taken," the wary

---

[28] *OR* 5, pp. 1036-1037.

[29] Ibid., pp. 1045-1046.

general mentioned, "not to reduce our force so much as to make its very weakness the inducement to the enemy's attack."[30]

To this effect, General Johnston issued a proclamation to the troops of the Department of Northern Virginia on February 4. He appealed to the soldiers' "indomitable courage already exhibited on the battle-field" to rally again to face the Federal horde "who has gathered up all his energies for a final conflict." He asked his men "to revolunteer at once, and thus show to the world that the patriots engaged in this struggle for independence will not swerve from the bloodiest path they may be called to tread."[31]

The situation was indeed serious as Johnston attempted to persuade his troops to extend their enlistment in the Confederate army. The paymaster for Virginia troops, for example, reported to the state's legislative branch in January that the one year term of service for some 527 Virginia artillery, cavalry, and infantry companies would expire by mid-1862. This meant that nearly 40,000 officers and enlisted men were eligible for discharge between April and July; virtually all of these troops served in the commonwealth and their loss threatened the ability of the Confederate army to defend Richmond. All of the state forces in Confederate service in Virginia faced the same predicament.[32]

This stark reality prompted the Confederate government and individual states to take further steps to preserve the army. On January 6 and 27, the war department published orders providing for a recruiting service to spur enlistments.[33]

Secretary of War Benjamin wrote to the governors of the 11 Confederate states on February 14 asking them to assist these recruiting parties in finding volunteers.[34]

---

[30] Ibid., pp. 1057-1058.

[31] Ibid., pp. 1060-1061.

[32] *OR* IV, 1, pp. 859-863.

[33] Ibid., pp. 833-834 and 925-926.

[34] Ibid., pp. 930-931.

As a sign of increasing desperation, Congress allowed the president on January 23 to call upon the several states for additional three years volunteers.[35]

The actual call by the government to the 11 Confederate states and Missouri for additional troops came on February 2. Richmond based its quota at 6 percent of the total white male population for each state as compared to the number of men from that state already in military service. The difference between the two figures would be the number of required soldiers. In the case of Virginia, the state needed to raise an additional 64,000 soldiers and 47 new regiments within a matter of weeks. The War Department promised to feed, clothe, and pay for all expenses of these new troops as well as to provide each soldier with a $50 bounty upon mustering into Confederate service.[36]

The central government received support from the states in the drive to strengthen the army in Virginia. John Letcher, the Old Dominion's governor, asked the legislature on February 11 to organize Virginia's manpower into two militia classes that could be pressed into military service in the event of emergency.[37]

Eventually, Letcher mobilized the Virginia militia to fill up shortages in the existing state volunteer units.[38] Governor Joseph E. Brown meanwhile issued a direct proclamation for volunteers "to sustain the high character won for Georgia by the valor of her troops in every contest where they have met their country's foe." Brown, at the same time, promised to draft men if insufficient numbers of volunteers stepped forward to fill the state's depleted ranks.[39] The governor of North Carolina employed similar tactics.[40]

While the governors wrestled with the problems of raising new troops, the 12-month volunteers showed little interest in reenlisting.

---

[35] Ibid., p. 869.

[36] Ibid., pp. 902-903 and 907.

[37] Ibid., pp. 923-925.

[38] *OR* 11, pt. 3, p. 683 and IV, 1, pp. 1009-1012.

[39] Ibid., pp. 918-921.

[40] Ibid., pp. 921-922.

James W. Old, a member of the 11th Virginia Infantry Regiment, told his folks from Centreville that "there was a auder red out at one time that wee could get furloughs 8 at a time ou[t] of a company[;] there was 8 of us got theres[,] one out of every letter[,] but they did not get off before the order was counter manded[;] no furloughs unless wee are sick or unless we enlist for the war[.] [S]o there is no chance for ous to get home," Old exclaimed, "and I dont care to reinlist untill I rest a while[.]"[41]

Even Captain Harrison of the 23rd Virginia expressed resentment at having to serve longer than a year. While at Winchester in mid-December, Harrison read about the Bounty and Furlough Act and told his wife, "I think a good many of my men will accede to the proposition & I would like for them all to do it as I then could come home." Harrison mentioned that he has "as much patriotism as ever but I told Col Taliaferro I could not & would not give up my family for country that it is unreasonable & uncalled for as I had discharged my duties faithfully & had never been sick or absent an hour since I came in the service."[42]

The possibility of transferring to another branch of service acted as the greatest single inducement to reenlistment in 1862. Marshall P. Frantz, a member of the 42nd Virginia Infantry Regiment, wrote his mother in April that "there is a good deal of anxiety among the boys to know whether they will be made to go in the same service that they are now in." Frantz believed that his comrades "are willing to reenlist— almost to a man, if they are allowed to go in any branch of service they choose." As for his plans, the Virginia soldier said, "I haven't reenlisted yet and don't know that I shall without they allow me to go in cavalry or Artillery."[43]

The first months of 1862 saw frenetic activity in camps throughout Virginia as officers tried to raise new outfits, especially artillery and cavalry commands. A member of the 44th Virginia, Private William E.

[41] Murray L. Brown, "The Civil War Letters of James W. Old," *Manuscripts,* vol. 42 (1990), p. 132.

[42] William F. Harrison to wife, December 14, 1861, Harrison Papers.

[43] Marshall P. Frantz to mother, April 13, 1862, Frantz Family Papers in private collection of Luther Mauney.

Isbell of Appomattox County, told his father in March that "I am very well satisfied that I am in for two years more for nearly all of our company have agreed to reenlist provided our Capt can get heavy artillery & we do not doubt his success."[44]

An officer in the same regiment even went so far as to write the secretary of war with the news that "very few will re-enlist if they are compelled to remain in the same company & Reg't., but all will if allowed to join wherever they wish."[45]

Section 4 quickly became the least desirable element of the Bounty and Furlough Act. Colonel John M. Brockenbrough of the 40th Virginia Infantry Regiment protested to Maj. Gen. Theophilus H. Holmes in March that the Confederate act and laws later enacted by the Virginia assembly weakened the army. Brockenbrough explained that he saw the "Virginia Legislature giving to men the privilege of raising new companies, and the Secretary of War, following its example, gives to men the authority of organizing new battalions, squadrons, and companies by recruiting even from the old organizations." The regimental commander went on to blast the men who spent their time raising these new units. "We find worthless, intriguing, politicians, and those who have been defeated in company elections, taking advantage of all these conflicting bills and unsatisfactory constructions, writing to and visiting our camps for the purpose of disorganizing, by inducing men to leave their old organizations and unite with them in forming new ones, using bribery, a great deal of flash plausibility, and arguments which any worthless demagogue is capable of making." Colonel Brockenbrough begged his commander "to put an end to this state of affairs."[46]

Another infantry regimental commander bitterly opposed the transfer of one of his companies to the artillery in a letter to his commander. The transfer, Lt. Col. James L. Hubard of the 44th Virginia wrote in March "has had a most unhappy effect upon this regiment. . . This act of

[44] William E. Isbell to father, March 10, 1862, Lewis Leigh Collection, U.S. Army Military History Institute, Carlisle, PA. Hereinafter cited as USAMHI.

[45] C. A. James to Secretary of War, March 15, 1862, Letter 58-J-1862, LSOW.

[46] *OR* 12, pt. 3, pp. 832-833; General Johnston protested against the same problems in a letter to President Davis on March 1, see *OR* 5, pp. 1086-1087, and the president's reply, *OR* 5, p. 1089.

the Sec of War is taking away one of the best companies in the whole service from my command, without supplying in its place [and] has given the regiment a shock that it will never get over. Unless something is done to stop this state of things and prevent companies, and individuals from leaving this command and entering other corps," Hubard warned, "the regiment will be ruined."[47]

There were mixed opinions about the value of using the militia to supplement the strength of the regular state units.[48] Private Frantz of the 42nd Virginia expressed his concerns about the governor's move. "Have all the militia gone sure enough? I was in hopes they were only called out to get Volunteers for the war. For if the men are called who is to make bread for the Army, what are we to do?"[49]

Jedediah Hotchkiss had served as a Virginia militiaman until he received an appointment on Thomas J. "Stonewall" Jackson's staff. On March 30, Hotchkiss told his wife that the governor's order drafting the militia into the volunteer units so as to bring all regular companies up to strength had arrived at Jackson's headquarters in the Shenandoah Valley. "Now there is much uproar among the militia," Hotchkiss observed, "this will throw all the officers into the ranks as privates—I am sorry for some of them for they are good men, but it will be a fine thing for some of them for they will thus learn what the duties of a soldier are." Hotchkiss added, "I am glad that I have made my escape from the militia."[50]

The idea of using militia draftees in the army displeased Private Isbell of the 44th Virginia, who told his father that "I can not reenlist unconditionally, for I know very few if any of our company will, besides if I rightly understand the law on the subject if only one man reenlist in a company enough men will be drafted to fill the company & he com-

---

[47] Letter located in file of James E. Robertson, Complied Service Records of Confederate Soldiers Who Served in Organizations from the State of Virginia, 20th Virginia Heavy Artillery Battalion, M324, RG 109, NA.

[48] *OR* IV, 1, pp. 1011-1012.

[49] Marshall P. Frantz to mother, April 13, 1862, Frantz Family Papers, Mauney Private Collection.

[50] Jedediah Hotchkiss to wife, March 30, 1862, Jedediah Hotchkiss Papers, LC; this same quotation is found in Jedediah Hotchkiss, *Make Me a Map of the Valley: The Civil War Journal of Stonewall Jackson's Topographer*, edited by Archie P. McDonald (Dallas, 1973), pp. 13-14.

pelled to remain in it, and the officers be appointed over them." Referring to the Virginia law which called for the drafting of militiamen to fill up the volunteer companies, Isbell complained that "he might as well be in a militia company & moreover men of the lowest character may be associated with him. Now I can not consent to this."[51]

Some soldiers, however, expressed satisfaction with Virginia's system of filling up the vacant ranks. Lieutenant Robert H. Miller of the 14th Louisiana Infantry Regiment, stationed near Yorktown, informed his mother that Louisiana "should pass a military bill similar to that of Virginia." Miller passed up the opportunity to go to Louisiana to recruit because he "found what a poor business it was I preferred not to go upon an errand which I considered entirely useless."[52]

Indeed, the reenlistment of the 12-months volunteers and the recruitment of new soldiers had mixed results. The adjutant general of Virginia reported in mid-March that some 13,000 men were still needed to bring companies up to the required strength of 100 soldiers. William H. Richardson stated that the militia act spurred enlistments so that "there is a fair prospect of the deficiency being filled up without a draft, or by a comparatively small one." At the same time, the mustering of the militia had proven less than satisfactory because many of the returns were "confused and imperfect."[53]

The state's acting assistant general was unable to provide a full report of the number of reenlisted Virginia troops by the end of March because returns were still "very meager."[54] Meanwhile, other states, such as South Carolina, also called up militiamen to fill its volunteer forces.[55] In late March, the Confederate army began to take steps to administer the exodus of men who refused to reenlist.

The War Department issued orders governing the payment of discharged troops and preparation of final muster rolls for those units that

---

[51] William E. Isbell to father, March 10, 1862, Leigh Collection, USAMHI.

[52] Forrest P. Connor, ed., "Letters of Lieutenant Robert H. Miller to his Family, 1861-1862," *Virginia Magazine of History and Biography* 70 (1962), pp. 70-71.

[53] *OR* IV, 1, pp. 1009-1010.

[54] Ibid., p. 1029.

[55] Ibid., pp. 973-976.

failed to reenlist.[56] The army also ordered commanders of discharged soldiers to retain for future government use all weapons turned in by the men.[57] By all indications, Confederate leaders expected to witness the dissolution of the Confederate army. This, of course, meant the early demise of the Confederacy and its bid for independence.

The Confederate Congress prevented the disbandment of the army with the passage of the "Act to Further Provide for the Public Defense," otherwise known as the First Conscription Act. In a message to all Southern governors and major commanders on April 15, the new Confederate secretary of war, George W. Randolph, stated the law's basic requirements. The act mandated military service for all white male residents of the Confederacy between the ages of 18 and 35, unless legally exempted. The law obligated the 12-month volunteers to remain in the service for an additional two years after the completion of their initial one year enlistment. Similarly, bounties and furloughs remained in effect for these soldiers although the act sharply curtailed the reenlistments of soldiers for other commands or branches. The Conscription Act retained the principle of unit elections and required all volunteer companies to hold unit elections within 40 days after the passage of the new law.[58]

The soldiers hotly debated the government's right to keep them in the army against their will although they reluctantly accepted the idea of serving another two years. Private John L. Holt of the 56th Virginia Infantry Regiment summed up the general attitude regarding the new law:

> I did not like [lack] but 2 years of getting off under the conscript act as I will be 33 the last day of this month But I do hope & trust that this unholy & unjust war waged upon us by Northern Vandals may soon be brought to a speedy termination. . . .I feel that we are fighting for all that is worth living for & this braces me up to bear the hardships of camp life[59]

[56] Ibid., p. 1046.

[57] Ibid., p. 1050.

[58] *OR* IV, 1, pp. 1061-1062 and 1095-1100. A full discussion of conscription can be found in Albert B. Moore, *Conscription and Conflict in the Confederacy* (New York, 1963), pp. 12-26.

[59] James M. Mumper, ed., *I Wrote You the Word: The Poignant Letters of Private Holt* (Lynchburg, 1991), p. 79. For an example of one junior officer's viewpoints concerning

Conscription had little immediate impact beyond keeping the 12-month volunteers in the army for another two years. The discharge of the overage and underage soldiers took time as did the receipt of new conscripts. The Conscription Act also contributed to further divisiveness in the army in Virginia; an effect that Congress had certainly not foreseen. The new law required only white men "who are residents of the Confederate states" to serve in the army. Soldiers from Kentucky and Maryland, as well as European immigrants, interpreted this clause to mean that they could still leave the service at the expiration of their one-year enlistments.

The army's interpretation of the act was also ambiguous and it devastated several companies from the District of Columbia and Maryland in the spring of 1862.[60] The 1st Kentucky Infantry Regiment had to be withdrawn from its positions near Yorktown and transferred to the west to keep the unit in Confederate service.[61]

The problems of the border state units proved to be an exception. Conscription kept the army together as Federal pressure increased throughout Virginia, on the Peninsula near Yorktown, at Fredericksburg, and in the Shenandoah Valley. The final dramatic scene of the Bounty and Furlough Act and the Conscription Act took place during the months of April and May as the soldiers reenlisted and elected new officers. A member of the 3rd Alabama Infantry Regiment, on duty near Norfolk in late March, described the reenlistment activities in his unit. The regimental commander, Col. Tennent Lomax, held a square formation in which he stood in the center and addressed his men. "For God Almighty's sake, men," Lomax thundered, "don't you know that by fighting the enemy in Virginia you prevent the possibility of the occurrence of such fiendish

---

conscription, see John T. Conrad to wife, April 17 and 24, 1862, John T. Conrad Papers, NCSA.

[60] For descriptions of these companies, see Lee A. Wallace, Jr., *A Guide to Virginia Military Organizations 1861-1865*, rev. 2nd ed. (Lynchburg, 1986), pp. 2, 83 and 91. For an analysis of the impact of the First Conscription Act on the 1st Maryland Infantry Regiment (C.S.), see Kevin C. Ruffner, *Border State Warriors: Maryland's Junior Officer Corps in the Union and Confederate Armies* (Ph.D. dissertation, The George Washington University, 1991), pp. 156-204.

[61] Edward P. Alexander, "Sketch of Longstreet's Division—Yorktown and Williamsburg," *Southern Historical Society Papers*, vol. 10 (1882), pp. 36-37.

scenes [committed by the enemy] in your own loved State." Lomax concluded his dramatic appeal by saying, "Boys, I don't pretend to be a saint but by-the-Gods, I *am* a patriot."

William A. Heirs, who recorded the colonel's speech, commented that "it is impossible for you to gain a single idea of the effect his remarks produced." The regiment soon replenished its ranks from soldiers inspired by their 41-year-old commanding officer. Two months later, Colonel Lomax was killed during the fighting at Seven Pines.[62]

The actions taken by commanders were not always so inspirational. Company H of the 3rd Virginia Infantry Regiment faced McClellan's Union troops near Lee's Mill on the Warwick River in mid-April. Many of the members of the company expressed dissatisfaction with the regiment because they disliked their commander, Col. Roger Atkinson Pryor. The men of Company H agreed to reenlist on the condition that they could transfer to other regiments. Pryor, a former U.S. congressman, mustered the company on April 20 and asked the men if they wanted to go home. One soldier replied that they only wanted to go to other units and were not seeking to avoid battle. This infuriated Pryor, who ordered the company to decide whether it would take orders from him or the regiment's major. When virtually every member of company opted to go into battle with Maj. Joseph V. Scott, Pryor disarmed the "mutineers" and marched them to Yorktown. A company of North Carolinians guarded the Virginians as Pryor put the men to work constructing earthworks. Within a matter of days, Pryor realized that he had made a mistake and he restored Company H to duty. The company, however, remembered the incident and declined to reelect its company officers.[63]

---

[62] "A Colonel Re-enlists his Regiment," *Civil War Times Illustrated*, vol. 19 (June 1980), pp. 20-21.

[63] Allan C. Hanrahan, "The Portsmouth National Grays: From 'Mutiny' to Glory," *Virginia Cavalcade*, vol. 24 (1974), pp. 88-95; and Lee A. Wallace, Jr., *3rd Virginia Infantry* (Lynchburg, 1986), pp. 22-23.

Most unit reenlistments proceeded without controversy. The elections of officers and non-commissioned officers, however, aroused passionate sentiment among the soldiers.[64] John T. Conrad of the 28th North Carolina Infantry told his wife about his company's elections:

> Last Saturday evening the Col. ordered our company to reorganize notwithstanding all of the company was not here. I found under the circumstances that there was no chance for me to be elected Capt. and so I never offered for that position but concluded it would be better for me to run for first Lt. to which position I was elected unanimously the Hon. J.C. Kelly only receiving 7 votes. I know you will not like it darling that I have condescended to accept a position under such a pusillanimous scoundrel.[65]

Richard W. Habersham of the Hampton Legion described the situation in his unit at Camp Peninsula near Yorktown in late April. "Our Company was re-organized yesterday. . . .the Captain I am not at all satisfied with. He had no opposition and [I] should have voted against him. Capt. M. [Habersham's former company commander] I have not heard from in some time and dont know where he is the last accounts I have of him he was in Richmond 'quite well.'" The soldier went on to explain that he did not vote for his former captain, "because I did not know that he deserved it, and voting would have been a mere farce."[66]

Five members of the 44th Virginia were so incensed at the election results in their company that they requested a transfer to Capt. Thomas D. Jeffress' Company G of the 56th Virginia Infantry Regiment. In their petition to the secretary of war, the privates detailed their reasons:

---

[64] For examples of results of various unit elections, see Richmond *Daily Enquirer,* May 3, 1862; a certification of election of William N. Ward, Jr. in the 47th Virginia Infantry Regiment is found in Ward Family Papers, LC; the returns of the 23rd North Carolina Infantry Regiment are located in the Jubal A. Early Papers, VHS.

[65] John H. Kenyon was elected captain of the company and is the "scoundrel" to whom Conrad refers. John T. Conrad to wife, April 14, 1862, Conrad Papers, NCSA.

[66] Richard W. Habersham to family, April 26, 1862, Habersham Papers, LC.

1st. That this company is composed of Rowdies, Drunkards, Thieves, Murderers, blackguards and every other kind of persons the world ever knew.

2nd. That in the elections which took place . . . some of the men who were elected were nothing but a set of whiskey sellers in camp and by this means got offices which they were totally unfit to fill. A few honorable exceptions with some who were elected.

3rd. That in Capt. Jeffress' company we have many friends & acquaintances with whom we wish to be during the war.

4th. That when the Company to which we now belong was made up we were acquainted with but few of them & in hopes we could remain with them 12 months. We have nearly done it & found them to prove worse than was ever anticipated by any person . . . for our reputation . . . grant [us] the much desired transfer.[67]

Unit elections throughout the army produced an almost entirely new officer corps; a corps untested on the battlefield and uncertain of its legitimacy. Disputes festered in many units even as the army fought for the capital's survival,[68] but the crucial fact is that Confederate government narrowly avoided a calamitous situation by passing the December 1861 Bounty and Furlough Act and the April 1862 Conscription Act. These acts preserved the Confederate army in Virginia at a critical juncture in the spring of 1862, saving the Confederacy from early defeat.[69]

Yet, the cost was great in terms of soldier morale and in the heavy casualties that the army suffered in the fighting around Richmond. The South lost over 20,000 men during the Seven Days Battles—outnumber-

[67] Soldiers to secretary of war, May 1, 1862, Letter 358-H-1862, LSOW.

[68] An example of the disputes that these elections created can be found in Brig. Gen. William Mahone's report about the field grade elections in the 16th Virginia Infantry Regiment, see Mahone to the adjutant general, June 21, 1862, Letter 1163-M-1862, Letters Received by the Confederate Adjutant and Inspector General, 1861-1865, M474, RG 109, NA.

[69] *OR* IV, 2, pp. 280-281.

ing total Union losses by nearly 5,000. An additional 7,000 Southerners became casualties at Williamsburg and Seven Pines. Historians have blamed the Confederate high command for the these losses, noting Gen. Robert E. Lee's willingness to attack and poor coordination among the different commanders on the field.[70]

But high losses can also be attributed to disaffection in the ranks and the inexperience on the battlefield of many lower-ranking officers. In a letter to Lee in early May—just as the campaign was about to open— General Johnston observed that his army was still "partially discontented at the conscription act and demoralized by their recent elections."[71]

The rawness of the officers was especially significant. The reorganization of the army in April and May created a new hierarchy of company and regimental commanders to face a well-trained and disciplined enemy. These officers were ill-prepared for the army's first rigorous campaign—a tragic fact reflected in the high Confederate toll on fields from Fort Magruder to Malvern Hill.

The Confederate army never again underwent such an extensive reorganization, partly because the government had learned a valuable, albeit costly, lesson in 1862. Appealing to Congress two years later to restrict unit elections, Brig. Gen. Henry A. Wise declared that "the reorganization, at the critical juncture of the spring of 1862, in its bad effects, was enough to account for many of our delays and disasters."[72]

---

[70] Lee's preference for the offensive is discussed in Grady McWhiney and Perry D. Jamieson, *Attack and Die: Civil War Military Tactics and the Southern Heritage* (University, AL, 1982).

[71] *OR* 11, pt. 3, pp. 502-503.

[72] Henry A. Wise to Confederate Congress, January 3, 1864, Jennings Wood Collection of Confederate Imprints, The George Washington University, Washington, D.C.

Edwin Cole Bearss

Ed Bearss received his M.A. degree in history from Indiana University and began his association with the National Park Service at Vicksburg, Mississippi, on September 28, 1955. While growing up on a Montana ranch, Bearss became fascinated with the Civil War after his father read him such works as John Thomason's *Jeb Stuart* and Lloyd Lewis' *Sherman: Fighting Prophet,* which prompted the captivated youngster to name the milk cows' calves after Civil War battles. Bearss, who is well-known as the nation's foremost Civil War battlefield tour guide, has written widely on the conflict. Among the score of books he has written is his monumental, three-volume work *The Vicksburg Campaign* (Morningside, 1985-1986). He is currently the chief historian of the National Park Service.

"... Into the very jaws of the enemy ... "

Jeb Stuart's Ride Around McClellan

PART 1
A DESPERATE VENTURE BEGINS

The afternoon of June 1, 1862, was an important hour in the history of our nation. On that date, Gen. Robert E. Lee assumed command of the dispirited and battered Confederate divisions that returned to the camps and staging areas whence they had confidently marched on the night of May 30. In the ensuing hours, they had fought on the eastern approaches to Richmond the battle of Seven Pines (Fair Oaks) against Maj. Gen. George B. McClellan's 100,000-man Army of the Potomac. The battle initially went well for the Confederates, despite delays and errors by senior generals. But the arrival of Union reinforcements and the wounding of Confederate commander Joseph E. Johnston at dusk on May 31 had checked the Southern advantage. Johnston's successor—Maj. Gen. Gustavus W. Smith—lost his nerve, and, when the Confederates botched an attack on the morning of June 1, he called off the battle, which had already cost the South more than 6,000 casualties. Smith withdrew, and the cautious McClellan did not accept the challenge to follow up his soldiers' success.

General Lee, in his first days as commander of what on June 1 he designated the Army of Northern Virginia, acted to restore morale and to assess the character of his senior officers and their troops. He also acted to ascertain the enemy's order of battle, strength and intentions. Lee's soldiers, with pick and shovel, threw up earthworks on the eastern approaches to Richmond, while Union pickets on the Williamsburg Road six miles from the Confederate capital listened to the city's church bells.

Lee established his headquarters close to the front at the Mary C. Dabbs House, on Nine Mile Road. Although he made daily reconnaissances of the Union lines, Lee encouraged his subordinates to express themselves about the strategic situation and listened intently to the advice of his junior officers at headquarters meetings. Throughout these days of adjustment to his new command, however, Lee kept his plans to himself.[1]

Among the subordinates who urged Lee to boldly seize the initiative was his chief of cavalry, Brig. Gen. James Ewell Brown Stuart, known throughout the army as Jeb. On June 4, Stuart penned a letter to Lee concerning the strategic situation. Introducing his subject, Stuart wrote: "The present imperilled condition of the Nation, I presume, will be sufficient apology for putting forth for your consideration, convictions derived from a close observation of the enemy's movements for months past, his system of war, and his conduct in Battle, as well as our own."

Stuart opined that General McClellan's Army of the Potomac would not resume its forward movement until it had fortified the area south of the Chickahominy. Consequently, "A pitched battle here [north of the Chickahominy] though a Victory, [would be] utterly fruitless to us." Stuart held that the proper course for Lee to follow was for him to mass his artillery and hold his left on the Chickahominy and attack south of that stream with the remainder of his army. Stuart continued:

> We have an army far better adapted to attack than defense. Let us fight at an advantage before we are forced to fight at disadvantage. It may seem presumption in me to give these views, but I have not thus far mistaken the policy and practice of the enemy. At any rate, I would rather incur the charge of presumption than fold my arms in silence and indifference to the momentous crisis at hand. Be assured, however, General, that whatever course you pursue you will find nowhere a more zealous and determined cooperator and supporter. . . .[2]

Lee did not seriously consider Stuart's plea to assail McClellan's hosts south of the Chickahominy. He fretted that if he adopted the action

---

[1] Douglas S. Freeman, *Lee's Lieutenants, A Study in Command*, 3 vols. (New York, 1942), vol. 1, p. 275; Burke Davis, *Jeb Stuart, The Last Cavalier* (New York, 1957), p. 109.

[2] Freeman, *Lee's Lieutenants*, 1, pp. 276-77; Davis, *Jeb Stuart*, p. 109.

Brig. Gen. James Ewell Brown Stuart

urged by Stuart—whom he first knew as a cadet when Lee was superintendent at the U.S. Military Academy and later got to know better in mid-October 1859 during John Brown's raid on Harpers Ferry—his army would be at a disadvantage. General Lee had a talent for knowing the enemy and had served with McClellan on Maj. Gen. Winfield Scott's staff during the Mexican-American War. All that he saw satisfied Lee that McClellan planned to capture Richmond and defeat the Confederates by first investing and then besieging the city. To counter a siege and bombardment, in which God would be on the side of the heaviest guns and battalions, Lee developed a counter-strategy. On June 5, the day after receipt of Stuart's proposal, Lee informed President Jefferson Davis:

> McClellan will make this a battle of Posts. He will take position from position, under cover of his heavy guns, and we cannot get at him without storming his works. . . .It will require 100,000 men to resist the regular siege of Richmond, which perhaps would only prolong not save it. I am preparing a line that I can hold with part of our forces in front, while with the rest I will endeavour to make a diversion to bring McClellan out.[3]

The diversion Lee contemplated was an all-out attack north of the Chickahominy. Part of the army would hold the earthworks north and south of the Williamsburg and Nine Mile Roads, while the rest crossed to the north bank of the Chickahominy near Mechanicsville and assailed McClellan's right flank corps. Such a maneuver would compromise McClellan's major supply line—the Richmond & York River Railroad, which extended northeast 14 miles from Savage's Station to White House Landing on the Pamunkey River. Such an offensive, Lee told President Davis, would compel McClellan to come out of his entrenchments and fight the Confederates on ground of their choosing, thus forestalling the projected siege.

[3] Douglas Southall Freeman, ed., *Lee's Dispatches: Unpublished Letters of General Robert E. Lee, C.S.A, to Jefferson Davis and the War Department of the Confederate States of America 1862-1865* (New York, 1957), pp. 5-7.

On June 10, Jeb Stuart received a summons to report to the Dabbs' house. This time, no grand strategy was discussed. Lee wanted to talk about a scheme he had been considering for the past several days. When he entered Lee's office, Stuart was introduced to an opportunity the likes of which he lusted for. Lee told Stuart of his plan to attack McClellan's army north of the Chickahominy. If the army were to take the offensive in this sector, Lee continued, he must first learn the whereabouts of the Union outposts. Specifically, Lee wanted to know the strength of McClellan's pickets patrolling the watershed separating the Chicka-hominy and Pamunkey rivers. Stuart's youthful enthusiasm boiled over as he listened. When Lee finished speaking, Stuart announced that "he could do more than ascertain the position of the Federal right; if the commanding General permitted, he would ride entirely around McClel-lan's army." Lee undoubtedly vetoed such a rash proposal.[4]

In a buoyant frame of mind, Stuart rejoined his command. Here was a choice mission for a 29-year-old who only 15 months before had been a captain in the 1st U.S. Cavalry. That evening, Stuart received addi-tional information from Lee concerning the Federals' dispositions. Ac-cording to the reports reaching army headquarters, the Union right was stronger than Lee had anticipated when he had spoken with Stuart ear-lier. If this were true, Stuart's forced reconnaissance could involve seri-ous fighting.[5]

* * *

Before noon on the next day, Wednesday, June 11, a staff officer galloped up on a lathered horse to Stuart's headquarters at Mrs. Morde-cai's. Reining up his mount, the courier handed Stuart instructions from Lee. Stuart was

> . . .to make a secret movement to the rear of the enemy, now
> posted on [the] Chickahominy, with a view of gaining intelli-

[4] Freeman, *Lee's Lieutenants*, 1, p. 277.

[5] Ibid., pp. 277-278.

gence of his operations, communications, etc., of driving in his foraging parties, and securing such grain, cattle, etc., for ourselves as you can make arrangements to have driven in. Another object is to destroy his wagon trains, said to be daily passing from the Piping Tree road to his camps on the Chickahominy.

The utmost vigilance on your part will be necessary to prevent any surprise to yourself, and the greatest caution must be practiced in keeping well in your front and flank reliable scouts to give you information.

Lee, recalling Stuart's words about riding around McClellan's army, cautioned:

You will return as soon as the object of your expedition is accomplished, and you must bear constantly in mind, while endeavoring to execute the general purpose of your mission, not to hazard unnecessarily your command or to attempt what your judgment may not approve; but be content to accomplish all the good you can without feeling it necessary to obtain all that might be desired.[6]

Lee recommended that Stuart "only take such men and horses as can stand the expedition, and that you take every means in your power to save and cherish those you do take." The cavalry leader was to leave behind sufficient cavalry to carry out the basic needs of the Army of Northern Virginia. Stuart was to "remember that one of the chief objects of his expedition was" to gain intelligence on which Lee could plan future operations.

Since, in Lee's opinion, success of the mission depended upon secrecy, he added a few words of caution for his aggressive cavalry chief. If Stuart discovered the Federals were moving toward his right or were

---

[6] U.S. War Department, *The War of the Rebellion: The Official Records of the Union and Confederate Armies*, 128 vols., (Washington D.C., 1890-1901), series I, vol. 11, pt. 3, pp. 590-591. Hereinafter cited as *OR*. All references are to series I unless otherwise noted.

so strongly posted as to render the "expedition inopportune," he was to return to his camps.[7]

Stuart turned to preparing his expedition. His staff drafted orders alerting the 1st and 9th Virginia Cavalry Regiments to get ready to take the field. Six companies of the 4th Virginia Cavalry and two squadrons of the Jeff Davis Legion also received marching orders. General Lee's nephew, 26-year-old Col. Fitzhugh Lee, a West Pointer, would lead the 1st Virginia, along with the four companies from the 4th Virginia. Col. Williams C. Wickham of the 4th Virginia was on sick leave, recuperating from the wound received on May 5 at the battle of Williamsburg. Col. William H. F. "Rooney" Lee, the general's 25-year-old second son, headed the 9th Virginia Cavalry. Two companies of the 4th Virginia were temporarily assigned to Rooney Lee's command. Lt. Col. William T. Martin, a 39-year-old Mississippi lawyer and planter, was to select 250 of the best men belonging to the Jeff Davis Legion. A section (two guns) from the Stuart Horse Artillery commanded by Lt. James Breathed would go along. In selecting his guns, Breathed chose a rifled 12-pounder Blakely and a 12-pounder howitzer. Stuart's striking force mustered about 1,200 officers and men.[8]

Tensions continued to build, especially when orders came for the men to prepare three days' cooked rations. Stuart's staff directed ordnance officers to issue to each man 60 rounds of ammunition. Lt. William T. Robins, Rooney Lee's adjutant, recalled that when these orders were given, there were many "surmises and conjectures as to our destination." Even so, Stuart kept his own counsel. Not even the staff officers knew the expedition's mission.[9]

---

[7] Ibid. Mrs. Mordecai's was three miles northwest of Richmond, and midway between the tracks of the Richmond, Fredericksburg & Potomac Railroad, and the Brook Turnpike.

[8] *OR* 11, pt. 1, pp. 1036, 1042-1044; Freeman, *Lee's Lieutenants*, 1, p. 278-279. The Jeff Davis Legion was composed of six companies, two from Alabama, one from Georgia, and three from Mississippi. *OR* 5, p. 1030. The Boykin South Carolina Rangers had been temporarily attached to the Legion. *OR* 11, pt. 1, p. 1095. At this time, Stuart's Cavalry Brigade included: the 1st North Carolina; the 1st, 3d, 4th, 5th, 9th, and 10th Virginia; Cobb's Georgia Legion Cavalry Battalion; two squadrons of Hampton's South Carolina Legion; the Jeff Davis Legion; 15th Virginia Cavalry Battalion; and the Stuart Horse Artillery.

[9] William T. Robins, "Stuart's Ride Around McClellan," in Robert U. Johnson and Clarence C. Buel, eds., *Battles and Leaders of the Civil War*, 4 vols., (New York, 1956), vol. 2, p. 271.

At 2 a.m. on June 12, Stuart awakened his staff by announcing, "Gentlemen, in ten minutes every man must be in his saddle." Inside of half the allotted time, the officers had mounted their horses. John Esten Cooke vividly remembered the start of the "Ride Around McClellan":

> As. . .[Stuart] mounted his horse on that moonlight night he was a gallant figure to look at. The gray coat buttoned to the chin; the light French saber balanced by the pistol in its black holster; the cavalry boots above the knee, and the brown hat with its black plume floating above the bearded features, the brilliant eyes and the huge moustache, which curled with laughter at the slightest provocation—these made Stuart the perfect picture of a gay cavalier, and the spirited horse he rode seemed to feel that he carried one whose motto was to 'do or die.'[10]

Stuart and his staff had spent the night several miles from where his regiments were camped. By the time the general reached the camps near Mrs. Mordecai's and Kilby's Station on the Richmond, Fredericksburg & Potomac Railroad, the officers and men were astir. Quietly and without undue noise, the long column took up the march. Bugle calls were forbidden. Men left behind bewailed their misfortune, while the troopers chosen to accompany the expedition were elated at the prospect of some excitement. As the troopers of the 9th Virginia rode out of their encampment, Lieutenant Robins heard one of the men shout, "Good-bye, boys; we are going to help old Jack drive the Yanks into the Potomac."[11]

After departing their camps, the Confederate horsemen turned into the Brook Turnpike. Rumors passed up and down the column that the expedition was headed for Louisa Court House. If true, the cavalrymen knew they were bound for the Valley, where General Jackson had recently won a series of startling victories. To cloak his mission in secrecy,

[10] John E. Cooke, *The Wearing of the Gray, Being Personal Portraits, Scenes and Adventures of the War,* (Bloomington, 1959), p. 166.

[11] The trooper's reference was to Maj. Gen. Thomas J. Jackson, whose army was operating in the Shenandoah Valley. Freeman, *Lee's Lieutenants*, 1, p. 282; Robins, "Stuart's Ride," p. 271; Davis, *Jeb Stuart*, p. 111.

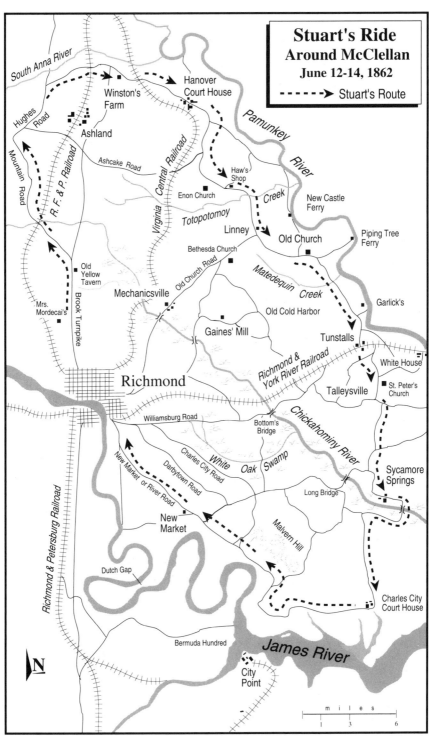

Stuart's Ride
Around McClellan
June 12-14, 1862

------➤ Stuart's Route

South Anna River

Winston's Farm

Hanover Court House

Hughes Road

Pamunkey River

Ashland

R. F. & P. Railroad

Mountain Road

Ashcake Road

Virginia Central Railroad

Haw's Shop

Enon Church

Creek

New Castle Ferry

Totopotomoy

Linney

Old Church

Piping Tree Ferry

Bethesda Church

Old Church Road

Old Yellow Tavern

Matedequin Creek

Brook Turnpike

Mrs. Mordecai's

Mechanicsville

Old Cold Harbor

Garlick's

Gaines' Mill

Tunstalls

Richmond

Richmond & York River Railroad

White House

Talleysville

St. Peter's Church

Williamsburg Road

Bottom's Bridge

Chickahominy River

Richmond & Petersburg Railroad

New Market or River Road

Charles City Road

Darbytown Road

White Oak Swamp

Long Bridge

Sycamore Springs

New Market

Malvern Hill

Dutch Gap

Charles City Court House

Bermuda Hundred

James River

N

City Point

miles

1   3   6

David A. Woodbury

Stuart purposely directed his march toward Louisa Court House. Some of the men, however, correctly guessed their objective.[12]

Most of the troopers in Stuart's column were familiar with the route. After passing Old Yellow Tavern, the head of the column turned into the Mountain Road and struck out in a northwesterly direction. Soon after they crossed the tracks of the Richmond, Fredericksburg & Potomac Railroad, the vanguard left the Mountain Road and took Hughes Road. Throughout the long, hot afternoon, the dusty horsemen continued their northward march toward the crossing of the South Anna River. To guard against a surprise encounter, Stuart covered his column with a strong advance guard, flankers, and a rear guard. Scouts rode east to see if they could ascertain the whereabouts of General McClellan's pickets. The area seemed devoid of the enemy. As the Confederate troopers pushed steadily ahead along deserted roads, they passed farms and houses, from which old men stared in admiration and women waved their handkerchiefs or aprons.[13]

Late in the afternoon, as the head of the column approached the South Anna River, Stuart turned east and crossed the Richmond, Fredericksburg & Potomac Railroad a second time. Shortly thereafter, the general called a halt. The troopers, having covered 22 miles since leaving the Richmond area, camped on the Winston farm, south of the South Anna River, near the post office of Taylorsville.[14]

Stuart ordered a "noiseless bivouac." There were no camp fires. The cavalrymen were warned to observe the strictest silence. After the troopers had bedded down, Stuart and Rooney Lee called on Colonel Wickham. Wounded and captured at Williamsburg, Colonel Wickham had been paroled by the Federals and had returned to his plantation, Hickory Hill, to await exchange. A five-mile ride brought the two officers to Hickory Hill. Rooney Lee visited with the Wickhams—who were his

---

[12] OR 11, pt. 1, p. 1036; Davis, *Jeb Stuart*, p. 112; Freeman, *Lee's Lieutenants*, 1, p. 282.

[13] Freeman, *Lee's Lieutenants*, 1, p. 282; Henry B. McClellan, *I Rode with Jeb Stuart, The Life and Campaigns of Major General Jeb Stuart* (Bloomington, 1958), pp. 53-54. OR 11, pt. 1, p. 1036.

[14] OR 11, pt. 1, p. 1036; Freeman, *Lee's Lieutenants*, 1, p. 282.

in-laws—until the wee hours. Stuart, after a few words with the injured colonel, slept in a chair.[15]

Rooney Lee aroused Stuart for a pre-dawn breakfast. The two officers then retraced their evening ride back to camp. As it had on the preceding morning, the command turned out "without flag or bugle-sound." Meantime, the scouts had returned, and told the general that the road to Old Church was unobstructed. To signal the start of the day's march, several rockets zoomed aloft, leaving trails of sparks. The head of the long column moved out, taking the road that led southeast to Hanover Court House. Colonel Will Martin's legionnaires and the gunners manning the 12-pounder howitzer brought up the rear.[16]

Stuart now made known his plans to his field officers. Already, many of the men had deduced their objective. Calling for his regimental commanders—the Lees and Will Martin—Stuart tersely explained the purpose of the expedition. The general wanted to ensure his chief subordinates' intelligent action and cooperation in whatever might occur. After listening to Stuart, the officers rejoined their commands.[17]

Pressing rapidly ahead, the Southern horsemen crossed the Virginia Central Railroad. The line of march led through a rolling sandy countryside. Among the pine forests were fields of corn, the stalks knee high. At 9 a.m. the vanguard sighted Hanover Court House, and John Esten Cooke recalled:

> We looked upon it [Hanover Court House] on that day of June—upon its old brick courthouse, where Patrick Henry made his famous speech against the parsons, its ancient tavern, its modest roofs, the whole surrounded by the fertile fields waving with golden grain. . .all this we looked at with universal interest.[18]

[15] Cooke, *Wearing of the Gray*, p. 167. Rooney Lee was married to Charlotte Wickham.

[16] *OR* 11, pt. 1, pp. 1036, 1044-1045; Robins, "Stuart's Ride," p. 271. It is uncertain whether the 1st or 9th Virginia had the lead when the expedition left Winston's.

[17] *OR* 11, pt. 1, p. 1036; McClellan, *I Rode with Jeb Stuart*, p. 54.

[18] McClellan, *I Rode with Jeb Stuart*, p. 54; Cooke, *Wearing of the Gray*, p. 167.

Stuart, riding at the head of the column, reined up his horse and studied the scene. The scouts reported that Union cavalry of undisclosed strength was in the village. Stuart made his dispositions accordingly, telling Fitz Lee to take his regiment, the 1st Virginia, and swing to the right. After bypassing Hanover Court House, Lee's Virginians would establish a roadblock on the far side of town. As soon as Fitz Lee's troopers rode off, Stuart had Rooney Lee and Will Martin mass their commands. When he judged sufficient time had elapsed to allow Fitz Lee's troopers to block the Federals' line of retreat, Stuart advanced the remainder of his force.[19]

The Federals—a 150-man patrol from the 6th U.S. Cavalry—did not wait for the Confederates to complete their dispositions. The Regulars mounted up and evacuated Hanover Court House. Stuart saw that the "blue birds," as his men had dubbed the foe, were pulling out of the village and, satisfied that he had waited sufficient time to allow Fitz Lee to get into position astride the Northerners' line of retreat, he waved his men to the attack. Surging forward, Stuart's troopers charged into the village. The Federals had a head start and disappeared in a cloud of dust down the road leading southward toward Mechanicsville. Having become entangled in a marsh, Fitz Lee's Virginians were unable to block the road. Except for the loss of one man—a sergeant who was captured—the Federal patrol escaped.[20]

---

[19] *OR* 11, pt. 1, p. 1036; McClellan, *I Rode with Jeb Stuart*, p. 54; Freeman, *Lee's Lieutenants*, 1, p. 284.

[20] Ibid.

Brig. Gen. Philip St. George Cooke

When the march resumed, Rooney Lee's 9th Virginia took the lead. Colonel Lee screened his advance by throwing forward a squadron under his resourceful adjutant, Lieutenant Robins. Since the Federals had escaped and would sound the alarm, Stuart determined to turn off the main Old Church Road. Some three miles beyond Hanover Court House, the head of Stuart's column left the main road. Marching by way of Taliaferro's Mill and Enon Church, the hard-riding Confederates headed for Haw's Shop, where they would regain the Hanover Court House-Old Church Road [21]

PART 2
STUART MEETS THE YANKEES

On the last day of May, Capt. William B. Royall of the 5th U.S. Cavalry received orders from his commanding officer, Capt. Charles G. Whiting to report to Brig. Gen. Philip St. George Cooke. In addition to being in charge of the cavalry assigned to the Army of the Potomac, the 53-year-old Cooke was Jeb Stuart's father-in-law. Cooke directed Royall to take the 2d and 4th squadrons, 5th U.S. Cavalry, and ride to Old Church.

Royall, in accordance with General Cooke's instructions, proceeded to Old Church. To guard the approaches to the right flank and rear of the Army of the Potomac, Royall established a picket line covering the routes to Old Church from the north and west. Daily, a company of the 5th U.S. undertook reconnaissance sweeps toward Hanover Court House. Scouts also checked out Confederate activity in the vicinity of the Richmond, Fredericksburg & Potomac Railroad.[22]

---

[21] *OR* 11, pt. 1, p 1037; McClellan, *I Rode with Jeb Stuart*, p. 54.

[22] *OR* 11, pt. 1, p. 1020. The 2d squadron was composed of Companies A and C, the 4th squadron of Companies F and H. Capt. James E. Harrison was in charge of the 4th squadron. Royall, a native Virginian, had seen service in the Mexican War as first lieutenant in the 2nd Missouri Infantry. Mustered out in October 1848, he rejoined the military on March 3, 1855, as a lieutenant in the elite 1st U.S. Cavalry and soldiered with Jeb Stuart in "Bleeding Kansas." As a captain in the 5th U.S. Cavalry, Royall was brevetted major for gallantry in the May 27, 1862 fight at Hanover Court House. As a lieutenant colonel of the 3rd U.S. Cavalry, he fought in the June 17, 1876 affair with the Sioux and Cheyenne on Rosebud Creek in Montana Territory.

At dawn on June 13, it was Company F's turn to patrol the Hanover Court House road. Lt. Edward H. Leib had his men in the saddle early. Lieutenant Leib, before leaving Old Church, reported to Captain Royall for instructions. Royall told the lieutenant that he was to proceed to Hanover Court House and "ascertain the strength and position of the enemy, should he be found in that quarter."[23]

At 6:00 a.m., Leib's patrol rode out of camp and a non-commissioned officer and eight privates constituted his advance guard. By 11:00 a.m., Leib's Regulars were one-half mile from Hanover Court House, and Leib saw horsemen approaching. Leib inched his way forward to identify the cavalrymen to his front and saw two squadrons of riders drawn up in a line. This force was covered by about 15 troopers deployed as skirmishers.[24]

Leib knew that a patrol from the 6th U.S. Cavalry was also operating in the area, so he was uncertain whether he was watching Confederates or Federals. He needed a closer look at the cavalrymen. As the lieutenant rode toward a small intervening stream, an officer and six or eight men advanced to meet him. The Southerners and Lieutenant Leib established one another's identity at the same time, and both the Confederates and the Union officer rapidly retraced their steps.[25]

Leib rejoined his advance guard and told his men of the large force of Confederates to their front. He informed the vanguard that they were now the rear guard and rejoined his main party. Upon doing so, he sent a message to Old Church. The courier was to tell Captain Royall that Leib's patrol had encountered two squadrons of Rebel cavalry. Leib then withdrew. Stuart's column marched by way of Taliaferro Mill, so the Federals were not followed as they fell back.[26]

---

[23] Ibid., p. 1021. Leib, after a two week stint as a private in the 25th Pennsylvania Infantry, was commissioned a second lieutenant in the 2nd U.S. Cavalry on April 26, 1861. Promoted to first lieutenant, he was reassigned to the 5th U.S. Cavalry. For his gallantry in the June 13 fight against Stuart, Leib was brevetted captain.

[24] Ibid., p. 1021.

[25] Ibid., pp. 1021-1022.

[26] Ibid., p. 1022.

At Haw's Shop, Leib halted. Questioning his rear guard and a scout who had been posted on a hill commanding a good view of the Hanover Court House-Old Church road, Leib learned that there were no Confederates in sight. Leib now sent Royall a second dispatch, notifying his captain that he had seen two Confederate squadrons, but the Southerners had not pursued the Federals when they returned to Haw's Shop. As soon as the messenger disappeared down the road, Leib had his rear guard retrace its steps. After proceeding about one and one-half miles toward Hanover Court House, the patrol stopped and established an outpost.[27]

Leib had been at Haw's Shop about an hour when orders came from Captain Royall to return to Old Church. Recalling his outpost, Leib started for camp. Before leaving Haw's Shop, Leib warned the pickets that Confederates were in the area. One mile east of Haw's Shop, Leib encountered Lt. William McLean and about 30 troopers from Company H, 5th U.S. Cavalry.[28]

Only one of the messengers sent by Lieutenant Leib to contact Captain Royall reached Old Church. It was 2 p.m. when the captain received a dispatch from Leib reporting that Confederates "were advancing in force from the direction of Hanover Court House." Royall also learned that Lieutenant Leib's patrol "was returning slowly toward camp." Royall then called out Lieutenant McLean and told him to ride to Leib's support with Company H. The captain planned to follow with the remainder of his command—Company C—as soon as it was relieved from picket duty. At the time that the emergency developed, one of Royall's companies was absent. Captain James E. Harrison, with part of Company A, was out with a flag-of- truce party.[29]

Leib briefed McLean and they determined to return to Old Church. McLean's company took the lead; Leib's brought up the rear. The Regulars rode about one-half mile before several excited pickets galloped up shouting "that the enemy were about a quarter of a mile back, advancing

[27] Ibid., p. 1022

[28] Ibid., p. 1022

[29] Ibid., p. 1020. General McClellan had signed the orders detailing Harrison to escort the flag-of-truce detail.

rapidly." Leib relayed this distressing news to Captain Royall and Lieutenant McLean. Not hearing anything from McLean, Leib halted and formed his company into line. The troopers took position under the brow of a hill on the side of the road. If the Rebel force was smaller than his, Leib would charge; if not, he would fight a delaying action.[30]

Near Haw's Shop, the Confederate vanguard sighted Union pickets. So efficiently did Lieutenant Robins manage his troopers that, although Lieutenant Leib had alerted the Federal sentries, the Southerners captured several with their horses. As soon as the prisoners had been disarmed and turned over to the provost guard, Robins continued the advance. Approaching the Totopotomoy Creek bridge, Robins' advance guard sighted Leib's Regulars. Both sides opened fire. Leib's Federals and Robins' Virginians banged away at each other for several minutes. Despite the expenditure of much ammunition, scant damage was done to life and limb. Leib reported that, while he lost several horses, only one of his men was hit. Robins' troopers, armed with rifles and shotguns, held a marked advantage over the pistol firing Federals. After his men emptied their pistols, Leib shouted for them to draw sabers, preparatory to charging.[31]

Stuart, with the rest of the 9th Virginia, thundered up. A glance convinced Stuart that the Federals had chosen their ground wisely. The road, at the point where Leib had formed his Regulars, passed through a deep ravine, the banks of which were fringed with laurel and pine. The only way the Confederates could get at Leib's men was up the road in column of fours.[32]

Leib's Federals started toward Robins' vanguard, and Stuart determined to beat the Regulars to the punch. "Form fours! Draw saber! Charge!" Stuart commanded. Rooney Lee's response was prompt and decisive. Capt. Samuel A. Swann, commander of the leading squadron, spearheaded the attack. Swann's troopers moved off at a trot. Rounding a

---

[30] Ibid., p. 1022.

[31] Robins, "Stuart's Ride," p. 271; McClellan, *I Rode with Jeb Stuart*, p. 55; *OR* 11, pt. 1, p. 1022. Leib opined that if his men had been equipped with carbines they "would have been able to do him [the foe] more injury and hold him longer in check."

[32] McClellan, *I Rode with Jeb Stuart*, p. 55; *OR* 11, pt. 1, p. 1037.

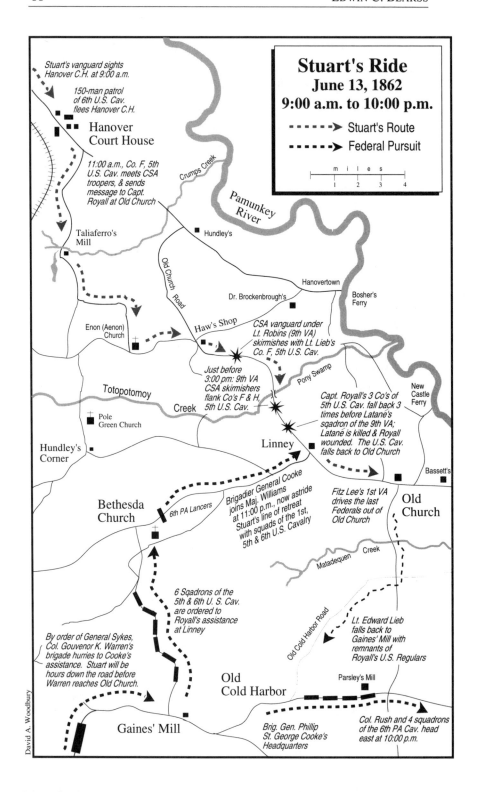

Stuart's vanguard sights
Hanover C.H. at 9:00 a.m.

150-man patrol
of 6th U.S. Cav.
flees Hanover C.H.

Hanover
Court House

11:00 a.m., Co. F, 5th
U.S. Cav. meets CSA
troopers, & sends
message to Capt.
Royall at Old Church

Stuart's Ride
June 13, 1862
9:00 a.m. to 10:00 p.m.

- - - - -▸ Stuart's Route
▬ ▬ ▬ ▸ Federal Pursuit

m i l e s
1   2   3   4

Crumps Creek

Pamunkey
River

Taliaferro's
Mill

Hundley's

Old Church Road

Hanovertown

Bosher's
Ferry

Dr. Brockenbrough's

Enon (Aenon)
Church

Haw's Shop

CSA vanguard under
Lt. Robins (9th VA)
skirmishes with Lt. Lieb's
Co. F, 5th U.S. Cav.

New
Castle
Ferry

Pony Swamp

Just before
3:00 pm: 9th VA
CSA skirmishers
flank Co's F & H,
5th U.S. Cav.

Totopotomoy

Capt. Royall's 3 Co's of
5th U.S. Cav. fall back 3
times before Latané's
sqadron of the 9th VA;
Latané is killed & Royall
wounded. The U.S. Cav.
falls back to Old Church

Pole
Green Church

Creek

Linney

Bassett's

Hundley's
Corner

Bethesda
Church

6th PA Lancers

Brigadier General Cooke
joins Maj. Williams
at 11:00 p.m., now astride
Stuart's line of retreat
with squads of the 1st,
5th & 6th U.S. Cavalry

Fitz Lee's 1st VA
drives the last
Federals out of
Old Church

Old
Church

Matadequen   Creek

6 Sqadrons of the
5th & 6th U. S. Cav.
are ordered to
Royall's assistance
at Linney

Old Cold Harbor Road

Lt. Edward Lieb
falls back to
Gaines' Mill with
remnants of
Royall's U.S. Regulars

By order of General Sykes,
Col. Gouvenor K. Warren's
brigade hurries to Cooke's
assistance. Stuart will be
hours down the road before
Warren reaches Old Church.

Old
Cold Harbor

Parsley's Mill

Gaines' Mill

Brig. Gen. Phillip
St. George Cooke's
Headquarters

Col. Rush and 4 squadrons
of the 6th PA Cav. head
east at 10:00 p.m.

David A. Woodbury

bend in the road, the Virginians sighted Leib's advancing Federals 200 yards away. Swann barked out the order to charge, and the men galloped forward. So sudden was the onset that the Regulars broke and retreated in confusion. One look at the onrushing Confederates was enough.

Leib, realizing that he was badly outnumbered, determined to fall back upon Lieutenant McLean's company. Wheeling their horses around, the Federals raced toward Totopotomoy Creek. The Northern troopers had a 200-yard head start, but the Rebel yell that broke upon the air lent the Federals wings. A few Regulars fell into Confederates hands, but the remainder of Leib's force escaped across the creek. The road as it approached Totopotomoy Creek narrowed and was bounded by thick brush, and Swann saw that he was in ambush country. He reined up his horse and told his bugler to sound recall.[33]

Stuart, at the head of the rest of the 9th Virginia, followed Swann's squadron. Fitz Lee and Will Martin likewise kept their units closed up. Several Union prisoners recognized Fitz Lee, who, in the days before the Civil War, had served in the 2d U.S. Cavalry, which had been redesignated and reorganized as the 5th on August 3, 1861. John Esten Cooke recalled:

> I could not refrain from laughter at the pleasure which "Colonel Fitz"—whose motto should be *"tou jours gai"*—seemed to take in inquiring after his old cronies. "Was Brown alive? Where was Jones? and was Robinson sergeant still?" Colonel Fitz never stopped until he found out everything. The prisoners laughed as they recognized him.
>
> It was difficult to believe that the Union prisoners and the dashing young colonel represented opposing armies mustered to slaughter each other.[34]

Stuart rode up to where Captain Swann was reforming his squadron and made a hasty reconnaissance. Several prisoners stated that the Federals would make a stand at the Totopotomoy, and Stuart grew cautious.

---

[33] Robins, "Stuart's Ride," p. 271; *OR* 11, pt. 1, pp. 1022, 1037, 1043.

[34] Cooke, *Wearing of the Gray*, p. 168.

The Confederate officers were satisfied that if the Federals chose to make a stand at the Totopotomoy bridge, Stuart's advance would be delayed long enough to force him to abort his mission. That the Northerners did not destroy the bridge reinforced Stuart's apprehension that they were planning a stand. After halting his column, Stuart had Rooney Lee dismount half a squadron. Deployed as skirmishers, these troopers advanced toward the bridge.[35]

After crossing the Totopotomoy, Leib's people rendezvoused with McLean's company, and the two officers posted their men to cover the bridge. Next, Leib sent to Captain Royall another report on the increasingly grave situation. The 9th Virginia skirmishers waded the creek on either side of the bridge, causing Leib to fear that his small command would be surrounded. He ordered his men to fall back.[36]

It was almost 3 p.m.; Old Church was four miles away. There, if anywhere, the Federals could be expected to make a stand. Stuart knew that the wagon trains from the big White House Landing supply depot passed through Old Church as they hauled supplies to McClellan's right wing. The Confederate commander also knew that his father-in-law, General Cooke, would not neglect to guard such an important and exposed position.[37]

As soon as a bridgehead had been established, Stuart sent Lieutenant Robins' horse soldiers across the stream. Robins, before crossing the bridge, dismounted his Virginians. Pressing resolutely ahead, Robins' vanguard harassed the Federals as they retired down the Old Church road. In his after action report, Stuart, officially commended the lieutenant, "On, on dashed Robins, here skirting a field, there leaping a fence or ditch, and clearing the woods beyond. . . ."[38]

It was mid-afternoon before all of the men from Company C, 5th U.S. Cavalry, had been relieved on the picket line. As soon as all the troopers from Company C had returned to Old Church, Captain Royall

---

[35] McClellan, *I Rode with Jeb Stuart*, p. 55; Freeman, *Lee's Lieutenants*, 1, p. 285; *OR* 11, pt. 1, p. 1037.

[36] *OR* 11, pt. 1, p. 1022-1023.

[37] Freeman, *Lee's Lieutenants*, 1, pp. 285-286.

[38] Robins, "Stuart's Ride," p. 271-272; *OR* 11, pt. 1, p. 1037.

called for Lt. Richard Byrnes, the company commander. Royall told Byrnes to take the field. The troopers saddled their horses and the wagoners harnessed teams. Byrnes was to be ready for any emergency that developed. After telling Byrnes that he was going to the point of danger, Royall rode off.[39]

Byrnes, following the captain's departure, mounted and formed his company astride the road at the blacksmith's shop. He also sent a seven-man patrol north down the road to Bosher's Ferry to learn of any Confederate activity along that road. Before the patrol returned, a courier galloped up with further orders from Captain Royall: Byrnes was to report to the captain with his company. Before leaving Old Church, Byrnes ordered Cpl. Cyrus C. Emory to return to camp and get the wagons ready to roll. Byrnes then led his company up the Hanover Court House-Old Church road. At Linney's, where the road to Mechanicsville branched off to the left, Byrnes found Captain Royall.[40]

Meantime, Lieutenants Leib's and McLean's companies had continued to retire in the face of Stuart's advance. At Linney's, the two lieutenants determined to hold this strategic junction "at all hazards." In addition, they felt confident that they would soon be reinforced. Captain Royall soon arrived, and Leib tersely told his superior that the Southerners were to his front. Before proceeding any farther, Royall decided to alert General Cooke and ordered Lt. Louis D. Watkins to carry the news of the Confederate advance to the general. Next, the captain sent a messenger to call up Lieutenant Byrnes' company.[41]

To get a personal impression of the strength and character of the foe, Royall determined on a forced reconnaissance. Royall placed himself at the head of McLean's company and started up the road toward the Totopotomoy Creek bridge. Leib's and Byrnes' companies followed

[39] *OR* 11, pt. 1, pp. 1023-1024. Ireland-born Byrnes, formerly sergeant-major of the 1st U.S. Cavalry, was commissioned a second lieutenant on May 14, 1861, and soon thereafter transferred to the 5th U.S. Cavalry. He became colonel of the 28th Massachusetts Infantry, a unit in the Irish Brigade, and died of wounds received while commanding a brigade in the June 3, 1864, Battle of Cold Harbor.

[40] Ibid., p. 1024. The patrol sent up the road to Bosher's Ferry was led by Sgt. Robert H. Montgomery.

[41] Ibid., pp. 1020, 1023, 1024.

McLean's troopers. Before Royall had gone far, he sighted Lieutenant Robins' Virginians and shouted for his bugler to sound the charge.[42]

Robins' troopers topped a hill and saw Royall's Regulars drawn up in column of fours, ready to attack. Hearing Royall give the command to "charge!" Robins yelled for his dismounted troopers to fall back. Before the vanguard had retired very far, Stuart cantered up. The general was accompanied by the 9th Virginia. Robins told Stuart of the Federals' presence. Stuart did not hesitate. He ordered Rooney Lee's leading squadron—under the command of 29-year-old Capt. William Latané —to clear the road.[43]

Latané led his men up the hill at a trot. As soon as he sighted the Northerners, Latané shouted "charge!" Lieutenant Robins' men, having secured their mounts, joined in the savage onslaught. The squadron, with a mighty shout, galloped forward. The attack was in column of fours, boot to spur, with saber. It was received by Royall's Federals deployed as skirmishers on the right of the road. Royall's Regulars blazed away at the Virginians with their pistols. After firing a few shots, the Federals bolted to the rear. The vigor with which Latané drove his charge home convinced Royall that the Confederates outnumbered him. Royall subsequently reported that he had been attacked by "six or seven squadrons of cavalry in front and on both flanks."[44]

The Federals retreated down the road intermingled with the head of Latané's squadron. In their rush toward the rear, the Regulars swept Latané's vanguard along with them. Latané and Royall met in a desperate hand-to-hand contest. Latané gashed Royall's arm and chest with his saber, but the Federal shot the Southerner from his saddle with his revolver.[45] Captain Latané died in his brother John's arms.

---

[42] Ibid., pp. 1020, 1023-1024. Byrnes' company reached Linney's just as Royall departed.

[43] Ibid., pp. 1037, 1043; Robins, "Stuart's Ride," p. 272. Latané's squadron was composed of Companies E and F, 9th Virginia Cavalry.

[44] Robins, "Stuart's Ride," p. 272; McClellan, *I Rode with Jeb Stuart*, p. 56; *OR* 11, pt. 1, p. 1020.

[45] McClellan, *I Rode with Jeb Stuart*, p. 56; Robins, "Stuart's Ride," p. 272; Davis, *J.E.B. Stuart*, p. 116.

Following Latané's fall, Lieutenant Robins and the six leading files of the dead officer's squadron were borne along by the retreating Regulars. The Confederates' situation worsened when they sighted Leib's troopers driving toward them. It looked as if they would be crushed between the two Union commands. But fortune smiled on Robins and his comrades. By the time they had covered a quarter of a mile, they somehow escaped. Lieutenant Robins made his get away by leaping his horse over a rail fence and into the field beyond.[46]

Mmes. W. Newton and W. B. Newton, and Mr. James Lowry, the overseer on the Newton farm, repaired to Mrs. Brockenborough's. The body of the captain was prepared for burial. The citizens procured a coffin after much difficulty. Since there was no cemetery on Dr. Brockenborough's plantation, the body was transported on the following morning—the 14th—to Summer Hill, residence of Capt. W.B. Newton, and was interred in the Page family burial ground. The ladies were not permitted to secure the services of a clergyman. At the request of Mrs. W. B. Newton, the burial service of the Episcopal Church was read at the graveside by Mr. R.E. Atkinson.[47]

News of Latané's death and burial made him an overnight Confederate hero. Richmond poet John R. Thompson wrote an elegy honoring the dead captain. The poem inspired painter William D. Washington to recreate with paint and brush the graveside scene, employing Richmond women as models. The painting—titled *The Burial of Latané*—was completed in 1864 and depicts the officer's grave surrounded by grieving women, children, and household slaves.[48]

Lieutenant Byrnes had heard the command "Draw Sabers!" Halting his company he had several of his troopers dismount and throw down the

---

[46] Robins, "Stuart's Ride," p. 272. John Latané of the 9th Virginia Cavalry remained with the body of his brother when Stuart's command passed on toward Old Church. He procured a cart to remove the body to Dr. Brockenborough's house. There, John Latané turned his brother's body over to Mrs. Catherine Brockenborough (or "Brockenbrough." *Confederate Veteran,* 40 vols. (Wendell, 1984), vol. 5, p. 49, vol. 9, p. 558, and vol. 10, p. 262. Since a Union outpost was stationed near the house, Latané could not remain. Proceeding to the residence of Capt. W. B. Newton, Latané obtained the necessary information to permit him to pass through Union lines.

[47] McClellan, *I Rode with Jeb Stuart,* p. 68.

[48] Editors of Time-Life Books, *Lee Takes Command, From Seven Days to Second Bull Run,* (Alexandria, 1984), p. 26.

fence on the right of the road and then led his men into a large field. Byrnes planned to keep pace with Royall's column, which was riding west along the road in column of fours. Before Byrnes' company drew abreast of Royall's column, Latané's Virginians attacked. At the sound of gunfire, Byrnes sent Cpl. Benjamin Evans and six men to explore the woods to his right and rear. Evans' patrol had not gone very far before many Confederates emerged from the woods and entered the field.[49]

Royall's bugler at this moment sounded the charge. Byrnes waved his men to the attack. Before Company C had advanced very far, Royall's troopers broke. The retreat was so rapid that advancing Confederates got between Byrnes and his superior. Unable to join Royall, Byrnes led his company across the field. Leaping their horses across a fence, the Federals entered the adjoining field, where Byrnes formed his troopers behind the fence. From the cover of the barrier, the Unionists opened fire on Latané's column as it swept down the road, but Byrnes' Federals at once saw another group of Southerners. This column was apparently trying to get between Company C and the woods. To keep from being cut off, Byrnes called retreat. The Federals reached the woods ahead of the Confederates. Detouring north of the Hanover Court House-Old Church road, Byrnes' command came into the road to Bosher's Ferry about 300 yards from Old Church. Byrnes, during the retreat, saw what he thought was a Rebel infantry column marching along a road that turned into the Bosher's Ferry road.[50]

When Captain Royall saw that reinforcements were at hand, he shouted for his cavalrymen to reform. The Regulars' discipline asserted itself. Within a few hundred yards of the place where the first clash occurred, they again wheeled into line. Leib's company thundered up. By this time, the rest of the 9th Virginia had come up in support of Latané's squadron. Before Leib committed his men, Royall ordered him to fall back. For a second time, McLean's company gave way in the face of the Virginians' slashing attack. In addition to McLean, the Southerners captured a number of Regulars. Royall succeeded in rallying the remnant

[49] *OR* 11, pt. 1, p. 1024.

[50] Ibid.

of McLean's company for another stand, and Leib's troopers took position alongside McLean's former command. Despite the hard-fighting captain's efforts, the best the outnumbered Federals could do was to slow the pace of Stuart's savage onset. Breaking a third time, the Northerners retired to Old Church.[51]

At Old Church, a badly wounded Royall turned over command of his detachment to Lieutenant Leib. Before doing so, he told the lieutenant "not to risk another attack." After sending a messenger pounding off to notify General Cooke of what had occurred, Leib sent several patrols to see what had happened to the Confederates. Lieutenant Byrnes' company, following its circuitous march, now reported to Leib. Leib, having deployed his command to cover the approaches to Old Church, called for two non-commissioned officers. One rode north to recall the pickets posted on the Pamunkey at New Castle Ferry; the other was to turn back any wagon trains then en route to the front from White House Landing. A third courier galloped down the road to Old Cold Harbor to ask for reinforcements at the first camp he passed.[52]

The attack on Royall's Regulars, in conjunction with the detachments necessarily made to protect the flanks, had dissipated the strength of the 9th Virginia. Stuart now brought Fitz Lee's 1st Virginia to the front. While Stuart regrouped his command, the Federals broke contact and withdrew to Old Church. Fitz Lee rode up with a request to make of his chief. From several of the Union prisoners, Lee learned of the 5th U.S. Cavalry's camp at Old Church. He begged Stuart to let him pay his former comrades a visit. Stuart gave Fitz Lee the green light, but conditioned it with the injunction that he must return as soon as possible. Fitz Lee, having secured Stuart's sanction, led his cavalrymen toward Old Church. The Virginians approached the strategic crossroads and saw the Regulars drawn up to protect their camp.[53]

Fitz Lee's troopers drove in the outposts. Leib, despairing of checking the Southerners, determined to evacuate Old Church. The Federals

[51] Ibid., p. 1021; McClellan, *I Rode with Jeb Stuart*, p. 56; Robins, "Stuart's Ride," p. 272; *OR* 11, pt. 1, p. 1021.

[52] *OR* 11, pt. 1, pp. 1021, 1023-1024.

[53] McClellan, *I Rode with Jeb Stuart*, p. 57; Robins, "Stuart's Ride," p. 272.

abandoned their position and retreated down the Old Cold Harbor road. Patrols from the 1st Virginia followed them to the crossing of the Matadequen. After fording the stream, the Federals saw no more Confederates, and continued on to Gaines' Mill without further incident.[54]

Lee's Southerners entered the Union encampment hard on the Regulars' heels. They found many deserted tents and an abundance of supplies—boots, pistols, whiskey, and other items. These were appropriated by the Virginians, and the tents set on fire amid wild shouts. John Esten Cooke pronounced the spectacle "animating." But, he recalled that, when a rumor started making the rounds "that one of the tents contained powder, the vicinity thereof was evacuated in almost less than no time." The Federals, except for a few stragglers, had escaped. Fitz Lee realized that nothing was to be gained by driving the Northerners back upon their supporting infantry, which could not be very far off.[55]

So far, casualties on both sides had been slight. Captain Royall reported four of his men killed and ten or twelve wounded. A number of Regulars had been captured. One of the Confederates, Captain Latané, was dead and about 15 or 20 wounded, mostly with saber-cuts. Stuart had surprised and beaten the Regulars in detail. At all points of contact, the Confederates had decisively outnumbered the Federals.[56]

The column halted briefly at Old Church. The people of the area,alerted to the approach of the expedition, flocked to greet the raiders and wished them Godspeed. Lieutenant Robins remembered that "Some of the ladies brought bouquets, and presented them to the officers as they marched along. One of these was given to General Stuart, who, always gallant, vowed to preserve it and take it to Richmond."

Stuart kept his promise.[57]

---

[54] *OR* 11, pt. 1, pp. 1021, 1023-1024.

[55] Ibid., p. 1037; Robins, "Stuart's Ride," p. 272; Cooke, *Wearing of the Gray*, p. 169.

[56] Robins, "Stuart's Ride," p. 272; *OR* 11, pt. 1, p. 1021.

[57] Robins, "Stuart's Ride," p. 272.

PART 3
STUART DECIDES TO RIDE AROUND
McCLELLAN AND BAFFLES THE FOE

At Old Church, Stuart was 17 miles from Hanover Court House. He had accomplished the principal objective of the expedition by ascertaining that there was no Union force of consequence deployed along the Chickahominy-Pamunkey watershed. Now the cavalry leader had to determine the best way to convey this vital news to General Lee.[58]

Two courses of action were open to Stuart. He could return the way he had advanced, or he could ride around the Army of the Potomac, crossing the Chickahominy at one of the lower fords. Stuart felt that the Northerners expected him to adopt the first alternative. If they were alert, the Federals would burn the Totopotomoy bridge. Should the Federals neglect to destroy the bridge, they would certainly watch the route along which the column had advanced. Recent rains had made the South Anna River unfordable, and the bridges had been burned, so Stuart would have to again pass through Hanover Court House. The presence of the Union outpost at Hanover Court House earlier in the day warned Stuart that a far larger body might be waiting to greet him on his return. Stuart concluded that if he retraced his steps, danger and perhaps disaster awaited him.[59]

Given his flair for the dramatic, it is possible that Stuart's after action report magnified the difficulties to be encountered if the column returned by way of Hanover Court House. But the targets that lured him deeper into the Federal rear were very real. Nine miles to the southeast was Tunstall's Station on the Richmond & York River Railroad. This railroad linked McClellan's army with its White House Landing supply depot on the Pamunkey. It would be a tremendous achievement, Stuart reasoned, if his cavalrymen cut this vital supply artery.[60] After wrecking the railroad at Tunstall's, Stuart's raiders could veer to the south and

---

[58] *OR* 11, pt. 1, p. 1038.

[59] Ibid.; Freeman, *Lee's Lieutenants*, 1, p. 288; McClellan, *I Rode with Jeb Stuart*, p. 58.

[60] Freeman, *Lee's Lieutenants*, 1, p. 288.

cross the Chickahominy at Forge Bridge. Stuart's scouts told him that the bridge had been burned but could be quickly repaired, and he believed that he could cross the river long before the Federals brought up infantry. After he had crossed to the Charles City County side, Stuart reasoned, General Lee could make a diversion in favor of the expedition. Such a move on General Lee's part would discourage Federal efforts to intercept Stuart from the direction of White Oak Swamp.[61]

When the expedition was planned, Stuart suggested that the cavalry ride around McClellan's army. Lee had rejected Stuart's suggestion. Perhaps the youthful cavalryman wanted to prove Lee wrong. Despite Stuart's confidence, there were imponderables. Foremost of these was that the Federals might have sufficient infantry posted along the railroad to defeat Stuart's troopers. One thing in Stuart's favor was that McClellan would not expect the Confederates to ride around his army. Since the Federals were not anticipating such a move Stuart believed he might get away with it. Whatever the risk, there was a chance, as Stuart would write in his report, of "striking a serious blow at a boastful and insolent foe, which would make him tremble in his shoes."[62]

Stuart made his decision and disclosed his plans to several of his officers in a "brief and frank interview." While none of these men gave their full assent to Stuart's daring plan, all of them assured the general of their support. Their misgivings hardened Stuart's resolution. To deceive the Federals as to his future actions, Stuart inquired of several farmers the best route to Hanover Court House. Next, he selected guides from members of his command who came from the area he was about to enter. Pvt. Richard E. Frayser of the New Kent Company, who knew every road and byway between Old Church and Tunstall's, took charge of the scouts.[63] Stuart turned to John Esten Cooke and remarked, "Tell Fitz Lee to come along, I'm going to move on with my column."

"I think the quicker we move now the better," Cooke replied laughing.

---

[61] Ibid.; *OR* 11, pt. 1, p. 1038.

[62] Freeman, *Lee's Lieutenants*, 1, p. 289; *OR* 11, pt. 1, p. 1038.

[63] Ibid.; McClellan, *I Rode with Jeb Stuart*, p. 62.

"Right," Stuart answered, "tell the column to move on at a trot."[64]

Stuart touched the flank of his horse with his spurs and was off. The general recalled:

> There was something of the sublime in the implicit confidence and unquestioning trust of the rank and file in a leader guiding them straight, apparently, into the very jaws of the enemy, every step appearing to them to diminish the faintest hope of extrication.[65]

The captured Regular cantonment was in sight of the road. Fitz Lee was surprised to see the remainder of Stuart's column riding eastward toward Tunstall's. As he passed, Stuart called for Lee to follow when his work was completed.[66]

It was 2:50 p.m. when Captain Royall's messenger Lt. Louis D. Watkins galloped up to General Cooke's Gaines' Mill headquarters with news that Royall's command had been attacked by Confederates. Watkins made the news worse by giving Cooke the impression that the attackers numbered between 3,000 and 5,000, and "were close upon" the general's camp. Cooke had the cavalry alarm "To Horse" sounded. There were in camp were six squadrons of the 5th and 6th U.S. Cavalry, the 1st U.S. Cavalry and 6th Pennsylvania Cavalry. Cooke ordered Brig. Gen. William H. Emory to take the six squadrons of the 5th and 6th U.S. Cavalry and ride to Royall's assistance. Cooke relayed news of the attack on Royall Brig. Gen. George Sykes, commanding the nearest infantry division. Sykes' headquarters were near New Bridge.[67]

---

[64] Cooke, *Wearing of the Gray*, p. 170.

[65] *OR* 11, pt. 1, p. 1038.

[66] McClellan, *I Rode with Jeb Stuart*, p. 57.

[67] *OR* 11, pt. 1, pp. 1007-1008, 1010. General Cooke was in charge of the Cavalry Reserve of the Army of the Potomac. Cooke's command was divided into two brigades: the First, commanded by General Emory, and the Second, led by Col. George A.H. Blake. Emory's brigade consisted of the 5th and 6th U.S., and the 6th Pennsylvania; Blake's included the 1st U.S. and the 8th Pennsylvania. In addition, a second Union mounted force led by Brig. Gen. George Stoneman operated on McClellan's right. Stoneman's troopers picketed the countryside from Pole Green Church on the right to Chickahominy on the left. At Pole Green Church, Stoneman's outposts connected with the line of videttes from Cooke's command. Ibid., pp. 1006-1007.

General Emory, hearing the commotion, shouted for his men to saddle their horses. Seeing that the troopers of the 5th Cavalry were mounted, Emory started for Cooke's headquarters to get additional instructions. While en route to his superior's command post, Emory encountered one of Cooke's aides. The staff officer relayed Cooke's orders to Emory orders to rush the 5th and 6th U.S. Cavalry to Royall's support. Retracing his steps, Emory relayed this message to Captain Whiting of the 5th U.S. Cavalry. A staff officer rode with the same information to the commander of the 6th U.S. Cavalry, Maj. Lawrence Williams. Emory intended to give Williams further instructions when the 6th regiment passed brigade headquarters. Williams did not know this, and decided that, to overtake the 5th U.S., which had a head start, he would have to take a short cut. When Emory learned that he had missed Williams, he set off in pursuit of his "flying column." The general overhauled the Regulars at Bethesda Church as they were filing into the Old Church road.[68]

After telling Williams "to push on with all possible speed," Emory reined in his horse. The sergeant in charge of an outpost near Bethesda Church galloped up and told the general that Confederate patrols were on the road leading to Hundley's Corner. Just as Emory was preparing to detach a squadron from his "flying column" to investigate the reported Confederate activity in the direction of Hundley's Corner, Col. Richard H. Rush and his 6th Pennsylvania Lancers rode up.[69] The general told Rush to detach one of his five squadrons. This unit would patrol to the westward and watch the roads leading to Mechanicsville and Hundley's Corner. Colonel Rush with his four remaining squadrons took position in a field alongside the Old Church road, a short distance east of Bethesda Church. Emory would hold the 6th Pennsylvania in reserve, while he used the 5th and 6th U.S. to feel for Stuart's column. Following the arrival of the Lancers, the 5th and 6th U.S. moved off.[70]

[68] Ibid., p. 1015.

[69] Ibid.

[70] Ibid., pp. 1015-1016.

General Cooke wondered what had happened to General Emory and the 6th Pennsylvania. Neither Emory nor Rush had told Cooke that they planned to take the field. The 1st U.S. Cavalry by this time had reported to Cooke, and, accompanied by that regiment, the general started for Old Church. Beyond Bethesda Church, he found General Emory and Rush's Pennsylvanians. After Emory had explained the situation to him, Cooke decided to remain where he was until he could learn something about the Confederates' actions.[71]

As a result of having taken a short cut, the 6th U.S. Cavalry reached the Old Church road ahead of the 5th U.S. Cavalry. Major Williams, as ranking officer, took charge of all the squadrons of the 5th and 6th in the "flying column" as it marched to Captain Royall's relief. At Linney's, Williams' vanguard received fire from Confederates. The Federals returned fire, and the Southerners fell back toward Hanover Court House. Williams, before pressing on, halted to reconnoiter. The major questioned the man from whose house the Confederate pickets had fired. The farmer told the major that the Southern column—which he estimated at from 3,000 to 4,000 strong, supported by two to four pieces of artillery—"had passed about half an hour before." Williams forwarded this news to General Cooke. Since his force numbered only 380 sabers, Williams decided to remain where he was pending the arrival of reinforcements. As they waited at Linney's, Williams' Regulars were astride Stuart's line of retreat ready to meet him should he retrace his steps.[72]

Next, Williams called for Lieutenant Watkins. The lieutenant was familiar with the area, so Williams told him to ride out into the woods and seek out Captain Royall's detachment. Watkins was to tell Royall that Williams' column was at Linney's. If Royall were attacked, he was to swing to the south and fall back on Williams' command. Watkins carried out his hazardous mission with speed and precision. Within a few minutes, he returned with the distressing news that Royall's camp had

---

[71] Ibid., p. 1010.

[72] Ibid., pp. 1019, 1025. Williams, in his after-action report, claimed that he discounted the farmer's estimate of the strength of the Confederate column. He commented that he did not think the Rebel force numbered more than 1,000 officers and men, supported by two guns. But, in his dispatch to Cooke, Williams wrote that "the enemy was in force (3,000 to 5,000), artillery, infantry, and cavalry." Ibid., p. 1006.

been burned. The Southerners, he continued, had passed beyond Old Church and were headed toward White House Landing. To keep track of the Confederates' movements, Williams called for Lt. Christian Balder. The lieutenant was to take his platoon and shadow the Rebel column and gauge their strength.[73]

Soon thereafter, Lieutenant Byrnes entered Williams' lines and told the major that he had seen five regiments of Rebel infantry on the Bosher's Ferry road, about one mile northeast of Linney's. Major Williams relayed this information to General Cooke.[74]

When reports finally reached General Cooke's Bethesda Church command post, they flooded in. First came the courier with the message that Major Williams had found the foe "in great force between him and Royall's position" at Old Church. Next, several of Royall's men galloped up on sweat-flecked horses and reported that they had retreated by way of Old Cold Harbor. Then came Byrnes' report of "about five regiments of the enemy's infantry." Finally, one of General Sykes' aides rode up and told the general that Col. Gouverneur K. Warren would soon report to him with his brigade and one battery.[75]

Cooke also kept in touch with Brig. Gen. Fitz John Porter, commander of the V Army Corps. It was dusk when Porter received from Cooke a copy of Major Williams' message, listing the Confederate strength as between 3,000 and 5,000. Finally, Cooke informed Porter that the cavalry would attack at daylight. In reply, Porter cautioned Cooke "to be on his guard." General Sykes, Porter pointed out, had been directed to join Cooke in time to participate in the attack on Stuart's raiders. Cooke, in the meantime, was to ascertain the Confederates' position "and act according to circumstances." The cavalry would await Sykes' arrival before attacking. Porter wanted to see either Cooke or Emory by 8 p.m.[76]

---

[73] Ibid., p. 1025.

[74] Ibid.

[75] Ibid., pp. 1010, 1015-1016.

[76] Ibid., p. 1006.

After sending an officer to tell Major Williams to hold his position and await the arrival of reinforcements, Cooke ordered Emory to see General Porter. When Emory left for Porter's headquarters, he carried with him Major Williams' and Lieutenant Byrnes' reports of the Old Church situation.[77]

It was 5 p.m. when Colonel Warren received the order from General Sykes to turn his men out under arms. Warren's brigade was camped on the north side of the Chickahominy, near New Bridge. Warren was to have his troops ready to repel a Confederate attack on the right flank of the Army of the Potomac. The alert was so sudden and the danger so imminent that the commissary officers were unable to supply the soldiers with the designated two days' rations. At Gaines' Mill on the line of march, Warren received orders to report to General Cooke at Bethesda Church. Warren's brigade was now reinforced by Company I, 5th U.S. Light Artillery.[78]

While awaiting Warren's brigade, Cooke made a distressing discovery: Colonels. Richard H. Rush of the Lancers and George Blake of the 1st U.S. Cavalry approached the general and explained that their units were short of rations and forage. Cooke, realizing that his men would be in the field for at least 24 hours, authorized the two regiments to return to their nearby camps. As soon as the troopers drew their rations and forage, the two regiments were to rejoin the general. While en route to their Gaines' Mill camps, the troopers encountered Warren's infantry.[79]

Upon the departure of the Lancers and the 1st U.S. Cavalry, Cooke sent a message to Emory directing him to send a wagon load of rations to the 5th and 6th U.S. Cavalry. This request was complied with. Pending the arrival of Warren's infantry and the return of the 1st U.S. and the Lancers, Cooke returned to his headquarters. Not feeling well, the general desired a cup of coffee. Cooke, while at Gaines' Mill, received orders from General Porter to have four squadrons of the Pennsylvania

---

[77] Ibid., pp. 1010, 1016.

[78] Ibid., p. 1029. Warren's brigade was composed of three regiments—the 5th and 6th New York Infantry, and the 1st Connecticut Infantry.

[79] Ibid., pp. 1010, 1016, 1026-1027. Colonel Blake's other regiment—the 8th Pennsylvania—was on outpost duty.

Lancers report to General Sykes. The cavalry general relayed this dispatch to Colonel Rush.[80]

It was getting dark when General Cooke returned to Bethesda Church. Before proceeding very far, the general overtook Warren's hard-marching infantry. He told Warren to continue up the Old Church road, and rode on. It was 10 p.m. when Cooke joined Major Williams' command at Linney's. Williams told the general that, except for an outpost guarding the Totopotomoy bridge, all his people manned the roadblock. At first, Cooke wanted to push on toward Old Church. But, when Williams told him that he was unable to obtain any information regarding the Confederates' strength, Cooke decided to await Warren's infantry.[81]

By the time that Colonel Warren's foot soldiers reached Linney's, the cavalry leaders had shaved their estimates of the strength of Stuart's mounted column to 600 troopers and two guns. In addition, Warren did not put much faith in Lieutenant Byrnes' tale of seeing five regiments of Rebel infantry. Warren, familiar with the area, did not believe that the lieutenant could have seen the reported number of regiments in the heavily wooded countryside. In his after action report, Warren wrote he "never for a moment believed we had any evidence of an infantry force."[82]

Without waiting for instructions from General Cooke, Warren ordered the 1st Connecticut to proceed to Old Church. The general then asked Warren, a former officer in the Topographical Engineer Corps, to prepare a sketch map of the area. While the colonel was doing this, he and the general discussed the strategic situation. As soon as the map was completed, Warren asked Cooke to let him proceed to Old Church with his entire brigade. From Old Church, Warren planned to march to New Castle Ferry. The possession of New Castle Ferry, Warren explained, would enable his infantry to command the roads by which Stuart was expected to return to his base. Cooke told Warren to proceed.[83]

---

[80] Ibid., p. 1010.

[81] Ibid.

[82] Ibid., pp. 1029-1030. Warren's infantry brigade had been stationed at Old Church for several weeks before being transferred to the New Bridge sector.

[83] Ibid., pp. 1011, 1030.

It was midnight before Warren was ready to resume the march. The moon was shining brightly, and Warren anticipated little difficulty in carrying out the proposed movement. Just as Warren's rear regiment, the 5th New York, was starting down the road, General Cooke had a change of heart. He determined to deploy the Zouaves to screen the rear of his mounted column when it rode forth, and Lt. Col. Hiram Duryea of the 5th New York was told to post his men and send one company to relieve the cavalry outpost at the Totopotomoy bridge. Subsequently, Cooke again changed his mind. At 2 a.m., June 14, he instructed Duryea to proceed to Old Church. Another hour elapsed before Duryea's Zouaves rejoined Warren.[84]

Warren, in the meantime, had reached Old Church. Several blacks told the colonel that the Southerners were holding New Castle Ferry. He thought that this was likely, because he felt that Stuart would escape across the Pamunkey River, and he relayed this intelligence to Cooke. Almost immediately thereafter, several bedraggled Federals straggled up the road from Garlick's Landing, and excitedly told Warren that Stuart's raiders had visited the landing late the previous afternoon. The raiders had left Garlick's about sunset, headed in the direction of White House Landing. One of these men, Pvt. Blanchard of the 1st Cavalry, was given a horse by Warren and sent to General Cooke's command post at Linney's.[85]

* * *

News that the Confederates were striking for White House Landing caused Warren to change plans. He would not march to New Castle Ferry. Instead, he let his tired infantrymen get a few hours' sleep, before pushing on to White House. Except for the soldiers assigned guard duty, the troops lay down with their arms.[86]

After Warren's departure for Old Church, a trio of messages reached General Cooke from General Porter. The first notified the cavalry leader

---

[84] Ibid. The company which had been sent to guard the bridge was also recalled. This company, however, did not overtake the regiment until after it had reached Old Church.

[85] Ibid., p. 1030.

[86] Ibid., 1030.

that General Sykes had been placed in charge of the efforts to bag the raiders. Sykes would join Cooke in the morning with a large force of infantry and artillery. A communication received at 11:10 p.m. requested Cooke to forward any information in his possession to Fifth Corps headquarters. Ten minutes later, a third staff officer reached Linney's, and Cooke learned that Porter did not want him to attack a superior force. He was to hold his position. When he had drafted this communication, Porter did not know that Warren had already joined Cooke. Cooke was to have two of his squadrons report to General Sykes as soon as possible.[87]

The first news Cooke received from Warren was favorable. The infantry commander pinpointed the Confederates near New Castle Ferry. Based on this information, Cooke sent a dispatch to Sykes stating that he hoped "to strike the enemy" at daylight. Cooke also informed Sykes that he had been unable to obtain any fresh data regarding the Rebel infantry seen by Lieutenant Byrnes. Shortly thereafter, Private Blanchard reached Linney's with word of the attack on Garlick's Landing. Since Blanchard had traveled to Linney's by way of Old Church, Cooke knew that the intelligence Warren had received placing the Confederates at New Castle Ferry was incorrect.[88]

While the 6th Pennsylvania Cavalry drew forage and rations, Colonel Rush received an order from General Porter to send a squadron to patrol the Old Church-Old Cold Harbor road. Before Rush acted on this order from Porter, he received a second, directing him to report to General Sykes with his entire regiment. One squadron had been left on outpost duty at Bethesda Church, so Rush hastened to Sykes' headquarters with his four remaining squadrons. At 9 p.m., when Rush reached Sykes' headquarters, the general was absent. After sending a squadron to picket the Old Church-Old Cold Harbor road, Rush directed his Lancers to relax, pending Sykes' return.[89]

---

[87] Ibid., p. 1011.

[88] Ibid. A second teamster reached Linney's close on Private Blanchard's heels.

[89] Ibid., pp. 1016-1017.

Within an hour of his arrival at General Porter's headquarters, General Emory received his marching orders. Porter told the cavalryman to take four squadrons of the 6th Pennsylvania Cavalry and proceed with all speed to Tunstall's Station. Porter had learned that the Confederate column was striking for the vital Richmond & York River Railroad. Riding to Sykes' encampment, Emory relayed Porter's instructions to Colonel Rush. The Lancers were in the saddle, and were ready to take the field on a moment's notice. As the column moved off, Rush glanced at his watch: the time was a little before 10:00 p.m. Marching by way of Old Cold Harbor, Parsley's Mill, Mount Prospect Church, and Hopewell Church, the Lancers headed rapidly east.[90]

Troopers of the 1st U.S. Cavalry had likewise returned to their Gaines' Mill camp to procure provisions. Before leaving for the point of danger, General Cooke had told Colonel Blake that his command was to be ready to take the field at 11 p.m. When the designated hour arrived, Blake ordered the 1st U.S. Cavalry into the saddle. In accordance with Cooke's instructions, Blake planned to rendezvous with the 5th and 6th U.S. Cavalry. The regiment had not traveled more than one mile before Blake received orders from General Porter to detach two of his squadrons under Capt. Marcus A. Reno and send them to General Sykes. After Blake had carried out this order, it reduced his command to two understrength squadrons. Continuing up the Old Church road, the 1st U.S. Cavalry proceeded to Linney's, where Colonel Blake reported to General Cooke early on the 14th.[91]

* * *

PART 4
STUART'S ADVENTUROUS AND HAZARDOUS RIDE

The Confederates' line of march, upon their departure from Old Church late on the afternoon of June 13, skirted the Pamunkey River. To

---

[90] Ibid.

[91] Ibid., pp. 1026-1027. Captain Reno, a major in the 7th Cavalry in the mid-1870's, was a principal and controversial player in the Little Bighorn drama of June 25, 1876.

the south, the country was more populous. To the north and northeast a number of great plantations extended down into the meadows and swamps bounding the Pamunkey. As the column trotted past, women, girls, and old men at every farm and plantation turned out to greet the first Southern soldiers they had seen in weeks. One young lady threw her arms around a brother she had not seen for some time and alternately sobbed and laughed with joy.[92]

Questioning the jubilant civilians, the Confederate officers were unable to learn much about either the Federals' strength or position. Ships lay at Garlick's Landing; wagon trains passed frequently; a detachment of Union soldiers guarded at Tunstall's Station. These were the fragments of information Stuart secured. As the Southerners rode onward, they could see a large tent city far to the southwest. Rumors passed up and down the column, identifying these tents as the nerve center of the Union Army—McClellan's headquarters.[93]

One-half mile beyond Tignor's house, the head of the column reached a fork in the road, and scout Frayser turned into the right fork, which led southeastward toward Tunstall's. Bone weary though the men were, they straightened up expectantly: New Kent County troopers cautioned their comrades that the column was getting closer to the area where the Northerners must be waiting.[94]

Stuart realized that the Union cavalry was, in all probability, in hot pursuit. He knew that his rear had now become important as his front. That capable Will Martin—an officer in whose judgment and skill he had the utmost confidence—was watching the rear of the column with his Jeff Davis Legion made Stuart feel better. Nevertheless, Stuart determined to alert Martin. Calling to Lt. John Esten Cooke, Stuart said, "Tell Colonel Martin to have his artillery ready, and look out for an attack at any moment."

Cooke spurred to the rear of the column and delivered this order to Colonel Martin. While Cooke was returning to the head of the column,

---

[92] Freeman, *Lee's Lieutenants*, 1, pp. 289-290; Cooke, *Wearing of the Gray*, p. 172.

[93] Freeman, *Lee's Lieutenants*, 1, p. 290; *OR* 11, pt. 1, p. 1038.

[94] Freeman, *Lee's Lieutenants*, 1, p. 290. The left-hand road led to Piping Tree Ferry.

the cry, "Yankees in the rear!" came from behind. The reaction was instantaneous. Sabers flashed; troopers formed into fours and wheeled about. A roar of laughter then swept along the column. Someone had cried "wolf!" As soon as the alert had passed, the horse soldiers slumped back in their saddles, but not too comfortably. Next time, they knew, the alarm might not be false.[95]

Late that afternoon, 25 non-commissioned officers and men of the 5th U.S Cavalry hailed Colonel Martin. One of the Federals brandished a white flag. Mistakenly believing that they were surrounded, the Federals handed over their arms and horses to the astonished Confederates.[96]

As he approached the road leading to Garlick's Landing and Putney Ferry, Stuart organized a combat patrol. Satisfied by reports that the stores at Garlick's were guarded by a small force, Stuart felt that two squadrons could effect their destruction. He sent one squadron from the 1st Virginia and one from the 9th Virginia to take Garlick's, Capt. O. M. Knight of the 9th Virginia in command. After torching to the stores, Knight's raiders were to bring off all captured horses. Following the departure of the patrol, the main column swept on toward Tunstall's.[97]

Early that morning, a small train (14 wagons and one ambulance) had left the Gaines' Mill encampment of the 1st U.S. Cavalry en route to Garlick's Landing. It was guarded by a ten-man patrol commanded by Lt. Joseph S. Hoyer. The train reached Garlick's without incident by 2 p.m. As soon as the quartermaster's department had loaded the wagons with the requisitioned supplies, Lieutenant Hoyer—in accordance with his orders—had his men unsaddle and unharness their horses and teams. They would camp for the night on the Pamunkey River and return to Gaines' Mill in the morning. In addition to the wagons of the 1st U.S. Cavalry, the supply train belonging to the 17th and 44th New York Infantry Regiments stood at Garlick's. The New Yorkers' wagons were

---

[95] Cooke, *Wearing of the Gray*, p. 171; Freeman, *Lee's Lieutenants*, 1, p. 290.

[96] *OR* 11, pt. 1, pp. 1038, 1045.

[97] McClellan, *I Rode with Jeb Stuart*, p. 60; *OR* 11, pt. 1, p. 1038. Captain O. M. Knight led the squadron from the 9th Virginia, Capt. George N. Hammond of Company B the one from the 1st Virginia.

guarded by a 15-man detail. Three supply schooners loaded with hay and forage were tied up at Garlick's Landing.[98]

It was 6:00 p.m. when the Confederates swept down on the landing and caught Lieutenant Hoyer's troopers eating supper. So sudden was the Southerners' attack that the Regulars were unable to mount, and Hoyer shouted for his men to form into line. Moments after the Federals had scrambled into position, Knight's skirmishers called upon them to ground arms. The Unionists refused the demand and opened fire. The Southerners recoiled on their supports. As soon as all their men were up, the Virginians charged, and the Federals scattered into the underbrush.[99]

Meantime, the Virginians had forced the detachment escorting the New Yorkers' supply train to surrender. Two of the three schooners at anchor were also captured; the crew of the third cast off in time. Freed of her moorings, the vessel drifted out of the Confederates' reach. In a futile effort to prevent the escape of the schooner, the butternuts opened fire, killing a sergeant from the 83d Pennsylvania.[100]

After setting fire to the wagons—many of which were loaded with fodder—and the two captured schooners, Captain Knight rounded up the prisoners and reformed his units. The combat patrol then moved off, having successfully accomplished its mission at Garlick's Landing. Since they had to overtake Stuart, Captain Knight set a brisk pace as he led his Virginians southeastward.[101]

Following departure of the two Garlick's Landing-bound squadrons, the main column pushed on toward Tunstall's. The road showed signs of heavy travel and gave evidence that news of the Confederates' coming had preceded them. Overturned wagons and spoils of all sorts lay by the road, abandoned by the panicky Federals. Perhaps at Tunstall's, which

[98] *OR* 11, pt. 1, pp. 1027-1028, 1032, 1034. The 17th New York Infantry was assigned to Brig. Gen. Daniel Butterfield's brigade, the 44th New York to Brig. Gen. John H. Martindale's brigade.

[99] Ibid., p. 1038. Among the 15 teamsters and 10 guards assigned to the train, ten escaped. On June 15, Lieutenant Hoyer reported that, of the rest, three had surrendered and 11 were still missing.

[100] Ibid., pp. 1032, 1034.

[101] Ibid., pp. 1033, 1038. The Confederates estimated the number of wagons burned at 75, the Federals at 30.

was only two miles away, Federal infantry might be deployed athwart the raiders' line of march.[102]

Stuart accordingly ordered Breathed's rifled Blakely to the head of the column. Breathed, however, was engaged in a desperate contest with "General Mud." Both the rifled gun and the 12-pounder howitzer were mired to their axles in deep Virginia mud. Despite the lashing and swearing of the drivers, the horses could not budge the pieces. "Gott! Lieutenant," swore a sergeant of German stock to Lt. William McGregor, "it can't be done."

The sergeant shifted his gaze and glanced at an ambulance, which, with a treasured keg of whiskey, had been found in the Federals' abandoned encampment at Old Church. Struck by inspiration, the sergeant added, "just put that keg on the gun, Lieutenant, and tell the men they can have it if they only pull through!" Lieutenant McGregor thought the experiment was worth a try. Chuckling, he had the keg placed on the gun, and the sturdy gunners leapt into the knee-deep slime. Their eyes focused on the keg, the artillerists seized the wheels of the guns and the heavily loaded limbers. One mighty effort sufficed and the guns and limbers rose out of the mud hole. The cannoneers claimed their reward and headed for the front.[103]

While the redlegs[104] wrestled with the field pieces, Private Frayser galloped up to Stuart and reported that he had approached to within a short distance of Tunstall's. Approaching the Richmond & York River Railroad, Frayser saw one or two companies of Federal infantry. A Union officer "politely beckoned" to Frayser and called in a broad German accent "Koom yay!" Disregarding this invitation to surrender, Frayser wheeled his horse about and reported to Stuart.[105]

As soon as Frayser finished speaking, Stuart prepared to attack. Stuart again called upon Lieutenant Robins, and told him to take 30 picked men and cover the advance. Robins' vanguard was to precede the

---

[102] Freeman, *Lee's Lieutenants*, 1, pp. 290-291.

[103] *OR* 11, pt. 1, p. 1045; Cooke, *Wearing of the Gray*, pp. 172-173.

[104] Both Union and Confederate artillerymen wore red piping on their uniforms.

[105] Cooke, *Wearing of the Gray*, p. 173.

main column by one-half mile. When Robins' troopers reached the road linking White House Landing with the mills, they would stop long enough to cut the telegraph wire then push on to Tunstall's Station. Stuart cautioned Robins that Frayser had seen infantry at Tunstall's. After dispersing the infantry, Robins' men were to cut the telegraph and block the railroad. The Confederates knew that, until they crossed the railroad, the Federals could employ the rolling stock to throw infantry astride their line of march. Once across the track, this danger would be passed.[106]

Pushing forward at a trot, Robins' combat patrol swept up a few stragglers and, upon reaching the road connecting the mills with White House Landing, overtook an ordnance wagon loaded with canteens and Colt's revolvers. The wagon was stuck in a mud hole. The driver cut his team loose from the traces and escaped. An irate Union sergeant remained with the wagon and was captured. Revolvers and canteens were scarce in the Confederacy, so this was a valuable prize. To save time, Robins handed one of his men an ax. This man cut the telegraph, while his comrades plundered the wagon.[107]

Just then a mounted Union patrol rounded a bend in the road. The previous evening—the 12th—a company of the 11th Pennsylvania Cavalry, based at White House Landing, had been sent to Garlick's. Early on the 13th, the Pennsylvanians started up the south bank of the Pamunkey. At Bosher's Ferry, the Pennsylvanians encountered Captain Royall, who reported "all quiet in front." When its mission had been accomplished, the patrol returned and halted near Garlick's and a provost guard was sent to arrest a Rebel sympathizer. Before the patrol returned, a sergeant and four enlisted men of the 5th U.S. Cavalry rode up on lathered horses and informed the Pennsylvanians that Royall's command had been overwhelmed by a powerful column. Remounting, the Pennsylvanians prepared to contest the Confederate advance. As they rode toward Tunstall's, the Northerners chanced upon Robins' vanguard.[108]

---

[106] Robins, "Stuart's Ride," pp. 272-273. Among the men assigned to Robins' patrol were Redmond Burke, William D. Farley, and John S. Mosby, all of Stuart's staff.

[107] Robins, "Stuart's Ride," p. 273; *OR* 11, pt. 1, p. 1044.

[108] *OR* 11, pt. 1, p. 1031.

The surprised Union officer momentarily was at a loss as to what to do. Within a few seconds, he recovered his wits and had his troopers draw sabers, preparatory to a charge. The Confederates had by this time cut the telegraph and rifled the wagon. Robins and his men remounted, formed into column of fours, and drew sabers. For the next several minutes, the Virginians and the Pennsylvanians sat their horses, eyeing one another. Before either group made a hostile move, the head of Stuart's main column thundered into view, whereupon the Northerners wheeled their horses and retreated down the road to White House Landing.[109]

One of the Federals did not accompany his comrades. Instead, he raced for Tunstall's as fast as his horse could carry him to warn the Tunstall's garrison. Robins, subsequently learned that the flying Pennsylvanian galloped through Tunstall's without stopping. When one of the guards yelled at him, "What's to pay?" he dashed madly along, calling out, at the top of his voice, "Hell's to pay."[110]

The skedaddle of the Pennsylvanians cleared the road, so Robins' vanguard resumed its advance. The Federals, loitering around the depot, appeared to be oblivious of the Confederates' proximity. As they approached the station, Stuart's men let loose a "Rebel yell" and charged. The greater part of the Northerners took to their heels, the Confederates in hot pursuit. Lieutenant Robins struck boldly for the depot. There he found the commander of the garrison and 13 of his men. The Unionists were unarmed, and only one of them seemed eager for combat. Racing for the station platform and the firearms stacked there, he picked up a rifle-musket. Before the soldier could ram a cartridge home, the sweep of a saber close to his head caused him to throw down his piece. Jumping into a ditch, the dogged infantryman escaped through a culvert, over which the railroad passed.[111]

Robins had no time to press his pursuit. Turning to the Union officer, Robins accepted his surrender. While several of his men took axes and

---

[109] Robins, "Stuart's Ride," p. 273.

[110] Ibid., p. 273.

[111] Ibid., p. 273.

chopped down telegraph poles, Robins sought to turn the switch, but found it locked. Undaunted, Robins had several troopers fell a tree across the track. An oaken sill, about a foot square and 14 feet long, was placed athwart the rails. The work was completed none too soon, because hardly had Robins' men finished their task before their lookout saw a train approaching from the southwest.[112]

Just as the locomotive chuffed into view, General Stuart reached the station with the 9th Virginia. The engineer saw the obstructions on the track, and, suspecting that something was amiss, put on a full head of steam. The train which had been slowing down began to pick up speed. Observing this, Stuart shouted for his men to dismount and take cover. Confederates posted themselves on a high bank overlooking a cut through which the railroad passed east of the station.[113]

The locomotive approached the obstructions, and several of the Confederates called at the engineer to stop. He refused; the train continued to pick up speed. Plowing into the obstructions, the locomotive pushed them aside and held the track. Confederates leaped from places of concealment and blazed away at the train with their pistols. Aboard the flatcars, startled Federals scrambled for cover. Men not cut down by this galling fire hugged the beds of the cars. A paymaster leaped off the accelerating train, leaving $125,000 in cash behind. Will Farley took Capt. Heros von Borcke's carbine and rode after the accelerating train. Drawing abreast of the locomotive, Farley shot and killed the engineer. The fireman took over, and the train continued to gain speed. Within a matter of minutes, the train was out of range. Perhaps if the artillery had been at the head of the column and not bogged down, the Confederates might have derailed and captured the train, but now that it had escaped there was nothing for the disappointed troopers to do except round up the Northerners who had fled the station or jumped off the flatcars.[114]

[112] Ibid.; *OR* 11, pt. 1, p. 1044.

[113] *OR* 11, pt. 1, pp. 1039-1044; Robins, "Stuart's Ride," p. 273; McClellan, *I Rode with Jeb Stuart*, pp. 60-61; Cooke, *Wearing of the Gray*, p. 174; Freeman, *Lee's Lieutenants*, 1, pp. 292-293.

[114] Freeman, *Lee's Lieutenants*, 1, pp. 292-293. The Federals reported that aboard the train two men were killed and eight wounded. *OR* 11, pt. 1, p. 1032.

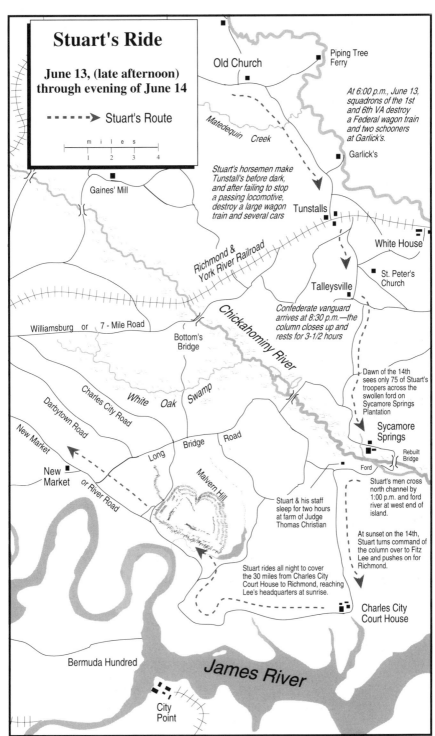

Stuart's Ride

June 13, (late afternoon) through evening of June 14

- - - - ▶ Stuart's Route

m i l e s
1 2 3 4

Old Church

Piping Tree Ferry

At 6:00 p.m., June 13, squadrons of the 1st and 6th VA destroy a Federal wagon train and two schooners at Garlick's.

Matedequin Creek

Garlick's

Gaines' Mill

Stuart's horsemen make Tunstall's before dark, and after failing to stop a passing locomotive, destroy a large wagon train and several cars

Tunstalls

White House

St. Peter's Church

Talleysville

Richmond & York River Railroad

Confederate vanguard arrives at 8:30 p.m.—the column closes up and rests for 3-1/2 hours

Williamsburg or 7 - Mile Road

Chickahominy River

Bottom's Bridge

Charles City Road

White Oak Swamp

Darbytown Road

Dawn of the 14th sees only 75 of Stuart's troopers across the swollen ford on Sycamore Springs Plantation

Sycamore Springs

New Market

Long Bridge Road

Rebuilt Bridge

Ford

New Market

or River Road

Malvern Hill

Stuart's men cross north channel by 1:00 p.m. and ford river at west end of island.

Stuart & his staff sleep for two hours at farm of Judge Thomas Christian

At sunset on the 14th, Stuart turns command of the column over to Fitz Lee and pushes on for Richmond.

Stuart rides all night to cover the 30 miles from Charles City Court House to Richmond, reaching Lee's headquarters at sunrise.

Charles City Court House

Bermuda Hundred

James River

City Point

David A. Woodbury

For a second time that afternoon, Stuart was confronted by a dilemma. The general asked himself whether he should continue his march toward the Chickahominy and make for his own lines, or advance down the railroad and try to capture the great Union supply depot at White House Landing. White House, Stuart knew, would be an invaluable prize. If it could be destroyed, McClellan would be compelled either to change his base or retreat.

But, on further reflection, Stuart realized that the escape of the train and the presence of the Union scouting party that Robins had encountered prior to the attack on Tunstall's made it certain that the Federals at White House knew of his approach. The presence of large portions of the Army of the Potomac encamped within five or six miles of Tunstall's made prospects for a successful attack on White House Landing even smaller. McClellan, by using the railroad, could rush a large force of infantry to the endangered sector. Thus, if the alerted White House garrison could delay the Southern horsemen, the arrival of fresh infantry on their rear would ensure the destruction of Stuart's command.

In addition, the two squadrons sent to Garlick's Landing had not rejoined the column. Stuart could not, even if he wished, move against White House until they returned. Billowing smoke clouds from the northwest indicated to Stuart that the two squadrons had carried out their assignment. Stuart accordingly decided not to move against White House Landing. Perhaps he recalled General Lee's admonition: "Be content to accomplish all the good you can without feeling it necessary to obtain all that might be desired."[115]

Darkness approached. Before pressing on, the Confederates must destroy the public property that had fallen into their hands at Tunstall's. Many army wagons loaded with corn and forage stood abandoned around the station. Troopers also discovered a large train parked in the nearby woods and several cars on the Tunstall's spur, also filled with corn and forage. Because many troopers had eaten the rations carried in their haversacks, they plundered several sutler's wagons. Finally, just before resuming the march, the Southerners torched the wagons.

---

[115] McClellan, *I Rode with Jeb Stuart*, p. 61; Cooke, *Wearing of the Gray*, p. 174; Freeman, *Lee's Lieutenants*, 1, p. 293; *OR* 11, pt. 3, p. 590.

While the demolition teams carried out their tasks, the two squadrons sent to Garlick's reported to Stuart. Meantime, Lt. Redmond Burke had taken a detail and set fire to the Black Creek railroad bridge. Another detachment worked felling telegraph poles for a considerable distance on either side of the station.[116]

By the time the main column was ready to resume the march, it was dark. Stuart reported that "the burning of the immense wagon train and the extricating of the teams involved much labor and delay and illuminated the country for miles." Stuart had no fresh reports of pursuit, but he knew that the reflections from fires and the reports spread by the trainmen would direct powerful pursuing forces toward Tunstall's Station. At Old Church, Stuart had reasoned that the worst of the dangers would be behind him after he had passed Tunstall's. Now, he was not so sure that his return march would be unmolested.[117]

When the column left Tunstall's, Lieutenant Robins again commanded the advance guard. Near St. Peter's Church, the Confederates turned into the road leading southward to Talleysville. The road, badly cut up by wagons, was the worst that the expedition had yet encountered. Lieutenant Breathed's artillery had an especially difficult time, but the vanguard entered Talleysville at 8:30 p.m. Stuart found a Federal hospital containing 150 patients in the town, but deemed it humane not to molest it or disturb the doctors and hospital stewards.[118]

The horse soldiers of the vanguard had not shared in the captured stores at Tunstall's, and they were delighted to discover that an enterprising Yankee had set up shop at Talleysville. This sutler hoped to capitalize on Union soldiers passing between McClellan's army and White House Landing. Crackers, cheese, canned fruits, sardines, and many other dainties dear to a cavalryman stood stacked on his shelves.

---

[116] McClellan, *I Rode with Jeb Stuart*, pp. 601-662; *OR* 11, pt. 1, p. 1039; Freeman, *Lee's Lieutenants*, 1, p. 294.

[117] Freeman, *Lee's Lieutenants*, 1, p. 294; *OR* 11, pt. 1, p. 1038.

[118] *OR* 11, pt. 1, p. 1039; Robins, "Stuart's Ride," p. 273.

Lieutenant Robins recalled that "in the brief hour spent with. . .[the sutler] we of the advance were made new men. I fear little was left to cheer and to invigorate those in the rear."[119]

Stuart remained at Talleysville 3 1/2 hours to rest his men and horses and allow the column to close up. It was midnight before the artillery and Colonel Martin's rear guard overtook the main column. As soon as Stuart learned of Martin's arrival, he ordered the march resumed. It was eight miles from Talleysville to Forge Bridge on the Chickahominy. According to Stuart's schedule, the last of his horse soldiers would be across the river by daybreak on June 14. To expedite the march, Union prisoners were mounted on captured horses and mules. Since there were more Federals than surplus horses and mules, a number of Northerners rode double.[120]

Long before the Southerners left Talleysville, a full moon rose. Lieutenant Robins' detachment again took the lead as the column struck southward toward Mount Olivet Church. Lt. Jonas Christian, whose home was Sycamore Springs near Forge Bridge, led the way. Lieutenant Robins recalled that the "moon lighted our way and cast weird shadows across our path. Expecting each moment to meet the enemy, every bush in the distance looked like a sentinel, and every jagged tree bending over the road like a vidette."[121]

Many participants recalled the ride from Talleysville to the Chickahominy as the hardest part of the raid. The 9th Virginia, in the advance, became separated from the 1st Virginia. This caused Stuart anxious minutes. Calling to Lieutenant Cooke, Stuart inquired, "Where is Rooney Lee?"

"I think he has moved on, General," the staff officer replied.

"Do you *know* it?" Stuart asked in an agitated tone.

"No, but I believe it," Cooke answered.

"Will you *swear to it? I* must know! He [Rooney Lee] may take the wrong road, and the column will get separated!" Stuart exclaimed.

---

[119] Robins, "Stuart's Ride," p. 273.

[120] *OR* 11, pt. 1, p. 1039; Freeman, *Lee's Lieutenants*, 1, pp. 294-295; McClellan, *I Rode with Jeb Stuart*, p. 63.

[121] Robins, "Stuart's Ride," p. 273; McClellan, *I Rode with Jeb Stuart*, p. 62.

Cooke told the general that he would ascertain if Rooney Lee's regiment was in front.

Stuart told Cooke to go ahead, but to take care or he might be captured. Before Cooke had ridden 200 yards, he heard the clatter of hooves coming toward him. Reining in his horse, Cooke called, "Halt! Who goes there?"

A courier from Rooney Lee, came the reply. Questioning the messenger, Cooke learned that the 9th Virginia was a mile up the road. Before the two cavalrymen had finished their conversation, Stuart rode up. On learning that Rooney Lee's regiment had not wandered off, the general drew a deep breath, and exclaimed, "Good!"[122]

The pace of the march told on the troopers. Entire companies napped in their saddles. Stuart was no exception. After locating the 9th Virginia, the general relaxed. He threw one knee over the pommel of his saddle, folded his arms, dropped the bridle, and rested his chin on his chest. Stuart's plumed hat drooped over his forehead. The general's aides watched as Stuart snatched a few minutes of sleep. To keep the general from falling off his mount, Cooke rode at his side and steadied him in the saddle.[123]

Shortly before the head of the column reached the Chickahominy, Lieutenant Christian informed Stuart that he knew the location of a ford on Sycamore Springs plantation that was nearer than Forge Bridge. Stuart was delighted by this news. He believed his command could slip across the river at the ford and avoid wasting precious hours repairing the partially dismantled bridge. If the Federals were pursuing, they could be expected to press on to Forge Bridge in ignorance of the seldom-used ford.[124]

Day was breaking when the vanguard turned off the main road and into the lane which led past Sycamore Springs and down to Long Reach Ford. To their consternation, Robins' people found the Chickahominy swollen by recent heavy rains. The banks were overflowed, and a muddy

---

[122] Cooke, *Wearing of the Gray*, pp. 174-175.

[123] Ibid., p. 177.

[124] Freeman, *Lee's Lieutenants*, 1, p. 295.

torrent rolled madly by. Lieutenant Christian was shocked. Never within the young officer's recollection had the normally placid Chickahominy looked like this. Neither man nor beast could get across the river without swimming. To make matters worse, the north bank approach to the crossing was below the point on the far side where the Confederates would emerge from the flood-swollen river. The riders, should they try to swim their horses across, would breast a powerful surging current. Mud made it impracticable for the horses to approach the river except by way of the road leading to the ford.[125]

Rooney Lee was the first ranking officer to reach the crossing. He decided to give it a try. Accompanied by several of his men, Rooney Lee urged his horse into the angry water. After a fierce struggle with the river, Lee and his companions reached the south bank. Not only were the cavalrymen buffeted by the strong current, but the feet of the horses became entangled in tree roots. Only with much difficulty did the horse-men rescue these animals. Colonel Lee, however, would not consent to being separated from his regiment. Stripping off his clothes, he swam back across the river.[126]

His experiment satisfied Rooney Lee that "the passage in this man-ner was impracticable for the command." Next, Lee had his Virginians procure axes. The Southerners then tried to span the river by felling trees, upon which they hoped to lay a temporary bridge. As soon as the cavalrymen toppled a tree, it was swept downstream.[127]

While the 9th Virginia vainly sought to bridge the river, Stuart reached the ford. Staff officer John Esten Cooke called to Rooney Lee, "What do you think of the situation, Colonel?"

"Well, Lieutenant," Lee replied, "I think we are caught."

A glance satisfied Cooke that the men of the 9th Virginia shared their colonel's sentiments. The jig was up! Many of the troopers sprawled on the ground in every conceivable posture. Half asleep, they held their bridle reins over their arms, to be ready to mount at the first

---

[125] McClellan, *I Rode with Jeb Stuart*, p. 63; Robins, "Stuart's Ride," p. 273; Freeman, *Lee's Lieutenants*, 1, p. 296.

[126] McClellan, *I Rode with Jeb Stuart*, p. 64.

[127] Ibid.

alarm. Some remained on their horses, their drooping shoulders evidence that they dozed. Others munched the delicacies taken from the sutler's store. Gloom was written on their countenances.[128]

Every face had an anxious cast except Stuart's. As the commander rode down to Long Reach Ford, he did not say much. He knew that the Federals would soon be closing in. One look told him that the river, in all probability, could not be crossed without serious loss. After ordering Rooney Lee to resume his efforts to get his regiment across the river, Stuart called for Cpl. Turner Doswell. He asked the corporal if he thought he could reach the other side. When Doswell said he could, Stuart handed him a dispatch addressed to General Lee. Besides informing General Lee of his predicament, Stuart wanted him to make a diversion in his favor on the Charles City road.[129]

Rooney Lee's troopers resumed felling trees. As before, the timber was too short to bridge the swollen Chickahominy, and it was swept downstream. Mustering their ingenuity, several cavalrymen tried to fashion a crude ferry. In place of rope, they used bridle reins and halters to bind together a number of rails taken from a nearby fence. Aboard this raft, they piled their equipment and pushed it into the river. The raft promptly capsized and the cavalrymen lost their gear.[130]

Time was wasting and the June sun had risen over the eastern horizon. Rumors swept through the Confederate ranks that a strong force of Union infantry was closing in. Stuart knew that, if he were to save his command, a faster way of getting his people across the river must be found. In two hours only 75 men and their mounts had gained the south bank.

Several New Kent County horse soldiers now approached the general. They told him that the raiders might cross at the site of Forge Bridge. This was where Stuart had originally intended to cross the Chickahominy. This bridge was one mile below Sycamore Springs on the road from Providence Forge to Charles City Court House. Stuart's

---

[128] Cooke, *Wearing of the Gray*, pp. 177-178; Freeman, *Lee's Lieutenants*, 1, p. 296.

[129] *OR* 11, pt. 1, p. 1039; McClellan, *I Rode with Jeb Stuart*, p. 64.

[130] Freeman, *Lee's Lieutenants*, 1, p. 297.

informants said that at Forge Bridge a large island divided the Chickahominy into two channels. The bridge across the north channel was
reported to be partially destroyed. But, the New Kent men continued,
enough of the bridge remained to facilitate reconstruction of the span. At
the western end of the island was a little-used ford which could be used
to reach the south bank in an emergency.[131]

After directing Lt. Col. Richard C. Beale of the 9th Virginia, the
ranking man on the far side of the river, to make his way downstream,
Stuart ordered his troopers to Forge Bridge. Stuart found the conditions
there as described. The river ran deep and narrow between steep banks.
Stone abutments faced each other 40 feet apart. Between the abutments
was an "arching void" which it was necessary for the Confederates to
bridge. As soon as he had established a line of outposts covering the
approaches to the crossing and posted his artillery, Stuart placed Lt.
Redmond Burke and Cpl. Henry Hagen in charge of building an emergency bridge.[132]

The Southerners found a skiff and moored it in mid-channel to serve
as a pontoon just upstream from the abutments. A working party began
tearing an old barn to pieces and laying the planks across the gaps
between the banks and the pontoon boat. As soon as the fatigue party
had completed the bridge, the officers ordered their men to dismount.
Troopers unsaddled their horses and started carrying their gear across the
swaying structure. After they had deposited their equipment on the island, the cavalrymen retraced their steps. The horses were formed into
column of fours and driven into the rain-swollen river. Since the approach to the crossing was farther upstream then the exit, the horses
swam across without breasting the current.[133]

About one-half of the men and their mounts crossed in this fashion.
Stuart realized that the movement must be expedited, for there were still

---

[131] McClellan, *I Rode with Jeb Stuart*, p. 64; Robins, "Stuart's Ride," p. 274; Freeman, *Lee's Lieutenants*, I, pp. 297-298; *Atlas to Accompany the Official Records of the Union and Confederate Armies*, Plate XCIV.

[132] Cooke, *Wearing of the Gray*, p. 178; *OR* 11, pt. 1, p. 1039; Freeman, *Lee's Lieutenants*, 1, p. 298.

[133] Cooke, *Wearing of the Gray*, pp. 178-179; Robins, "Stuart's Ride," p. 274.

many men and two field pieces to cross, which Stuart had no intention of abandoning. Knowing that they needed a more substantial bridge, Stuart suggested Burke secure the sills and joists from the barn and see if they were long enough to span the river from the abutments. Troopers wielding sledge hammers demolished the barn, and Burke's working party carried the heavy timbers of the framework to the bank of the river. Another group ferried one end of each of the great timbers across the stream. Lifting them, the Confederates cheered when they found that the ends rested easily on the abutments. With the stringers in position, the Confederates floored the bridge with thick planks.[134]

The general watched the work from the small boat. Cooke recalled:

> Stuart worked with the men, and as the planks thundered down, and the bridge steadily advanced, the gay voice of the General was heard humming a song. He was singing carelessly, although at every instant an overpowering force of the enemy was looked for, and a heavy attack upon the disordered cavalry.[135]

It took Burke's detail three hours to complete the bridge. As soon as the structure was declared open for traffic, the guns rolled across. While the rest of the command passed over, Stuart called in his rear guard. By 1:00 p.m., all of the Confederates had reached the island. Fitz Lee was the last man to leave the north bank. The column, in the meantime, had pushed on toward the opposite side of the island. Before riding off, Stuart called for the ubiquitous Lieutenant Robins. The lieutenant was placed in charge of the rear guard. After all the troopers had crossed, Robins was to burn the bridge.[136]

Reaching the south side of the island, Stuart found the channel running deep and swift. Lieutenant Cooke volunteered to test the ford and urged his mount into the muddy water. Cooke found that the water was

---

[134] Cooke, *Wearing of the Gray*, p. 179; Freeman, *Lee's Lieutenants*, 1, pp. 298-299; McClellan, *I Rode with Jeb Stuart*, p. 65.

[135] Cooke, *Wearing of the Gray*, p. 179.

[136] Robins, "Stuart's Ride," p. 274; McClellan, *I Rode with Jeb Stuart*, p. 65.

"just deep enough to swim a small horse." Recrossing the channel, Cooke reported to the general that the ford was difficult, but not impracticable. The prisoners and their escort crossed first. Since many of the Northerners were riding double, their mounts had a hard time. In passing through the swamp beyond, many of the horses and mules lost their footing in "treacherous mud-holes." As the beasts scrambled to recover their balance, some Federals tumbled into the ooze. Later, when a third swamp loomed across their route, one of the disgusted Federals called out, "How many damned Chickahominies are there, I wonder, in this infernal country?"[137]

When the wheels of one of the limbers bogged down, the team jerked and the pole snapped. Time was vital, so Stuart ordered his cannoneers to abandon the limber. Except for this loss, the column successfully negotiated the far channel of the Chickahominy.[138]

Meantime, Colonel Beale's detachment had rebuilt the bridge across the southern channel. Stuart, however, did not know of this accomplishment. If he had, his command would not have been compelled to use the ford, and the limber in all probability would not have been lost.[139]

When Stuart stood on the south bank of the Chickahominy, the worst was behind him. But his difficulties were not over. The raiders were 35 miles from Richmond. Twenty of these miles lay within the Federal picket lines. Until Stuart had marched this distance, he could not feel secure against attack. Union gunboats patrolled the James River, and Stuart knew that a portion of his planned line of march lay within sight of that river. Worse, Brig. Gen. Silas Casey's Federal IV Corps division held the line covering White Oak Swamp. Casey's infantry was within easy striking distance of the roads leading to Richmond, and Stuart was only too aware that it would be easy for Casey to throw a strong force across his route.

---

[137] Cooke, *Wearing of the Gray*, p. 179.

[138] McClellan, *I Rode with Jeb Stuart*, p. 66; *OR* 11, pt. 1, p. 1039.

[139] Freeman, *Lee's Lieutenants*, 1, p. 299.

These dangers, however, seemed insignificant in comparison with those from which the Confederate cavalrymen had just escaped.[140]

Part 5
The Yankees Fail To Bag The Raiders

The raid came at an unfortunate time for General McClellan. On Thursday, June 12, as Stuart and his horse soldiers rode first north and then east to camp in the Winston fields south of the South Anna, McClellan transferred his headquarters from Dr. William Gaines' plantation, near New Bridge, to Dr. Trent's place on Grapevine Bridge road. The shift of army headquarters from north of the rain-swollen Chickahominy engrossed McClellan's attention. Consequently, coordination of efforts to intercept and pursue the daring raiders was left to his favorite corps commander, Fitz John Porter. At this time, three of the five corps—Brig. Gens. Edwin V. Sumner's II, Samuel Heintzelman's III, and Erasmus D. Keyes' IV—constituting the Army of the Potomac were south of the Chickahominy and north of White Oak Swamp. Another corps—Brig. Gen. William B. Franklin's VI—was being redeployed from its camps north of the Chickahominy to occupy commanding ground on Golding's farm south of the river and on Sumner's right.[141]

General McClellan had placed one of his trusted subordinates, Lt. Col. Rufus Ingalls, in charge of the White House Landing depot. Late on the afternoon of June 13, Colonel Ingalls received a telegraphed message signed by Brig. Gen. Randolph B. Marcy, McClellan's chief of staff, apprising him of the Confederate attack on Captain Royall's command. Shortly thereafter, several of Ingalls' scouts reached White House Landing with additional information concerning the fighting at Old Church. Before Ingalls acknowledged Marcy's communication, the telegraph

---

[140] McClellan, *I Rode with Jeb Stuart*, p. 65. McClellan was mistaken in his account. General Casey's division of the IV Corps—not Joseph Hooker's III Corps division—guarded the White Oak Swamp crossing. *OR* 11, pt. 3, pp. 229, 234.

[141] *OR* 11, pt. 1, pp. 1032, 243-246; pt. 3, p. 324; *OR* 51, pt. 2, pp. 637, 676, 682. McClellan designated the headquarters area Camp Lincoln.

went dead. The colonel suspected that the wires had been cut by Confederate raiders, and he ordered the garrison turned out under arms.[142]

Soon, the patrol from the 11th Pennsylvania—which had sighted the Confederates as they approached Tunstall's—and a number of stragglers from the 5th U.S. Cavalry reached the depot. Both the Pennsylvanians and the Regulars warned Colonel Ingalls that "a large rebel force" was in "pursuit and already very near the depot." Ingalls now feared that an attack on the big Union base was imminent.[143]

At the time of "Stuart's Ride Around McClellan," the force charged with the defense of White House Landing did not exceed 600 men. When the alarm was raised, cannoneers of Company F, 1st New York Light Artillery, unlimbered their four 3-inch ordnance rifles on the plain. From this position, the gunners commanded the roads along which it was reported that the Southerners were advancing. A battalion of the 93d New York Infantry and two companies of the 3d U.S. Infantry took positions in support of the artillerymen.

Some 250 convalescents, a number of guards, and civilian employees of the quartermaster's department volunteered their services. Colonel Ingalls saw that these men were armed and stationed near the wharves and hospital. Colonel Josiah Harlan of the 11th Pennsylvania Cavalry was directed to have his troopers in the saddle. Leaving behind the company which had just returned from the Bosher's Ferry patrol, Harlan took the field. The Pennsylvanians were to reconnoiter the railroad and wagon road leading to Tunstall's. If his men encountered the foe, Harlan was to keep Ingalls posted as to their movements.[144]

In addition to forming the garrison, Ingalls called upon the navy for assistance. Lieutenant Alexander Murray, the commander of the gunboat flotilla operating on the York and Pamunkey Rivers, placed his five gunboats in front of the depot. Murray trained his guns to sweep the plain of any hostile force. To assist the sailors in registering on their

---

[142] *OR* 11, pt. 1, p. 1032.

[143] Ibid., pp. 1031-1032.

[144] Ibid., p. 1032.

targets, Ingalls stationed Lt. F. W. Owen, his signal officer, on one of the chimneys on the White House.[145]

Ingalls, having made these dispositions, awaited the Rebel attack. At dusk, the White House Federals saw two pillars of smoke. One of these was in the direction of Tunstall's; the other appeared above Garlick's Landing. Throughout the night, Ingalls, not knowing that the Confederates had turned aside and were heading for the Chickahominy, kept his men at battle stations.[146]

Harlan's Pennsylvanians were not aggressive. By the time they had penetrated to within a mile of Tunstall's, the Confederates were on their way to Talleysville. Harlan's troopers did not know this. Not wanting to chance a night engagement, Harlan's command bivouacked. Daybreak would be soon enough to investigate what had happened at Tunstall's and Garlick's.[147]

Word of the Rebel attack on Tunstall's was not long in reaching Brig. Gen. George A. McCall's headquarters at Dispatch Station. McCall's division had, during the past 48 hours, been transferred by boat from Fredericksburg, Virginia, to White House Landing. Under orders to report to Fitz John Porter's V Corps, McCall had massed his command at Dispatch Station. In accordance with orders from Chief of Staff Marcy, General McCall issued marching orders to Brig. Gen. John F. Reynolds, one of his three brigade commanders. Reynolds was to take his brigade and proceed up the railroad to Tunstall's Station, seven miles away.[148]

It was midnight before the head of Reynolds' column approached Tunstall's. If the Confederates were still present, Reynolds hoped to take them by surprise, so he cautioned his men to be quiet. One regiment filed

[145] Ibid., pp. 246, 1032. The five gunboats assigned to Murray's flotilla were *U.S.S. Sebago, Marblehead, Corwin, Chocura,* and *Currituck.* White House plantation, where George Washington had wooed the widow Martha Dandridge Custis, was owned by Rooney Lee.

[146] Ibid., p. 1032.

[147] Ibid., p. 1033. Only three companies on the 11th Pennsylvania accompanied Colonel Harlan on his reconnaissance.

[148] Ibid., p. 1028; *OR* 11, pt. 3, pp. 219, 223, 225. Reynolds' brigade included the 1st, 2d, 5th, 8th, and six companies of the 13th Pennsylvania Reserves.

to the right to occupy the hill commanding the area; a second regiment fell out and moved into the woods on the left of the road. Reaching the depot, Reynolds' found the Confederates gone.[149]

Tunstall's Station was a picture of desolation. The Black Creek railroad bridge and a carload of corn on the spur smoldered; telegraph poles had been chopped down and the wire cut. Details extinguished the fires, saving the bridge and part of the corn. Union patrols, fanning out through the area, found the bodies of two men. Reynolds believed the dead men to be laborers. Several Federals, who had been prisoners but had escaped from the Confederates, wandered into Reynolds' lines and told the general that their guards had left in great haste, shortly before his infantry arrived.[150]

General Emory and the 6th Pennsylvania Lancers arrived at Tunstall's about 2 a.m. After discussing the situation with General Reynolds, Emory decided to wait until daybreak before following the Confederates' trail. He told Colonel Rush to let his Pennsylvanians catch a few hours of sleep and rest their horses. Captain Reno's squadron of the 1st U.S. Cavalry, which had been directed to report to General Sykes, had also been ordered to Tunstall's. Day was breaking when Reno's troopers arrived at the station.[151]

It was between 3 and 4 a.m., on June 14, before General Cooke completed his preparations and was ready to ride. A detachment was detailed to guard the bridge across the Totopotomoy, and Cooke left Linney's and headed for Old Church. Companies from the 1st, 5th, and 6th U.S. Cavalry Regiments rode with the general. Meantime, General Warren roused his brigade. By the time that Cooke's Regulars reached Old Church, Warren's infantry was formed and mustered.[152]

---

[149] *OR* 11, pt. 1, p. 1028.

[150] Ibid., pp. 1028-1029. When Surgeon James King examined the bodies of the two men found dead at Tunstall's, he found that one of the men had been shot in the head. The other man had been run over by a train. Two members of the 8th Pennsylvania Cavalry were arrested by Reynolds' pickets. Subsequently, Reynolds sent the two cavalrymen to White House with a request that they be turned over to their regiments as deserters.

[151] Ibid., pp. 1014, 1017, 1029.

[152] Ibid., pp. 1011, 1030.

Cooke, as senior officer present, took charge of the pursuit. The head of the column soon reached Bassett's—where the road to New Castle Ferry branched off to the left—and Warren asked to speak with General Cooke. Warren urged the general to detach his infantry brigade and part of Company I, 5th U.S. Light Artillery, and post them at the junction. Here, Warren said, his command would be positioned to intercept the raiders if they sought to retrace their steps. Warren told Cooke that his infantry was too exhausted to have any hope of keeping up with "an efficient cavalry pursuit."[153]

Cooke replied that the reports reaching him had "invariably" placed the strength of the Confederate column as from 1,000 to 2,000 strong, with artillery. Cooke was also concerned about the Southern infantry, which the unfortunate Lieutenant Byrnes had said he had seen. If the Confederates retraced their steps, Cooke knew that his column must soon meet them, and he reasoned that if the enemy horsemen were supported by infantry, his 500 cavalrymen would be brushed aside. Warren disagreed with the general. He was confident that no infantry accompanied the enemy cavalry.[154]

Cooke was not swayed by Warren's arguments. He would not leave the infantry behind. In addition, Cooke knew that the Southerners had been at Garlick's Landing 10 hours before, and realized that, if the foe did not return as expected, it would be impossible for his troopers to overtake them.[155]

Cooke, having made up his mind, sent a dispatch to General Sykes. Besides notifying Sykes that he was starting after the enemy, Cooke informed the infantry general that he was leaving "the rear toward Hanover Court House to his care. . . ."[156]

Cooke ordered the march resumed. The sun came up, and the day turned hot and sultry. In spite of the heat and the "heavy" road, the infantry bore up well as far as the Matadequen. After crossing that

[153] Ibid., pp. 1011-1012, 1030.

[154] Ibid., pp. 1011, 1030.

[155] Ibid., p. 1011.

[156] Ibid. Cooke also informed Sykes that he could not consider as binding the orders to maintain his position.

stream, the foot soldiers straggled badly, and some fainted from exhaustion or sunstroke.[157]

By the time the head of the column neared Garlick's Landing, General Cooke knew that the White House depot had not been attacked, but he could only guess at the raiders' movements. The Federal cavalry rode on to Tunstall's, and Cooke directed Warren to halt his infantry at the first water. It was noon before Warren found a suitable camp site near Tunstall's, and the fagged out men learned that their forced march had been in vain. The Confederates had left Tunstall's 12 to 14 hours before. In his after action report, Warren criticized Cooke's handling of the pursuit:

> I deem it my duty to say that I do not believe from the way in which General Cooke conducted the operations that the enemy would have been prevented from returning to Hanover CourtHouse by taking the road along the Pamunkey River. It was impossible for the infantry to overtake him, and as the cavalry did not move without us it was impossible for them to overtake him.[158]

Cooke's cavalry, its advance screened by two squadrons of the 1st U.S., gradually pulled away from Warren's infantry. Cooke rode with Warren, so Colonel Blake, as ranking officer, led the cavalry. It was 9:30 a.m. when Blake's troopers reached Tunstall's Station. Pending Cooke's arrival, Blake reported to General Emory. After telling Warren to halt his brigade, Cooke hastened on to Tunstall's.[159]

---

[157] Ibid., p. 1030

[158] Ibid., p. 1030-1031. Warren's brigade was ordered to return to New Bridge on the following day, June 15. To take advantage of the moonlight and the cool of the night, Warren advanced his scheduled hour of departure to midnight. After loading the sick and exhausted aboard flatcars, Warren's troops retraced their steps, reaching their camp at 7:00 a.m. Between 5:00 p.m. on the 13th and 7:00 a.m. on the 15th, Warren's troops had marched 41-1/2 miles.

[159] Ibid., pp. 1008, 1012, 1014, 1026-1027. A short distance beyond Old Church, the cavalry traveled the lower road. At Turner's Store, the troopers turned back into the main Old Church-Tunstall's Station road.

At Tunstall's, General Emory could obtain no definite information from General Reynolds regarding the strength of the Rebel column. Worse, no one seemed to know where the Southerners had gone. A sergeant in the infantry, eyewitness to the attack on Tunstall's, told Emory that about 150 Confederates had swept down on the station about sunset. In an effort to find out where the Confederates had disappeared to, Emory called for Colonel Rush of the 6th Pennsylvania and told him to have one of his squadrons sweep through the countryside east of the railroad. Rush gave the assignment to Maj. Robert Morris.[160]

By 5:00 a.m. on the 14th, Morris' troopers had gobbled down a hurried breakfast and saddled their horses. While Morris' men squared their gear away, Colonel Rush told the major to reconnoiter the roads leading toward White House and St. Peter's Church. Houses were to be searched, and any white man found at home was to be arrested and sent to General Emory's command post. If Morris came across the Confederates' trail, he was to notify Emory and press the pursuit. Rush promised to send reinforcements if necessary.[161]

A mile east of the station on the St. Peter's road, Morris halted his squadron and sent a squad to explore the road that branched off to White House Landing. The march resumed. Morris' next stop was at the Rice house. After ransacking the house and outbuildings and not finding any Confederates, Morris questioned Mrs. Rice. She told the major that she had not seen any Southern cavalrymen. But, Mrs. Rice continued, she had heard horses passing her house during the night.[162]

About a quarter mile beyond the Rice house, the condition of the road, which had been badly cut up by wagons, improved. In the mud, the Northerners saw the tracks of many horses. The Pennsylvanians had found the trail. Major Morris asked a citizen if he had seen any Confederates. "Yes!" the farmer said. He reported that "the enemy, about 10,000 strong, had been passing all night, commencing at about 8 o'clock."

---

[160] Ibid., pp. 1014, 1017.

[161] Ibid., p. 1018.

[162] Ibid.

After arresting the man and sending him to Emory's headquarters, Morris searched his house.[163]

Morris' troopers followed the Confederates' trail until they reached the intersection of the White House-Talleysville and Tunstall's Station-St. Peter's Church roads. The intersection had been churned into a bog by the passage of many animals. To make matters worse, a drove of cattle was passing through en route from White House to Talleysville. The man in charge of the herd told Morris that the Southerners had not attacked White House. After sending a scout to recall the men sent to scout toward White House, Morris started for Talleysville.

A short distance down the road, the major encountered a black man, who revealed that the Confederates, about 2,000 of them, had been at Talleysville the previous evening. The Southerners, after plundering the store, had started for the Chickahominy. This was the first concrete information Morris had obtained regarding the raiders' activities, and he sent two messages to General Emory. The first was verbal, and simply told the general that the Pennsylvanians were on the Southerners' trail. In the second, which was written, Morris informed Emory that the Confederates had been at Talleysville and were headed for the Chickahominy. Morris wanted Emory to send another squadron to reconnoiter the Talleysville road. At the same time, Morris would examine the road leading from New Kent Court House to the river at Forge Bridge.[164]

It was now a little after 7 a.m. Resuming the march, Morris' squadron followed a clearly defined trail as far as St. Peter's Church. Here, the horses' tracks turned off to the right. Questioning two local women—Mrs. Christian and Mrs. Apperson—Major Morris was unable to learn anything concerning the Confederates' movements.[165]

News that Morris had found the Confederates' trail reached General Emory about 8:00 a.m. Emory now focused on helping Morris. Colonel Rush was to speed reinforcements to Morris. Because one of his two remaining squadrons was also out on patrol, Rush had only one squadron

[163] Ibid.

[164] Ibid.

[165] Ibid., p. 1019.

available. This squadron, with a detachment of the 11th Pennsylvania that had just arrived from White House Landing, was ordered to take the field.[166]

Soon after the Pennsylvanians headed forth, a Confederate deserter was hustled into General Emory's command post. The Southerner told the general that Stuart had four regiments of cavalry and a battery of artillery. Emory knew that his small pursuing force would be helpless in the face of such formidable odds, and he called upon General Reynolds for assistance. Reynolds made available to the cavalry officer one of his infantry regiments, the 8th Pennsylvania Reserves. In addition, Reynolds promised to see if he could prevail on Colonel Ingalls to release the 11th Pennsylvania Cavalry.[167]

At daybreak, Colonel Harlan of the 11th Pennsylvania had his men in the saddle. Looking to the northwest, the Federals saw a pall of smoke still hanging over Garlick's Landing. In spite of having camped within a mile of Tunstall's, Colonel Harlan decided to investigate the fire. While Garlick's Landing was only two miles away as the crow flies, it was seven by road. The sun was well up in the sky before the Pennsylvanians reached the landing. On doing so, they discovered that the smoke came from a pile of still smoldering hay. The charred remains of 30 wagons and two schooners gave further evidence of the Confederates' visit. Seeing that there was nothing to be done at the landing, the colonel placed Maj. Samuel Wetherell in charge of three companies and instructed him to return to White House Landing. Upon his return to the supply depot, the major received orders from Colonel Ingalls to report to Colonel Rush. At dawn, when no attack developed, Colonel Ingalls suspended the alert. The troops charged with the defense of the Union base returned to their quarters, so Ingalls had no objection when Reynolds asked for the 11th Pennsylvania.[168]

Meantime, Major Morris' patrol had been strengthened. In addition to the squadron of Lancers sent by Colonel Rush, the detail that had been

---

[166] Ibid., pp. 1014, 1017.

[167] Ibid., p. 1014.

[168] Ibid., pp. 1033-1034. Harlan's troopers found the body of a sutler at the landing.

reconnoitering toward White House rejoined the major. Morris also received Emory's order disapproving the plan to divide the patrol, and he moved his entire command to Talleysville.

At Talleysville, the Federals found hoof marks from large numbers of horses. A black man, just escaped from the Confederates, told Morris that there were about 1,500 Southerners in the column, now camped at Forge Bridge. While in the Southerners' hands, he had heard them speak of "Charles City Court-House and the Chickahominy." Mounting the black man on a horse and turning him over to one of his sergeants, Morris sent him to see General Emory.[169]

Morris turned his column toward Forge Bridge. It was 9:30 a.m. when the Federals left Talleysville, their horses so badly jaded the Lancers held them to a walk. By the time the Pennsylvanians had approached to within four miles of Forge Bridge, Morris received an order from Emory to halt his command, pending Colonel Rush's arrival.[170]

Colonel Rush, accompanied by a detachment of the 11th Pennsylvania, had left Tunstall's about 10:00 a.m. It was noon before Rush overtook Morris' combat patrol and ordered the pursuit resumed. The Federal troopers reached Sycamore Springs, to see smoke rising from the woods to the southeast. Colonel Rush sent Major Morris and eight carbineers racing ahead to investigate.[171]

Following Stuart's departure, Lieutenant Robins directed his four men to dismantle a rail fence. The rails were piled on the bridge and torched. While waiting for the bridge to burn, the Confederates lounged on the north bank of the island. Soon, there was hissing and a cloud of steam as the temporary span burned through, and the timbers fell into the turbulent waters. Major Morris and his 8-man patrol now galloped into view on the opposite side of the channel. Throwing his carbine to his shoulder, Morris shot at the Confederates, but he was wide of his mark.

---

[169] Ibid., p. 1019.

[170] Ibid.

[171] Ibid., p. 1017.

Robins and his four comrades secured their horses concealed in the bushes and took off.[172]

As soon as the Confederates had disappeared, Morris' patrol retraced its steps and reported to Colonel Rush what had happened. The colonel still had hopes of capturing Confederate stragglers. For the next hour, he kept his men reconnoitering the woods about Sycamore Springs and Providence Mill, but they were unable to find any Confederates. Rush, now satisfied that all of the Southerners had escaped across the Chickahominy, prepared to return to Tunstall's Station. Just as the Lancers were leaving Sycamore Springs, three companies of the 11th Pennsylvania Cavalry joined them. Colonel Ingalls had ordered them to report to Colonel Rush.[173]

General Cooke reached Tunstall's about noon and hurried to General Emory's headquarters. Emory informed his superior that Major Morris' combat patrol had found and was following the Rebels' trail. Before pressing on, Cooke decided to let the tired troopers of the 1st, 5th, and 6th U.S. Cavalry rest. Emory, however, would not wait any longer; he took a section of Company I, 5th, U.S. Light Artillery, and rode to Rush's assistance.[174]

Emory and the artillerists soon overtook the 8th Pennsylvania Reserves. At Talleysville, one of Colonel Rush's couriers hailed Emory and told him that the Lancers had chased the Rebels across the Chickahominy. Whereupon Emory halted his column, pending the receipt of additional information from Colonel Rush. Colonel Rush's command soon appeared. After Rush corroborated the messenger's statement, Emory led his column back to Tunstall's.[175]

In the meantime, General Cooke had again taken the field. It was 3 p.m. when the general rode away from Tunstall's at the head of his Regulars. Before the troopers proceeded very far, Cooke received a mes-

---

[172] Ibid.; Robins, "Stuart's Ride," pp. 274-275.

[173] *OR* 11, pt. 1, pp. 1017, 1034.

[174] Ibid., pp. 1012, 1014.

[175] Ibid., p. 1014.

sage from Emory telling of the Confederates' escape, and he reversed his line of march.[176]

By late afternoon on the 14th, all the columns (Cooke's, Emory's, and Rush's) were back at Tunstall's Station, where they spent the night. The next morning, Cooke led his Cavalry Reserve back to its Gaines' Mill base. General Reynolds' infantry brigade returned to Dispatch Station on the 15th.[177]

Colonel Warren was not the only infantry officer unimpressed by the showing made by the Union cavalry in its efforts to cope with Stuart's lightening-like thrust. Corps commander Porter had harsh words for General Cooke and, to a lesser degree, General Emory. Porter informed McClellan on June 19:

> . . . General Cooke seems to have regarded his force as a reserve for the day of battle, and not therefore expected to perform any picket duty; at least no picket duty had been performed by it until ordered by me, except by Captain Royall's command. General Cooke seems to have confined his protection of our flank to scouting with one squadron from Pipingtree Ferry to the point on Pole Creek [Green] Church road where rested General Stoneman's pickets.
>
> I can only express surprise that General Cooke or General Emory did not join earlier their comrades in front and there act as circumstances required, and that when General Cooke did pursue he should have had his legs tied with. . .[Warren's] infantry command.
>
> I have seen no energy or spirit in the pursuit by General Cooke of the enemy. . . [nor has he] exhibited the characteristics of a skillful and active guardian of our flanks.[178]

Stuart, after crossing the Chickahominy, led his column up the south bank. He and his staff stopped at the home of Thomas Christian, where they lay down on a carpet spread on the grass and slept for two hours. It

---

[176] Ibid., pp. 1012, 1026-1027.

[177] Ibid., pp. 1012, 1027, 1029.

[178] Ibid., p. 1006.

was Sunday afternoon; the officers—except for the brief nap that they had taken while in the saddle—had not had any sleep since Friday night. Upon awakening, the famished staff ate Mr. Christian "out of house and home."[179]

While the general and his staff rested, the column pushed steadily on, toward the James River. Lieutenant Robins recalled that the march from the Chickahominy to the James was made "as vigorously as the jaded horses were able to stand." The troopers, though bone weary and hungry, were in good spirits, and jubilant over the successful crossing of the Chickahominy. Overtaking his command, Stuart rode to Judge Isaac Christian's plantation near Charles City Court House. Once again, the general and his staff were royally entertained. The rest of the column stopped at Buckland, a plantation belonging to Col. J. M. Wilcox. The horses grazed in a clover field, and the dozing troopers allowed their mounts to eat their fill. At twilight, the men kindled camp fires to cook rations the foragers had gathered.[180]

At sunset, Jeb Stuart turned over the command to Fitz Lee. The commanding general wished to carry his report of the success of the expedition to General Lee. Before leaving Judge Christian's, Stuart told Fitz Lee that the march to Richmond would be resumed at 11 p.m. Accompanied by Frayser and one courier, Stuart set off for the capital. It was 30 miles from Charles City Court House to Richmond. For two-thirds of the way, the riders were in danger of encountering Union scouting parties. Stuart was undaunted. He made only one stop during the long, hard ride, halting briefly at Rowland's Mill to get a cup of coffee. The sun was peeping over the eastern horizon on Sunday, June 15, when Stuart rode up to Lee's headquarters at the Dabbs house. After reporting to the general the results of the expedition, and having received his congratulations, Stuart rejoined his command.[181]

While en route to General Lee's headquarters, Stuart had sent Private Frayser to inform Mrs. Stuart and Governor John Letcher of Vir-

---

[179] McClellan, *I Rode with Jeb Stuart*, p. 66; Cooke, *Wearing of the Gray*, p. 180.

[180] McClellan, *I Rode with Jeb Stuart*, p. 66; Robins, "Stuart's Ride," p. 275.

[181] McClellan, *I Rode with Jeb Stuart*, p. 66; *OR* 11, pt. 1, p. 1039.

ginia of the safe return of the command. In recognition of Stuart's services to the Confederacy, Letcher subsequently presented the cavalry
leader with a handsome saber.[182]

Fitz Lee, in accordance with Stuart's instructions, had the cavalrymen in their saddles at 11 p.m. The omnipresent Lieutenant Robins was
again placed in charge of the vanguard. A full moon lighted the column's
line of march as it pushed up the River road. "Although in the saddle and
in motion, and aware that the safety of the expedition depended on great
vigilance in case the enemy should be encountered," Lieutenant Robins
found it difficult to keep awake. He repeatedly fell asleep and woke up
with a start just as he was starting to fall off his horse.[183]

At frequent intervals, the cavalrymen caught sight of the James
River off to their left. This caused shudders of apprehension to pass
along the column, because it was common knowledge that dreaded Union gunboats cruised the river. Early on June 15, the riders passed in
succession the "Double Gates," "Strawberry Plains" and "Tilman's
Gate." At Tilman's, the Confederates sighted a forest of masts and spars
on the river. Fortunately for the Southerners, the Union tars did not keep
a sharp lookout, and the raiders passed unobserved.

Soon thereafter, a sharp cry, "Who goes there?" rang out. The Confederate vanguard reined in their horses. Robins' people were relieved to
discover that they had been challenged by an outpost of troopers from
the 10th Virginia Cavalry commanded by Col. J. Lucius Davis. After
exchanging greetings and accepting Colonel Davis' congratulations, the
column moved on. The troopers forded Baileys Creek, passed the "Drill-
Room," and ascended New Market Heights. Having arrived well within
the Confederate defense lines, Fitz Lee halted his column about a mile
beyond the heights. After the men had rested and eaten, Fitz Lee permitted the regiments to return at an easy pace to their camps northwest of
Richmond.[184]

---

[182] McClellan, *I Rode with Jeb Stuart*, pp. 66-67.

[183] Robins, "Stuart's Ride," p. 275.

[184] Ibid., p. 275.

The tangible results of the expedition were considerable. Stuart turned over 164 prisoners to the provost-marshal when the column reached Richmond; 260 captured horses and mules went to the quartermasters of the various units constituting Stuart's command.[185] In addition, a large amount of public property belonging to the Army of the Potomac had been destroyed. Colonel Ingalls, the commandant of the great White House Landing supply depot, reported:

> So far as this depot was directly concerned it lost two schooners and some forage—amount unknown—and in all not to exceed 75 wagons. There were more trains lost, probably, but they were in possession of brigade quartermasters, serving with the army in front . . . We are daily recovering wagons and animals which the rebels were unable to carry away.[186]

Even more remarkable, the Confederates lost only one man killed in their three-day, 100-mile ride around McClellan's army. Captain Latané had been slain, "with his back to the ground and his feet to the foe."[187] Several other butternuts had been wounded.

More important than the capture and destruction of the public property was the information about conditions behind the Union lines gleaned by Stuart's expedition. Stuart reported to Lee that the roads around Tunstall's Station were worse than those behind the Confederate front. Lee was encouraged by this news because it meant that the roads would hinder McClellan's movements. Stuart told his chief the Federals were using wagon trains to supply the right flank of their army. There was no indication that McClellan planned to shift his base from White House Landing to James River. Lee welcomed this intelligence, for if the troops in his projected offensive turned the Federal right, they would cut McClellan's supply lines.[188]

---

[185] *OR* 11, pt. 1, p. 1039.

[186] Ibid., p. 1032.

[187] McClellan, *I Rode with Jeb Stuart*, p. 67.

[188] Douglas S. Freeman, *R.E. Lee, A Biography*, 4 vols.(New York, 1934), vol. 2, pp. 100-101.

Stuart had also collected invaluable data concerning the condition of affairs on the right of the Army of the Potomac. Except for cavalry patrols, the Federals had no troops guarding the Totopotomoy-Pamunkey watershed. There was nothing, insofar as Stuart could determine, to prevent the Confederates from turning Porter's formidable position behind Beaver Dam Creek. Fitz John Porter's right flank was not anchored on a formidable topographic feature—it was "up in the air" in military parlance—and vulnerable. This news was of momentous importance. In Lee's opinion, "It justified all the risks that Stuart had taken."[189]

The key to Lee's planned offensive was Stonewall Jackson's 15,000-man Valley Army, which in the heady days since its June 8 and June 9 victories at Cross Keys and Port Republic had been resting and regrouping at Mt. Meridian. Lee wanted Jackson to bring his two divisions east of the Blue Ridge and, by rapid marches, turn the right flank of Porter's Beaver Dam Creek line north of the Chickahominy. Lee, as soon as he heard Jackson's guns, was to cross the Chickahominy with a powerful host and, attacking from west to east, crush Porter's V Corps and destroy McClellan's White House Landing depot.

Aside from these strategic considerations, the "Ride Around McClellan" boosted "the *morale* not only of the cavalry, but of the whole army." Lee's confidence in his youthful cavalry leader and Stuart's "confidence in himself were confirmed." McClellan's prestige in the North was shaken by Stuart's success.[190]

In his congratulatory order to his men dated June 17, Stuart referred to himself as "The general of cavalry." Writing of the expedition in his after action report filed on the same day, Stuart was not reserved in describing his accomplishments.

At the same time, Stuart forwarded a letter to Lee enumerating and recommending for promotion those of his subordinates who had distinguished themselves on the expedition:[191]

Stuart's letter to Lee reads as follows:

---

[189] Ibid., p. 101.

[190] McClellan, *I Rode with Jeb Stuart*, p. 67; Freeman, *Lee's Lieutenants*, 1, p. 301.

[191] *OR* 11, pt. 1, pp. 1036, 1041; Freeman, *Lee's Lieutenants*, 1, p. 310.

General R. E. Lee,
Commanding Department of Northern Virginia:

General: I have the honor to append to my report of the Pamunkey expedition the following recommendations, which were suggested more particularly by the distinguished service rendered there:

1. Col. Fitzhugh Lee, First Virginia Cavalry, for promotion as brigadier-general of cavalry. In my estimation no one in the Confederacy possesses more of the elements of what a brigadier of cavalry ought to be than he.

2. Col. W. H. F. Lee, rivaling his cousin in the daring exploits of this expedition, establishing a like claim to the same grade.

3. Lieut. Col. W. T. Martin to have Shannon's and two other companies added to the Legion, so as to be colonel; a grade which he has fairly won.

4. Assist. Surg. J. B. Fontaine to be surgeon of his regiment (Fourth Virginia Cavalry), now without one. Dr. Fontaine is a man of signal military merit and an adept in his profession.

5. M. Heros von Borcke, a Prussian cavalry officer, has shown himself a thorough soldier and a splendid officer. I hope the Department will confer as high a commission as possible on this deserving man, who has cast his lot with us in the trying hour.

6. First Lieut. Redmond Burke to be captain, for the important service rendered by him on this occasion.

7. Capts. W. D. Farley and J. S. Mosby, without commission, have established a claim for position which a grateful country

will not, I trust, disregard. Their distinguished services run far back toward the beginning of the war, and present a shining record of daring and usefulness.

8. First Lieut. W. T. Robins, adjutant Ninth Virginia Cavalry, would be a valuable addition to the Regular Army.[192] Lee replied with a General Order, announcing to the Army of Northern Virginia that he took "great pleasure in expressing his admiration of the courage and skill so conspicuously exhibited throughout by. . .[General Stuart] and the officers and men under his command."[193]

This boost to Confederate morale was partially counterbalanced by the repercussions it had on McClellan's game plan. McClellan for some time had been concerned about the security of the railroad linking White House Landing with his forward Savage's Station supply depot. Stuart's raid confirmed its vulnerability, and McClellan determined to relocate his principal depot for receipt of the matériel of war from the North and their stockpiling from White House Landing to Harrison's Landing on James River.

On June 18, the day that Franklin's VI Corps completed its redeployment from north of the Chickahominy to Golding's Farm, the first supplies left White House by boat for the new base on James River. Porter's V Corps, the strongest numerically following the addition of the newly arrived division of George McCall, would remain north of the Chickahominy for the time being to guard the approaches to White House Landing while the change of base was effected.

---

[192]   *OR* 11, pt. 1, p. 1041.

[193]   Ibid., p. 1042.

This period illustration of Stuart and his men captures the
romantic imagery associated with the ride around McClellan.

Richard J. Sommers

A native of Hammond, Indiana, Dr. Richard Sommers received his B.A. degree from Carleton College in 1964 and his Ph.D degree from Rice University in 1970. He has written numerous articles and book reviews on the Civil War, and is best known for his award-winning study *Richmond Redeemed: The Siege of Petersburg* (Doubleday, 1981), which earned him the first biennial Bell Wiley Prize from the National Historical Society for the best Civil War book of 1980 and 1981. Since 1982, he has been a member of the Editorial Advisory Board for the multi-volume *The Papers of Jefferson Davis*, and since 1986 has been a member of the Board of Directors of the Society of Civil War Historians. Dr. Sommers taught at the U.S. Army War College from 1983-1985, and is currently the Chief Archivist-Historian at the U.S. Military Institute, Carlisle, Pennsylvania.

"They fired into us an awful fire"

The Civil War Diary of Pvt. Charles C. Perkins,
1st Massachusetts Infantry Regiment, June 4 - July 4, 1862

The Peninsula Campaign established the reputations of many Civil War generals—including R. E. Lee, John B. Hood, Joseph Hooker, and Fitz John Porter—ruined the reputations of others—such as G. W. Smith, John B. Magruder, Silas Casey, and Erasmus D. Keyes—and left the reputations of still others seriously in doubt—chief among them, "Stonewall" Jackson and George B. McClellan.

Yet the campaign involved more than just the exercise of high command. Approximately 200,000 junior officers and soldiers fought in that campaign between March and August, 1862. One of them was Charles C. Perkins, a private serving as bugler of Company K of the 1st Massachusetts Infantry Regiment.

Born and raised in Salem, Massachusetts, he was working in Boston as a civil engineer for the firm of Shedd & Edson when Civil War erupted. He promptly enlisted in the 1st Massachusetts, May 24, 1861, 23 days short of his 20th birthday. Ahead of him lay a full three years of service, from Blackburn's Ford to Spotsylvania. With his surviving comrades, he returned to Boston for the muster-out of the regiment on May 25, 1864. The remainder of his life was spent in the Bay State, much of it in his native Salem. Death came on March 28, 1915.

Countless soldiers, North and South, had similar experiences. What sets Perkins apart is that he was intelligent (high school valedictorian, member of the surveying party for the cog railroad up New Hampshire's Mount Washington), observant, and descriptive. Most diarists would have used four volumes to record the events of 36 months of service over four calendar years. Perkins, however, needed 13 volumes to set down his experiences. Three volumes had already been filled before the

Peninsula Campaign even began. He devoted the equivalent of two more to those operations. The result is an amazingly full recounting of the details of soldier life in camp, on the march, and in battle.

These diaries survived the war and the disastrous Salem fire of June 25, 1914, which destroyed hundreds of buildings, including Perkins' home. Through the generosity of his grandson, Mr. Frederic P. Clark, a copy of Charles Perkins' diaries has been made and preserved at the U.S. Army Military History Institute as part of the *Civil War Times Illustrated* Collection.

The following diary entries come from Volume IV-A . They cover the arrival of the 1st Massachusetts at the front near Richmond on June 4, 1862, just after the Battle of Seven Pines, and continue for a month through the Seven Days Battles until McClellan's Army of the Potomac reached the James River at Harrison's Landing. Recounting those 31 days would have taken an ordinary diarist 10 diary pages, which could be transcribed onto perhaps three legal-sized pages.

For Perkins, the transcript for that month runs to 27 legal-sized pages, single spaced. Even that extensive account represents his own abridgment, for when he re-transcribed his original entries into a different volume on December 31, 1863, he acknowledged that he would "only write principal items as there is not room for all." What he omitted is not known, but what remains, in the richness of its detail, provides an excellent record of one soldier's experience of the tedium and terror of war on the Peninsula.

Here, then, is Charles Perkins' day-by-day account of the decisive month in the campaign for Richmond:[1]

---

[1] The biographical information on Private Perkins comes from Mr. Clark. A special expression of gratitude is due to Mr. Clark for sharing the diaries with researchers through the Institute. He loaned the volumes for copying. Too faint to be photocopied, they were transcribed. Some words and passages remain illegible; fortunately, there are few such gaps in the entries printed in this article. Particular credit goes to Ms. Valerie Metzler, formerly the archives technician of the Institute, for her diligence in transcribing almost all of the diary. Gratitude also goes to Mr. Michael P. Musick, Civil War specialist of the National Archives, for his exceptional—but, from him, characteristic—helpfulness in making available the holdings of his repository, which he knows so well. The entries are printed virtually as written, including occasional lapses of spelling and capitalization; the obtrusive use of the word "sic" is avoided. The only change is the occasional insertion of a period, a comma, or a semicolon for clarity; brackets are not used around those inserted punctuation marks.

Wednesday, June 4th, 1862: Up at the magic call. Beans, Co. K, and they were tip top. Still saying men had to stand under arms this morn & got wet through. Took bugle from guardhouse. Road all washed away in places nearly 3 feet deep. Still raining very hard. Flat below hill all covered with water. Commenced letter home yesterday. Added to it today. Inclosed 36 C.C.P., did not get chance to send it.[2] Orders to pack up about 10. In few moments had permission to wait 2 hours and cook grub. Fresh meat served out and plenty of crackers. Started about 12, fine rain, showery. Marched towards Richmond about 7 or 8 miles and camped near the battleground of Saturday.[3] Heavy rain just as we arrived. Pitched our tents; passed the Jerseys and Sickles and are about 1/2 mile from the picket.[4] Near 7 Pines about 1/2 mile to south of R.R. Dead bodies of Rebels lying round, any quantity of them, all alive with magots. Bad smell. Trees all felled on battlefield. Went about a mile for water and turned in; ate no supper, awful tired. Casey's Div. took our place at Poplar Hill.[5] Rained in night.

Thursday, June 5th, 1862: Rheumatism in legs and knees, awful pains in night, could not sleep much. Regt. up at 3 or 4, packed up, struck tent and left for picket. I did not go. Thought I was not able. J. Y. J. Clark, Chase, Cooks

---

[2] The term "36 C. C. P." refers to the 36th installment of his diary which he transcribed and mailed home. Similar references appear all through his diary, cf. June 6, June 7, June 9, June 11, June 20, June 24, June 27. Charles C. Perkins Papers, *Civil War Times Illustrated* Coll., U.S. Army Military History Institute, Carlisle Barracks, PA. The collection and repository are hereinafter cited as *CWTI* and USAMHI, respectively.

[3] The Battle of Seven Pines raged on Saturday, May 31, and Sunday, June 1, 1862.

[4] Prior to the Battle of Seven Pines, Brig. Gen. Joseph Hooker's Second Division of the III Corps refused the Federal left rear by facing southward atop Poplar Hill, the high ground which overlooked the principal crossing of White Oak Swamp at White Oak Bridge. As the course of that battle grew increasingly ominous on May 31, Hooker led Brig. Gen. Daniel Sickles' Second (Excelsior) Brigade and half of Col. Samuel H. Starr's Third (Second Jersey) Brigade toward the front. They arrived too late to fight on Saturday but were heavily engaged on Sunday. Meantime, Brig. Gen. Cuvier Grover's First Brigade, in which Perkins served, remained on Poplar Hill to secure the left rear. Only on the afternoon of June 4 did Grover rejoin Hooker at the front. The remaining two regiments of the Jersey Brigade, which had held the Williamsburg Road crossing of the Chickahominy River at Bottom's Bridge, would return to the Second Division on June 5. U.S. War Department, *War of the Rebellion: A Compilation of the Official Records of the Union and Confederate Armies*, 128 vols. (Washington, D.C., 1880-1901), series I, vol. 11, pt. 1, pp. 818-824, 835-838. Hereinafter cited as *OR*. All references are to series I unless otherwise noted.

[5] Brigadier General Silas Casey's Second Division of the IV Corps had put up a brave fight and endured a terrible beating on May 31. Crippled and distrusted, it was relegated to a quiet rear sector at Poplar Hill and Bottom's Bridge, so that all of Hooker's men—battle-tested veterans of Yorktown and Williamsburg—could take over its former sector at the front.

and some 6 or 8 others stayed behind.[6] 2nd N.H. & 11th Mass. went on picket last night. 26th went with 1st this morning.[7] Cloudy morn but sun out occasionally. Breakfast: dipper of tea & crackers and my fresh meat. Awful muddy roads yesterday. In one place over boots in water. This morn tongue is coated. Am pretty well played out. Capt. C. had rheumatics and had to remain behind at Poplar Hill. Lieut. C. in Comd.[8] Laying round all day. Cloudy & sun by spells. Dinner: salt beef and dipper of tea made myself. In P.M. went with Chaplain and about 1/2 dozen others to bury the Rebel dead near camp.[9] Covered them over with dirt. Got a S.C. button from one.[10] Exposed parts of bodies black; skins of hands white & tight like close-fitting gloves. Buried 7 in all. Cannonading at right in A.M. Supper: tea, crackers and salt junk.

Friday, June 6th, 1862: Chaplain says balloon folks report the evacuation of Richmond taking place rapidly. Reinforcements coming to us every train.[11] Regt. came in about dusk last eve, relieved by Sickles' men. Up early, raining

---

[6] Sergeant John Y. J. Clark of Roxbury served with Company K from May 24, 1861, until transferred to the Veteran Reserve Corps, July 1, 1863; he lost his life in an accident, September 8, 1863. Another original member, Benjamin F. Chase of Boston, was one of Perkins' tent mates. He was still a private but would be a sergeant when his three years expired on May 25, 1864. Massachusetts Adjutant General, *Massachusetts Soldiers, Sailors, and Marines in the Civil War*, 9 vols. (Norwood, Mass., 1931), vol. 1, p. 61. Hereinafter cited as *Mass. Soldiers*.

[7] Grover's brigade consisted of the 1st and 11th Massachusetts, 2nd New Hampshire, and 26th Pennsylvania Infantry Regiments.

[8] "Capt. C." was Abial G. Chamberlain of Roxbury, who had commanded Company K since it was organized in the spring of 1861, ranking from May 22. On November 10, 1863, he would be discharged from the 1st Massachusetts to become lieutenant-colonel of the 37th U.S. Colored Infantry Regiment. His first lieutenant was Frank W. Carruth of Roxbury. Originally Company K's second lieutenant, he had been promoted one grade as of May 8, 1862. By the time the regiment mustered out, he would be captain of Company H. *Mass. Soldiers*, 1, pp. 60-61.

[9] Warren H. Cudworth of East Boston not only served as regimental chaplain for all three years but also wrote the history of the unit. In that book, he dwelt upon the horrors of the Seven Pines battlefield and of the burial detail there. Ibid., p. 2; Warren H. Cudworth, *History of the First Regiment (Massachusetts Infantry)*. . . (Boston, Mass., 1866), pp. 195-196.

[10] The fallen soldier must have belonged to Brig. Gen. Richard H. Anderson's South Carolina Brigade, which had battled heavily around the Williamsburg Road, May 31.

[11] Among the units to arrive was the 2nd New York Infantry Regiment, which reached the Army of the Potomac on June 5 and which was assigned to the Third Brigade of Hooker's division on June 6. The colonel of the 2nd, Joseph B. Carr, outranked Starr and thus had command of the brigade through the upcoming Seven Days Battles until the assigned commander returned to duty on July 4. Frederick H. Dyer, *A Compendium of the War of the Rebellion* (New York, N.Y., and London, U.K., 1959), p. 1405; Frederick Phisterer, *New York in the War of the Rebellion*, 6 vols. (Albany, N.Y., 1912), vol. 2, p. 1707; *OR* 11, pt. 2, pp. 149-152.

Pvt. Charles C. Perkins
Bugler, Company K, 1st Massachusetts Infantry Regiment

Capt. Abial G. Chamberlain
Perkins' company commander

1st Lt. Frank W. Carruth
Perkins' acting company commander

Acting Sgt. Nathaniel Averell
Perkins' non-commissioned officer

Chap. Warren H. Cudworth
Chaplain and
historian of Perkins' regiment

fine, misty. Coffee, salt junk and crackers. Added to mother's letter and put it in the office. Recd. letter from Father & Mother, 9 stamps, also 2 heralds and gazette[12] & letter from E. M. P.[13] Went over to 19th just beyond R. R. Saw Lieut. Hill & Capt. Batchelder, Co. C; Lieut. Reynolds, Co. D, was left behind sick.[14] Little rain this forenoon. Dinner: salt junk & crackers. Answ'd. father's and enclosed 37 C. C. P. Carrying off the wounded today on R. R.[15] Dead not yet all buried. Awful, terrible. Reading &c. in P.M. Cloudy. Supper: tea & crackers. Turned in early. Stench from the battlefield is awful to breathe; wind blows this way.

Saturday, June 7th, 1862: Up early. Pleasant. Men shooting cattle waked us. Coffee and crackers. Letter to Mother & enclosed 38 C. C. P. & sent 39 C. C. P. Warm forenoon. Dinner: soup, very good. Recd. letter from E. P. Burnham.[16] Answ'd. E. M. P.'s & sent Magnolia bud & rose. Reading &c. Thunder shower coming up. Cannonading up to right.[17] Orders to march in light order at 3 o'c. Heavy rain. Served out coffee, sugar & fresh meat & dozen crackers. Whit put his knapsack in mine and made one knapsack of the 2 & left them in tent.[18]

---

[12] The "herald" was presumably the *Boston Herald*. If the "gazette" came from his parents, as the sentence suggests, it was probably the *Salem Daily Gazette*. It could, however, have been the *Roxbury Gazette* if E. M. P. sent it. Winifred Gregory, comp., *Newspapers, 1821-1936* (New York, N.Y., 1937), pp. 275-276, 280, 298.

[13] His parents were Edward Burnham Perkins and Elizabeth Barrett Perkins of Salem, Massachusetts. "E. M. P." was Mrs. Elizabeth M. Pickering. She and her husband, Daniel ("Mr. P."), rented to Charles Perkins a room in their home at 18 Eliot Street in the 10th Ward of Boston, just south of the Common. He was living with the Pickerings when he enlisted in May, 1861. Throughout his military service, they faithfully corresponded with him. Information comes courtesy of Mr. Frederic P. Clark and is in the Perkins Papers, *CWTI* Coll., USAMHI; U.S. Census of Boston, Suffolk County, Massachusetts, 1860, reel 523, p. 184, National Archives, Washington, D.C. Hereinafter cited as NA.

[14] The three officers—Capt. George W. Batchelder, 1st Lt. John P. Reynolds, and 2nd Lt. William A. Hill—all hailed from Salem. The two senior officers had joined the 19th Massachusetts Infantry Regiment on August 22, 1861; Hill went into that outfit on February 19, 1862. The 19th was part of Brig. Gen. John Sedgwick's division, which occupied a sector of works to the north of Hooker, with the other division of the II Corps between them. *Mass. Soldiers*, 2, pp. 428, 439, 451.

[15] All references in this article to a railroad pertain to the Richmond and York River Railroad.

[16] Emily P. Burnham, a frequent correspondent, may have been related to Perkins through his father or to the soldier's girl friend, Eunice G. Burnham, or both.

[17] Confederate artillery tried unsuccessfully to disrupt Northern efforts to build two additional bridges across the Chickahominy River. Skirmishing also erupted that day as Federal pickets pushed back their Southern counterparts about a mile. *OR* 11, pt. 1, p. 46.

[18] "Whit" was Pvt. Harrison Whittemore of Andover. He was perhaps Perkins' best friend in the regiment. They had worked together in civil engineering before the war, had enlisted together, and had tented together through the Siege of Yorktown until Whittemore was wounded at the Battle of Williamsburg. They were bunking together again in June. Still a private since May 24, 1861, he

Line was formed and we marched in rain to relieve Jersey Brig. on picket. Only rained little while took position. Behind earthworks on right of Fort, 2nd N. H. on left.[19] Artillery was also relieved at same time. Men divided into 3 reliefs. Those on duty keep muskets in hand all time. I made some tea for supper. Made a bed of logs of wood. Slept nearly all night. Men roused up once in a while but 'twas a scare, dogs barking on right. All up at 3 and under arms till daylight. Slept well. Somewhat of a stench arising from the dead horses &c. &c. But by the aid of a swamp magnolia I got asleep.

Sunday, June 8th, 1862: Made dipper of tea. Salt junk brought out to us, being only about 1/4 mile from camp. Cloudy morn. Firing off to right, pickets & vollies of musketry. Rebs throwing shells also. Near R. R. Our men chopping trees down. Dinner: salt junk &c. Cloudy & sunshine by spells today. Recd. Boston Journal from G. E. Bousley & 'twas directed G. C. Perkins.[20] Picket brought in prisoner with flag of truce, white rag on a willow stick, blind-folded. Gen. Heintzelman & Keyes & Hooker passed with distinguished visitors:[21] Gen. Prim, another Spanish Gen. and admiral.[22] Working party, 20 men from

---

would wear a sergeant's stripes when Company K mustered out three years later. *Mass. Soldiers*, 1, p. 65.

[19] The official name of this stronghold was Battery 3. Its garrison in June nicknamed it "Fort Hooker." But it is known to history as "Casey's Redoubt," the site of heavy fighting on May 31. *OR* 11, pt. 1, pp. 113-115; Martin A. Haynes, *A History of the Second Regiment, New Hampshire Volunteer Infantry* (Lakeport, N.H., 1896), pp. 88-91.

[20] George E. Bousley of Salem was apparently still a civilian in early June. On July 1, 1862, however, his Company B of the 7th Massachusetts Militia Regiment went on active duty for six months garrisoning Fort Warren in Boston harbor. *Mass. Soldiers*, 5, p. 334.

[21] Brig. Gen. Erasmus D. Keyes of Maine (born May 29, 1810) was graduated from West Point in 1832, served on General-in-Chief Winfield Scott's staff in the Old Army, led a brigade at First Bull Run, and commanded the IV Corps from March 1862 to August 1863. He resigned from the army in 1864 and passed away in 1895. Brig. Gen. Samuel P. Heintzelman of Pennsylvania (born September 30, 1805) was graduated from West Point in 1826 and served in the Regular Army until 1869, eleven years before his death. After commanding a division at First Bull Run, he had charge of the III Corps, March-October 1862. He subsequently commanded the XXII Corps and the Northern Department. Within the III Corps, the 1st Massachusetts served in the Second Division under Hooker. An 1837 graduate of the U.S. Military Academy, Hooker served as a staff officer in the Mexican War. Resigning in 1853, he re-entered military service in 1861 and went on to head a brigade and division, the I and V Corps, the Center Grand Division, and the Army of the Potomac itself at Chancellorsville. In the autumn of 1863, he took four divisions to Tennessee and subsequently commanded the XX Corps in the Atlanta Campaign. In October, 1864, he succeeded Heintzelman in charge of the Northern Department. He retired in 1868 and passed away October 31, 1879, just short of his 65th birthday. Ezra J. Warner, *Generals in Blue* (Baton Rouge, LA, 1964), pp. 227-228, 233-235, 264-265.

[22] The Northern generals were escorting a visiting delegation of six Spanish military observers, who arrived that day. Heading the delegation was Lt. Gen. Don Juan Prim y Prats, the Count of Reus and Marquis de los Castillejos, who had commanded the Spanish portion of the European

each co., detailed in P.M., more rifle pits at right; were relieved at about 4 or 5 [by] Jerseys. Supper: bean soup & tea & crackers. Turned in early.

Monday, June 9th, 1862: Up early. Tea, salt beef &c. Pleasant. Last night 'twas cool. Had to put my frock coat over me. Slept well. Letter to E. P. Burnham. One to Mother, enclosing No. 40 C. C. P. Pleasant in A.M. Dinner: boiled rice and sugar. Nap before dinner. Cool air today. Paid off this P.M. Recd. 6.00 March & April. Supper: coffee and crackers. Cool evening. Morn .00, Eve 6.00.[23] Turned in after reading by candle light some time. Chase, Holden, Huggins, & Rich were playing Bluff far into the night. Got up in night. Many tents lit up by gamblers probably.[24]

Tuesday, June 10, 1862: Rained last night and all today. Coffee & salt junk. In A.M. took long nap in blanket with boots off. Reading some, pretty cold. Dinner: soup, very good. In P.M. reading, sleeping & dreaming of home & surroundings. Supper: coffee and crackers. Regt. went off on picket at 3 P.M. I did not [pull picket duty]. Paid G. W. Burditt 1.50.[25] Paid 50 cts. which I subscribed for testimonial to Steward of Roxbury.[26] Morn 6.00, Eve 4.00. Reading Waverly Mag. which Holden lent me. Turned in early.

---

force which intervened in Mexico in December, 1861. Spain, however, had pulled out of Mexico in April, 1862, so by June the presence of these officers in Union lines was welcome—at least by the government in Washington (though McClellan soon grew tired of them). Prim's party included his chief of staff, Gen. Lorenzo Milans de Bosch; his aides de camp, Colonel Deutenre and Don Tasto San Miguel; the historian Perez Calvo; and the U.S. State Department escort, Mr. Sales. The naval officer in the party was not an admiral but the commander of the warship *San Juan de Ulloa*, which had brought Prim's delegation to America, a colonel whose name is variously rendered as "Cortasar," "Cortazen," or even "Castara." George B. McClellan, *The Civil War Papers of George B. McClellan*, edited by Stephen W. Sears (New York, N.Y., 1989), pp. 293-296; *New York Herald*, June 12, 13, 17, 1862.

[23] Perkins frequently recorded his expenses for the morning, H.N. (high noon), and evening.

[24] Sergeant John H. Holden and wagoner James M. Huggins, both from Roxbury, were original members of Company K. The teamster served all three years, but the non-com's military career was fast drawing to a close. Private Orange S. Richardson ("Rich") of Newton Corner served in Company K from June 11, 1861, until discharged for wounds on October 4, 1863. Richardson and especially Chase had tented with Perkins since May 15; the sergeant also tented with him several times in late May. *Mass. Soldiers*, 1, pp. 62, 64; Perkins, *Diary*, May 15, 17, 25, 1862, *CWTI* Coll., USAMHI.

[25] Fellow musician George W. Burditt of Company G, a resident of Boston, enlisted on May 23, 1861, and served a full three years. He had shared quarters with Perkins before the spring campaign began. Their relationship proved a strange mixture of friendship and feuding. *Mass. Soldiers*, 1, p. 40.

[26] This reference is not clear. There were no soldiers in the 1st Massachusetts named "Steward." Whether, indeed, "Steward" was the name of a civilian or the title of a civic official back in Roxbury is not known to the editor.

Wednesday, June 11th, 1862: Up early. Breakfast: salt junk, coffee & crackers. Loafing in A.M. Went over to R. R. Bought 3 oranges, 25 cts.; 10 ginger cakes for 25 cts. Dinner: soup, very good. Sent 1.00 home in letter to Mother, also my little bugle I wore on my cap, also 41 C. C. P. In P.M. reading &c. Recd. 4 papers E. M. P. Supper: coffee and crackers. Eve walking, full moon. Morn 4.00, Eve 2.50. Men came in from picket about 4 o'c. Pleasant day. Burditt gave me a segar and I smoked it like a damned fool. Borrowed Mr. Tidd's razor and shaved my mustache off, got the hang of it after awhile, cut my nose again. Men got their whiskey this eve; have not had it for some time.[27]

Thursday, June 12, 1862: Picket firing last night, about dozen shots. Eclipse of moon, saw it when just going on. Men playing bluff in tents. Salt junk, coffee and crackers. Pleasant morn. Went up to R. R., bought jar of apple jelly .50 & 25 cts. worth of Tamarinds. Ate most of them. Pickles of Col's cook .25.[28] Paper of pepper .07. Sent 1.00 home by letter to Mother. Morn 2.50, eve .18, ginger cakes .25 cts. for 10. Dinner: bean soup. Recd. letter from Father 29 & E. M. P. 31 (back mail). Fell into line this A.M. in light marching order. Pickets (Sickles' Brig.) advanced and expected fighting. Nothing happened and broke ranks.[29] P.M. very warm. Supper: (Coffee) crackers, butter from Whit. Drew my ration whiskey for Mr. Higgins.[30]

Friday, June 13: Up early. Artillery firing off to right pretty brisk.[31] Pleasant. Shooting cattle out in field other side of road. Regt. stacked arms in line. Morn .18, H. N. 2.38, eve 1.70. Sold Mr. Tidd 6 stamps .20 cts. Bought enve-

---

[27] Squires S. Tidd of North Woburn served in Company K from May 24, 1861, until discharged for disability on November 25, 1862. Although state and federal service records give his first name as "Square," his pension file, containing his own signature, makes clear that his first name was "Squires." Perkins, too, gives Tidd's first name as "Squires." *Mass. Soldiers*, 1, p. 65; Tidd, pension file, Record Group 94, NA. Hereinafter cited as "RG" for "Record Group."

[28] Private George W. Funk of Company A had been detailed as the colonel's cook since May 8, 1862. This resident of Brookline served a full three-year tour in the 1st Massachusetts. Muster roll of Company A, 1st Massachusetts Infantry Regiment, May-June, 1862, RG 94, entry 57, NA; *Mass. Soldiers*, 1, p. 6.

[29] Sickles' advance did provoke light skirmishing, but the Secessionists did not fight back in force. *New York Times*, June 17, 1862.

[30] James T. Higgins of Boston enlisted in Company K on May 24, 1861, as a wagoner; was promoted to sergeant on January 1, 1862; and served until the company mustered out on May 25, 1864. *Mass. Soldiers*, 1, p. 62.

[31] Southern artillerists shelled Brig. Gen. William F. Smith's Second Division of the VI Corps just south of the Chickahominy until his sharpshooters silenced them. George B. McClellan, *McClellan's Own Story* (New York, N.Y., 1887), p. 404.

lopes 20 for 18 cts. Bought 12 cakes for .25 cts., 2 lemons .25. Dinner: soup, very good. Patterson shaved me this A.M., chin & mustache.[32] Warm & sultry day. Letter from Mother & Father in one. 2 papers home & letter M. O. B. & E. M. P. with note for Mr. Gillespie.[33] Lemonade. Sugar at C. H. [cook house]. Over to R. R. in P.M. Whiskey in P.M. & A.M. Line formed in P.M. to go on picket. Drew whiskey for Mr. Tidd in P.M. Pay for sugar for my lemonade. Started for picket at 4 o'c. We had the outposts this time. Capt. C. on duty again. Men posted about 10 paces apart along edge of woods about 1/4 mile outside entrenchments. Capt. C. in command of left companies. Small reserve with him. I stayed near Capt. C. Cooks brought supper out: coffee, fresh meat and crackers. Spread rubber and laid down with no cover. Slept greater part of night. Reb pickets fired few shots when picket was relieved. None hurt within 100 yds. of our picket. Splendid moonlight night. Haversack for pillow.

Saturday, June 14th, 1862: Up before daylight & waked rest of reserve. Cavalry picket, 3 men, stationed here also.[34] Fine morn. Coffee & Salt Junk. No firing night. Reading papers on leisure time. Dan M. B. of Co. D slept with me last night. Heard Rebs beating tattoo last night: "Boom-Shag-i-diddle ditto, Boom Shag i ditto. How's your maum. Old drum going again this morn." Had quite a nap this A.M. Very warm & sultry. Reading &c. Burditt gave 1/2 quire note paper. Stewed beans for dinner & dipper of soup from Co. G, very good. Traveller from home.[35] Sent letters to Father & Mother in eve. Cavalry picket relieved every 12 hours. Were relieved at about 4 or 5. Supper: coffee & few beans (left). Walked with B in eve. Sold my ration of whiskey to Evans .10. Morn 1.70, Eve 1.80. Turned in early in shirt sleeves. Blanket, warm eve, slept well.[36]

[32] Private John Patterson of Roxbury served in Company K from September 27, 1861, until discharged for disability on March 16, 1863. *Mass. Soldiers*, 1, p. 64.

[33] "M. O. B." was Martha O. Barrett, probably a relative of Perkins' mother, Elizabeth Barrett Perkins. The identity of Mr. Gillespie is unclear. He may have been related to Pvt. Edwin C. Gillespie of Montpelier, Vermont, who served in Company F, 1st Massachusetts, from May 24, 1861, until he deserted on October 8, 1862. Ibid., p. 36.

[34] The 3rd Pennsylvania Cavalry Regiment was the mounted arm of Heintzelman's corps. Co.'s E and F of that regiment were on picket from the night of June 13 into the next day. William Brooke Rawle et al., *History of the Third Pennsylvania Cavalry* (Philadelphia, PA, 1905), p. 70.

[35] This newspaper was the *Boston Traveller*, which was also published as the *Boston Morning Traveller* and the *Boston Evening Traveller*. Gregory, p. 282.

[36] Private William Evans from Roxbury survived two wounds and served the full three years with Company K. "Dan M. B. of Co. D" is more difficult to identify. The only soldier in that company with a similar name was Daniel D. Macomber of Boston. Another possibility is Daniel M. Ayer of Company F, who hailed from South Boston. Macomber, who was a friend and a fellow

Sunday, June 15: Up early. Heard Rebs rev [reveille]. Warm morn. Rebs tore up some of our track & fired into cars yesterday. Took some of picket pris. and carried them off. Back some ways in rear.[37] Rice & molasses. Very warm day. Dinner: salt horse and tip top crackers. Rebs threw few shell over this morn near 16th, who arrived and (now) form part of this Brig. day before yesterday.[38] Letter from E. M. P. and 2 papers. Were turned out just before supper, picket firing heard.[39] Thunder shower before supper. Whiskey to Evans .10 cts. Morn 1.80, H. N. 1.90. Bought 10 cakes for 25 cts. 10 of raisins. Eve 1.55. Supper: made tea, good crackers with some of Whit's butter. Turned in early & slept well.

Monday, June 16th, 1862: C. C. P. 21 years old. About 3 o'c were turned out and line formed. Picket firing on right near R. R. Under arms until daylight. Then marched towards fortifications but were ordered back by Grover.[40] Stacked arms and broke ranks. Coffee and salt junk, good crackers & butter.

---

bugler, is probably the soldier to whom Perkins refers. The letter "B," for that matter, may well mean "Bugler" rather than relate to the soldier's name. *Mass. Soldiers*, 1, pp. 26, 34, 61.

[37] This refers to Brig. Gen. "Jeb" Stuart's first ride around the Army of the Potomac. June 13 was actually the date when the raiders cut the York River Railroad at Tunstall's Station and fired on a train. On "yesterday" (i.e., June 14), the Confederate horsemen were south of the tracks on their way back to the main army.

[38] Following the heavy fighting at Seven Pines, May 31-June 1, McClellan combed garrisons on the eastern Peninsula and at Norfolk, Portsmouth, and Suffolk for veteran reinforcements. Among the infantry regiments which were thus ordered to the front were not only Carr's 2nd New York but also the 16th Massachusetts under Col. Powell T. Wyman. That outfit reached White House Landing on June 10-11, got as far as the Chickahominy River on the latter day (Wednesday), and formally reported at Savage's Station on the 12th. But as Perkins makes clear, the regiment did not actually join Grover until June 13. Organized June 29, 1861, the 16th had served in southeastern Virginia since August. Although it had seen no action except for the seizure of Norfolk on May 10, its year in uniform had given it valuable military experience. Now, as one of the five regiments of Grover's brigade, it would soon broaden its experience to include combat. *OR* 11, pt. 1, p. 45, and pt. 3, p. 221, and 51, pt. 1, pp. 659, 663, 667; *Mass. Soldiers*, 2, p. 214; Charles R. Johnson to wife, June 15, 1862, from Fair Oaks Battle Ground, Charles R. Johnson papers, Harrisburg Civil War Round Table Collection, USAMHI.

[39] This firing marked a successful Confederate foray that drove in part of Sickles' picket line—to Hooker's great disgust and mortification. *OR* 11, pt. 1, pp. 1046-1052.

[40] Brigadier General Cuvier Grover of Maine (born July 29, 1828) was graduated from West Point in 1850 and remained in the Regular Army until his death in 1885. Promoted brigadier general of volunteers, April 14, 1862, he succeeded Brig. Gen. Henry M. Naglee in charge of the brigade originally commanded by Hooker himself (the First Brigade, Second Division, III Corps). Grover led this brigade through the Peninsula and Second Manassas Campaigns. He thereafter commanded various divisions of the XIX Corps in the Army of the Gulf and the Army of the Shenandoah. In 1865, his division garrisoned Savannah, Georgia, so that none of William T. Sherman's veterans would have to be left behind to hold that city. Warner, pp. 193-194.

Bought paper & sent it home for the map. Bought 10 ginger cakes 25 cts., sugar cakes .20, cakes .25, 4 specked "carrots" [?] .10. Morn 1.55, Eve .65, Paper .10. Morn reading &c. Dinner: soup, very good. Mended my pants. Major took the Regt. out today.[41] Great many trees felled [illegible]. We were out before McClellan, [who] took his cap off and saluted every man who saluted him. Beard growing now.[42] Turned in at 8 o'c with Whit, slept well but cool night. After dinner, reading &c. Line formed for picket at about 3 o'c. Relieved the 6th Jersey.[43] Capt. C. gone to White House. Lieut. C. out with Co. Pleasant day. Our position to left. 3 reliefs, 2 hours each. Nothing but Bugle out this time. Blankets, haversack & day's ration—salt junk, crackers & coffee—brought us for supper. Awful stench from the bodies which were not properly buried. McClellan came here with 3 Brigs. and other officers; visited the new fort they are building to the right of the 1st, to the left of which we are now posted.[44]

Tuesday, June 17th: Up at sunrise. Have got cold. Coffee & salt junk. Pleasant morn & day. Laid down but could not rest. Head pained me, so bought lemons & cakes; ate few and made some lemonade. Vomited towards night. Felt very sick for 2 or 3 hours. Went into woods 5 or 6 times. Morn .65. Bought 8 sugar cakes for 15 cts., 3 lemons 17, Eve 33. Ate no supper. Felt little better towards night. Turned in after supper and slept well. Waked up in night, felt tip top. Recd. letter from Mother with Father's & hers. 12 ct. stamp on it. Rebs threw few shell & one rifled shot yesterday, burst pretty near us too. One was

[41] The major of the 1st Massachusetts was Charles P. Chandler of Boston, who held that office from May 22, 1861, until he was killed in action at the Battle of Glendale, June 30, 1862. *Mass. Soldiers*, 1, p. 2.

[42] The previous day, McClellan wrote to his wife that, "I speak very confidently, but if you could see the faces of the troops as I ride among them you would share my confidence. They will do anything I tell them to do." The reference to "beard growing now" evidently applies to McClellan, not to Perkins. Less than four weeks later, a captain of the 16th Massachusetts would write, "Little Mac. . .has let his whiskers grow all over his face. They are bright yellow, and if you want [to] know what he don't look like you can look at his likeness as it is shown at shop windows." McClellan, *Own Story*, pp. 404-406; Charles R. Johnson to wife, July 11, 1862, from Harrison's Landing, Va., Johnson Papers, Harrisburg Civil War Round Table Collection, USAMHI.

[43] The 6th New Jersey Infantry Regiment belonged to Carr's brigade.

[44] The new fort was Battery 4, situated just north of the Williamsburg Road. The generals who accompanied McClellan have not been identified. Heintzelman can almost certainly be ruled out, since he does not mention the visit in his detailed daily accounts. Perkins' failure to name the officers may suggest that he did not recognize them. Hooker, Grover and presumably Sickles were known to him. Three staff officers at the headquarters of the Army of the Potomac—Brig. Gens. John G. Barnard, chief of engineers; Andrew A. Humphreys, chief of topographical engineers; and William F. Barry, chief of artillery—would have been interested in the new fort. Whether any of them were the officers in question has not been determined. Haynes, p. 90; *OR* 11, pt. 1, pp. 115-116; Samuel P. Heintzelman, *Diary, Journal,* and *Notebook,* June 16, 1862, Heintzelman Papers, Library of Congress, Washington, D.C. Hereinafter cited as LC.

Brig. Gen. Cuvier Grover
Perkins' brigade commander

Brig. Gen. Joseph Hooker
Perkins' division commander

Col. Robert Cowdin
Perkins' regimental commander

Brig. Gen. Samuel Heintzelman
Perkins' corps commander

spherical case, I reckon. Felt rather sick this A.M. and ate no dinner, had very bad headache after nap about noon. About 1 o'c P.M. Lieut. C. gave me permission to go to camp.

Wednesday, June 18th, 1862: Up early, well as ever. Breakfast: salt junk & crackers & coffee. Drew rice & sugar for Whit last eve. Drew my ration of whiskey last eve and gave it to Dan Kelley. Capt. came back yesterday in P.M. Pleasant morn. Yesterday heard heavy cannonading in direction of James River. At Fort Darling, reckon.[45] Letter to Mother, enclosed memo from June 11 to 16. At about 11 were roused by assembly blown at Brig. H. Q. Were in line in about 2 minutes. Marched towards earthworks & back to dinner: potatoes & salt junk. In P.M. 16th went out reconnoitering, lost few killed & several wounded.[46] Drew my whiskey for Holden. Supper: coffee & salt junk & crackers. Sent up as bugler at Brig. H. Q. Rain about dark. Slept with Wadsworth.[47]

Thursday, June 19th, 1862: Slept well. Up early, pleasant morn. Baked beans. Morn 33, bought ink .10, 1/2 doz. biscuit of Col's. cook .15, Eve .08. Stopped at Brig. H. Q. all day except meal times. Reading papers &c. Had nap. Dinner: salt junk. Recd. by mail new rubber envelope, 2 elastics & lead pencil Faber No. 3. Letter to E. M. P. Very warm day. Did not have to blow today. Brig. went on picket at 3 1/2 P.M. I stopped at H. Q. The other buglers were sent back. Supper: (tea, not very good), salt junk &c. Pleasant eve. Very little firing today. Turned in after reading & talking with Ben.[48]

---

[45] Fort Darling, atop Drewry's Bluff, provided the main defense against an advance by the Union Navy up the James River to Richmond itself. On May 15, 1862, that stronghold had turned back five Federal warships. Not only Perkins but even McClellan thought that the shelling on June 17 marked renewed fighting at the bluff. Actually, the combat took place downriver at City Point, where Confederate batteries picked a fight with the Northern navy and were soon silenced. *OR* 11, pt. 3, p. 232; U.S. Navy Department, *Official Records of the Union and Confederate Navies in the War of the Rebellion*, 31 vols. (Washington, D.C., 1894-1922), series I, vol. 7, pp. 485-486. Hereinafter cited as *NOR*. All references are to series I unless otherwise noted.

[46] The regiment's casualties were heavier than Perkins suggests: 17 killed, 28 wounded, and 14 missing, a total of 59—a measure of the unit's eagerness and of its lack of combat experience. *OR* 11, pt. 1, pp. 1062-1063; *Mass. Soldiers*, 2, p. 256.

[47] Private Daniel Kelley of Roxbury enlisted on May 24, 1861, and would be a sergeant when his three-year term expired. Private Benjamin Wadsworth of Framingham enlisted on June 13, 1861; was mustered in on August 17, 1861; and left the regiment on March 2, 1863, to become a second lieutenant in the 10th Corps D'Afrique Regiment (while serving with which he was mortally wounded at Port Hudson). *Mass. Soldiers*, 1, pp. 62, 65; 7, p. 312.

[48] Whether "Ben" was Chase or Wadsworth is not clear. Since Perkins did not rejoin his regiment but remained at brigade headquarters and since he had tented with Wadsworth there the preceding night, the latter soldier may well be the one to whom he refers.

Friday, June 20: Up at sunrise. Salt junk &c. Fine morning. Reading &c. In A.M. reading &c. Cannonading & picket firing to right of us. Very warm day. Letters from E. M. P., E. F. L., and Father.[49] 9 red stamps, 5 blue, also 3 papers E. M. P. Letter home and No. 44 C. C. P. Dinner: salt junk & crackers & pint of lemonade. Morn .08, Lemon .08, Eve .25. In P.M. reading, writing &c. Our battery fired several shots and rebels returned them. Clark, Co. D, shot through his boot accidently. Mr. P's letter contained photo of Ed. Pick.[50] Shaved my upper lip at Wadsworth's tent. Men in from picket in P.M. Met Harry Patch, 2nd N. H., Co. B. Supper: tea & rice. Recd. note from W. H. Ford by member of his Co. His camp about 2 miles from here. Sold Dodge my new rubber envelope .25.[51]

Saturday, June 21st, 1862: Up at sunrise. Any quantity of axemen chopping trees down in front of our earthworks. Heard them most all night. Little firing in night. Fine eve; fine morn. Sat up late reading newspapers. Letter to Ford, directed Camp Lincoln, Virginia.[52] Blue stamp, also to Mrs. P., E. F. L., Alice Luscomb, & H. T. Helmbold, Chemist, Phil., for medicine and advice, just for the fun of it.[53] Dinner: soup. In P.M. blew the assembly to alarm camp 3 times. Did not make out very well 1st time, could not get upper "G," but I blew it through. Next time I blew it pretty well. Firing in front. Neither of these times did the Regts. go out to fort. Last time had just finished supper at Co., heard picket firing and ran for bugle. Got there just in time as General was calling me.

---

[49] "E. F. L." was Ellen F. Luscomb, a frequent correspondent.

[50] On July 8, Edward N. Pickering of Boston, presumably the son of Daniel and Elizabeth Pickering, would enlist in the new 35th Massachusetts Infantry Regiment as sergeant of Company D. By war's end he would be a first lieutenant in the 114th U.S. Colored Infantry Regiment. *Mass. Soldiers*, 3, p. 670; 7, p. 307.

[51] The soldiers of Perkins' own regiment are Pvt. James A. Clark of Boston, who enlisted on March 17, 1862, and served until July 27, 1865 (with the 1st Massachusetts until its term expired and with the 11th Massachusetts for the final 14 months); and Wooster F. Dodge of Leominster, who served in the regimental band from May 23, 1861, until it was mustered out, July 27, 1862. The other two soldiers are Pvt. William Henry Harrison Patch, who had been born in Salem, Massachusetts, but who was living in Concord, New Hampshire, when he enlisted on May 13, 1861, and Cpl. William H. Ford of Worcester, who had served in Company D, 15th Massachusetts Infantry Regiment since July 12, 1861. Like the 19th Massachusetts, the 15th belonged to Sedgwick's Second Division of the II Corps. Ibid., 1, pp. 3, 24, 65, 795; 2, pp.157, 580; Haynes, roster p. 86; to establish that the injured soldier in Company D was Pvt. James A Clark, not Sgt. Seth F. Clark, check their respective compiled service records in RG 94, entry 519, NA.

[52] Camp Lincoln was the name which McClellan bestowed on his entire position south of the Chickahominy River, confronting the defenses of Richmond.

[53] Alice Luscomb was presumably a relative of Ellen Luscomb.

Was all out of breath but blew it nevertheless. Brig. was under arms & in line in about 2 minutes & marched off to fort. Firing pretty brisk. Soon our artillery opened. And then all quiet. Enemy out making reconnaissance in force.[54] Supper: tea & hard bread. After supper about dark men came back and I was relieved by a bugler in 16th. Had shirt and pair socks washed .10 cts. Bought 2 sticks licorice .05, Morn .25, Eve .10.

Sunday, June 22, 1862: Picket firing pretty often in night. Waked up several times. At about 3 o'c heard the 16th bugler try to blow 3 times but he could not make out. Appleton of Co. F, 1st Mass. took it up and blew it tip top. Camp was alarmed and went out towards forts. Breakfast was carried out to the men. I did not go. As buglers were sent in other day. Shall go out if there is a fight as no doubt there will be soon. Breakfast: coffee, crackers, salt junk, pan from cook house. Down to spring to right of Regt. & washed body & legs, shirt, socks, 3 handkerchiefs and towel & feel great deal better. Pleasant day. Dinner: potatoes & salt junk. Letter from E. P. B. & 2 papers home. P.M. reading. Regt. went on picket at usual time. I did not. No unusual firing today. Supper: tea & crackers. Crocker trimmed my hair. Answ'd E. P. B.'s letter in eve. Awful smoky in eve. Rained few drops. Bought 7 sugar cakes for 10 cts. Eve .00. Reading by candle-light all alone in tent in eve.[55]

Monday, June 23rd, 1862: Up early. Pleasant morn. Salt junk, coffee & crackers. In A.M. reading &c. Mr. Newton of Ford's Co. came to camp & I returned with him as Ford was sick and could not come over. Went to 15th Mass., then to Engineers camp.[56] Arrived about 12 1/2 o'c. Ford does not look well, head shaved close. Had a talk with him and ate dinner there: bean soup & 2 potatoes & preserve. Saw Chas Mansfield, has been sick also. I left about 1 P.M. with Ford & Newton's pass time changed from 12 M. to 2 P.M. Did not

---

[54] McClellan considered that this firing marked an unsuccessful Southern effort to drive in Hooker's pickets. However, a Federal engineer who was actually on the ground reported the firing was simply in response to two or three Confederate companies moving to the edge of the Union slashing. *OR* 11, pt. 3, p. 241, and 51, pt. 1, p. 686.

[55] Fellow musician Henry Crocker of Roxbury served with Company K from May 24, 1861, until discharged for disability, October 10, 1862. The soldier from Company F was Pvt. William H. Appleton of Boston, who enlisted on May 24, 1861, and who was mortally wounded at Gettysburg. *Mass. Soldiers*, 1, pp. 34, 61.

[56] The U.S. Engineer Battalion was camped with army headquarters around Dr. Trent's house, situated two miles northeast of Seven Pines and half a mile southwest of Sumner's upper bridge over the Chickahominy. *OR* 11, pt. 1, p. 117; Gilbert F. Thompson, *The Engineer Battalion in the Civil War* (Washington, D.C., 1910), p. 16.

have to show it after arriving at camp.[57] Little rain and much thunder. Shaved mustache & chin this A.M. Mr. Tidd's razor. Borrowed of H. Whit 50 & bought butter @ 40 per lb. 50, Eve .00. Ate some salt junk and crackers after getting back. Supper: tea, bean soup and crackers & butter. Finished last eve's letter to Mother, wrote for a dollar. Very warm at midday. Towards supper time, report came to camp that our picket had advanced and Rebs had retreated some two miles, also that Rebs had Jeff Davis in prison. After supper heard some of our artillery fire several shots and then skirmishing, pretty brisk for some time. Our Brig. was relieved about dark and returned. Penn. 26th lost 3 or 4 wounded, N. H. 2nd one or two. Reb brought in, ball through shoulder.[58]

Tuesday, June 24th, 1862: Up at daylight. Rained in torrents last night, thunder and lightning very severe. Camp alarmed by the buglers' assembly (Hiram W., Co. A, on Brig. now) about 3 or 4 o'c. I did not get up. Regts. soon broke ranks. 3 days ration in haversacks at C. H.: salt junk, coffee, sugar & crackers (Coffee I did not take). Drank dipper, though, for breakfast. Warm in A.M., cloudy part of the time. Dinner: rice and molasses. Reading &c. this A.M. Pain in bowels last night, today, owing I think to eating vinegar with salt beef. Borrowed of N. Averell .25: cakes .20, 2 apples .05. Letter from Mother, enclosing verses "Soldier's Mother."[59] Also letter from Mrs. P. Answd. both & 46 C. C. P. Reading &c. Rain in P.M. by spells, thunder. Supper: tea (very little). Firing today, only few shots. Over to see Patch, 2nd N. H. Heavy rain after supper. .00 in Eve.[60]

---

[57] Besides Cpl. William H. Ford in the 15th, Perkins had a friend in Company C of the U.S. Engineer Battalion, Artificer William H. Foss of Boston. The diarist's handwriting is so small that it is difficult to distinguish between "Ford" and "Foss." However, since Pvts. Charles P. Mansfield of Westboro and Oliver W. Newton of Worcester both served with Ford in Company D of the 15th, it is assumed that Perkins is referring to the corporal. The name of the sick soldier has, accordingly, been rendered as "Ford" in the text. *Mass. Soldiers*, 2, pp. 159-160, 555; 6, p. 51.

[58] Again this day, Hooker advanced his skirmishers. To the division commander's displeasure, Grover took it on himself to withdraw his brigade at night, lest the Confederates cut him off. The junior officer's pull-back left Hooker no alternative but to withdraw his entire skirmish line to its original position. *OR* 11, pt. 3, pp. 246-247.

[59] The three stanzas of "The Soldier's Mother" are printed in Frank Moore, ed., *The Rebellion Record*, 12 vols. (New York, 1861-1864), vol. 5, p. 16.

[60] Nathaniel Averell of Roxbury went to war with Company K in May, 1861, as a corporal. By late June of 1862, he was evidently acting as a sergeant, and he would be promoted to that grade as of July 1. By the time his three-year term expired on May 25, 1864, he would be the second lieutenant of Company E. The soldier of Company A was Pvt. Hiram Williamson of Boston, who enlisted on May 23, 1861, and mustered out on May 25, 1864. *Mass. Soldiers*, 1, pp. 10, 60; Perkins, Notes, August 13, 1862, *CWTI* Coll., USAMHI.

Wednesday, June 25th, 1862:[61] Up early. Men ordered to get breakfast & take one day's rations and blankets & be ready to fall in at 7. Tea for B. I got ready to go, but heard they were only going to go and lay in trenches, so shan't go unless specially ordered. Wheeler on sick list; Doctor Munroe wrote opposite "Fit for light duty, such as fighting."[62] Pleasant morn. Hiram bugler orderly at Brig. H. Q. Regt. left about 7 1/2 and we soon found out they were advancing. Firing commenced and soon there were vollies and sharp firing. And it continued until about noon. Seemed to be driving pickets. Lieut. Dalton was nearly first brought in and Sergeant (Commissary) Hinkley said they wanted more men to bring off the wounded. I was just thinking of going out with musket. But thought I might do as much good bringing off the wounded, and of course at same time not quite as liable to be hit & I went out with Hinkley; Bill Hall & Greer (Co. Cook) also went with me. Saw Capt. C. brought in, shot in mouth, jaw fractured. Went out to edge of woods. Met Capt. Wild[63] wounded in hand & Horace Whitfield, Co. A. Brought his things in for him. Finger shot off. To camp with him & then went out again & helped the musicians on stretchers &c.

Most of firing stopped about noon. Our men being [in] the edge of woods & holding their position. Further side of woods [was an] open field in front of them. Stopped by lookout tree some time, then back to camp. Ate little salt junk & cracker and about camp all rest of day. Pretty quiet in front of us all rest of

---

[61] June 25 marked the opening of the Seven Days Battles, with the engagement at Oak Grove. Although the smallest of the combats which the two armies fought over the ensuing week, it was for the 1st Massachusetts the bloodiest. The Federal army precipitated this fight about 8:30 a.m. as Hooker, eventually supported by portions of three other divisions, battled his way through the wooded swamp which had served as the no-man's land between McClellan's and Lee's forces. After overcoming heavy opposition, Hooker secured the woods and then became embroiled across an oat field which stretched westward from the forest to the main Confederate works astride the Williamsburg Road. Spearheading the fight for the forest was Grover's heavy skirmish line, consisting of the 1st Massachusetts on the right and the 11th Massachusetts on the left. *OR* 11, pt. 2, pp. 95-98, 108-110, 120-133; Cudworth, pp. 204-208.

[62] Francis LeBaron Monroe of Medway served as an assistant surgeon of the 1st Massachusetts from September 2, 1861, until transferring to the 15th Massachusetts, January 18, 1863. *Mass. Soldiers*, 1, p. 2.

[63] Edward A. Wild of Brookline had commanded Company A since May 22, 1861. This wound on June 25, which cost him the use of two fingers on his right hand (though they were not shot off or amputated), ended his service with the 1st but not his Civil War career. On July 24, 1862, he was promoted to major of the 32nd Massachusetts Infantry Regiment. The following month, he became lieutenant colonel of the 32nd and then colonel of the new 35th Massachusetts Infantry Regiment. Elevated to brigadier general on April 24, 1863, he subsequently commanded a brigade and a division of U.S. Colored Troops as well as heading the Freedmen's Bureau in Georgia during Reconstruction (until mustered out, January 16, 1866). His papers form part of the collection of the Massachusetts Commandery of the Military Order of the Loyal Legion of the United States at USAMHI. See also Thomas Wentworth Higginson, Massachusetts in the Army and Navy, 2 vols. (Boston, MA, 1895), vol. 2, pp. 201-202; Warner, pp. 557-558.

day. Some artillery firing & sometimes volleys. Any quantity of cheering; McClellan is in front, they say, riding along the lines.[64] Supper: coffee, salt junk and crackers. Great many killed & wounded. Stillings & Moran killed, Co. K. Kept bringing in wounded men. 1st seems to have suffered worse than any. Capt. C., severe wound; Sergt. Holden, slight in arm; Corpl. Richardson, severe, not expected to live; Priv. Lang, ditto; Priv. Bovard, ditto; Powers, wounded legs; Pioneer Ivers, severe shoulder; Partridge, two fingers; Finerty, slight in arm.[65] Borrowed of Hollis Wrisley .25: Cakes .15, Eve .10. In Co. A there were 17 out of 27 killed & wounded. Quartermaster said he had counted 65 killed & wounded.[66] In P.M. considerable artillery firing. Evening some sharp skirmishing, also in night. Capt. C. went to White House and Sgt. Wilkins.[67] Lang also sent off. Cars running all day. Stillings & Moran both buried in our Co. street in Eve by Mr. Hall & the boys. Chaplain made a prayer and remarks. Chase came in in evening and Whit about 10 o'c or so.[68]

---

[64] About 11:00 a.m., Brig. Gen. Randolph B. Marcy, chief of staff of the Army of the Potomac, telegraphed Hooker to break off fighting and withdraw to his works. However, III Corps commander Heintzelman delayed carrying out the instructions until McClellan himself could reach the front. On arriving about 1:00 p.m., the major general ordered Hooker to renew the battle. *OR* 11, pt. 2, pp. 96, 109; Cudworth, p. 207.

[65] Privates James K. Ivers and Thomas L. Moran of Roxbury and George M. Stillings of Alton, New Hampshire, were killed instantly; Cpl. George G. Richardson and Pvt. William Lang, both of Roxbury, died on the day of battle from their wounds; and Musician Frank Bovard of Roxbury lingered until July 3 before passing away. Three more Roxbury residents, Sergeant Holden and Pvts. Frank Partridge and John J. Powers, were wounded so severely that they were discharged within a year. All nine men were original members of Company K. However, the remaining enlisted casualty, Pvt. Thomas P. Finnerty of Roxbury, only joined the company on April 4, 1862. He was discharged six months later and joined the 29th Massachusetts Infantry Regiment. The wounded officer was Company B's second lieutenant, Joseph H. Dalton of East Boston, whose commission dated from May 29, 1862; he would be discharged for disability, May 18, 1863. *Mass. Soldiers*, 1, pp. 11, 60-65; Cudworth, p. 213.

[66] Final returns put the regiment's loss at 14 killed or mortally wounded and 51 others wounded. Company A's casualties were not quite as severe as Perkins apprehended: two killed and nine wounded. His own Company K fared worse, with three killed, three mortally wounded, and five others wounded—the most fatalities of any company in the regiment. *Mass. Soldiers*, 1, pp. 2-66; Higginson, 1, pp. 197, 443, 465; Cudworth, p. 213.

[67] On August 13, 1862, in "notes" summarizing the Seven Days Battles, Perkins elaborated that: "Sergt. Chas. E. Wilkins was [illegible] some trouble in his legs and in my opinion a good deal of it was playing off. When Capt. Chamberlain was brought in wounded, he flew round pretty well and waited on him & when Capt. C. went home, he went with him, no furlough at all: it was desertion, no more or less. July 6, we saw a notice of the part taken by the Company (K) in the recent fights & speaking of the fight of the 25th June it said Sergeant Wilkins, though sick with the black typhoid, was in the fight until 3 o'c or words to that effect. He was not there at all & would have given a good deal rather than have been there, in my opinion. He thus got more credit for his non-fighting than the poor fellows that were there & had to suffer." Wilkins, a resident of Boston, was an original member of the company; he would be discharged for disability on October 31, 1862. *Mass. Soldiers*, 1, p. 65.

[68] In addition to himself, the relief parties that Perkins mentions are regimental Quartermaster

Thursday, June 26th, 1862: Up early. Coffee, baked beans and crackers. Pleasant. Corpl. Rich [Richardson] died last night and after breakfast men buried him. Most of the men went out to fort this morn & lieut. says they are soon to be relieved. So I think I won't go out. Wrote a letter to Holden's wife last night at his request and dictation. Quiet this forenoon. By mail, paper & envelopes from home and letter from Ed dated April 6.[69] Dinner: soup with dried potatoes in it. In P.M. wrote letter to Mother. Cannonading commenced about middle of P.M. and continued until dark. At first one or 2 heavy guns. I took a nap and when I was waked up for supper it was a perfect roar and continued so till dark. Supper: coffee and crackers. H. J. Whitten of Co. G buried in eve. Borrowed of N. Averell .25, cakes .35, Eve .00. Warm day. 4 fights in Penn. 26th today, men drunk. Recd. whiskey ration this morn; gave 1/2 of mine to Sergt. Higgins, 1/2 to Chase. Sgt. Holden and rest of wounded left today, all but Ivers. Shaved me this eve. Heavy cannonading continued until 9 or 10 at night. After turning in, Adjt. General recd. despatch from headquarters, saying McClellan had attacked the Rebs in great force at Mechanicsville and they were badly beaten. Great cheering all along the lines for an hour or more, going from camp to camp. Cannonading must be this side of there.[70] Bands playing until

---

Lt. William P. Cowie of Boston, Commissary Sgt. Harrison Hinckley of Old Cambridge, Pvts. Charles K. Greer and William B. Hall, both Company K men from Roxbury; and Pvt. Horace E. Whitfield of Brookline, Company A. All five were original members of the 1st Massachusetts, but only Greer remained with the regiment when it mustered out. Perkins also refers to three other original members of Company K: Cpl. Hollis S. Wrisley of Boston (transferred to the Veteran Reserve Corps on August 4, 1863), Pvt. George H. Wheeler of South Boston (discharged November 14, 1862) and "Chase." The last soldier is probably Ben Chase, mentioned supra n. 6, but may be bandsman Charles A. Chase of Leominster (enlisted May 25, 1861; discharged July 27, 1862). "Mr. Hall" is presumably not Bill Hall the cook (whom Perkins detested and would hardly have referred to in respectful terms of address), nor was he Sgt. Maj. James W. Hall of East Boston, who was back in the Bay State on recruiting duty. There is no reason why Lt. Peter G. Hall, the adjutant of the 26th Pennsylvania, would perform such duty. The reference may be to Sgt. Lewis H. Hall of Company F, a Bostonian who served a full three years in the regiment. Ibid., pp. 2-3, 6, 9, 36, 62, 65; Perkins, *Diary*, January 17, 1862, Perkins Papers, *CWTI* Collection, USAMHI.

[69] The lapse of 13 weeks in receiving the letter makes clear that "Ed" was Perkins' older brother, Quartermaster Sgt. Edward F. Perkins of the 3rd California Infantry Regiment. He entered service on October 4, 1861, and was stationed at Benicia Barracks when he wrote on April 6. By the time the letter reached the Peninsula, the 3rd had moved to Stockton. It continued east to guard the Overland Mail Route and reached Fort Ruby, Nevada Territory, on September 4. There, Edward Perkins contracted typhus and died on September 28, 1862. California Adj. Gen., *Records of California Men in the War of the Rebellion* (Sacramento, CA., 1890), pp. 506, 522, 531; Compiled Service Record of Edward F. Perkins, 3rd California Infantry Regiment, RG 94, entry 519, NA.

[70] The cannonading that Perkins heard indeed took place south of the Chickahominy, but much of the artillery firing occurred north of the river as part of the Battle of Mechanicsville. This combat opened Lee's effort to envelop the Union right flank. Just as McClellan's dispatch reported, the Southerners were bloodily defeated. The setback came, however, through the repulse of their onslaughts, not through a Federal attack.

late at night.[71]

Friday, June 27, 1862: Men were up before light at 3 or 4 o'c. Under arms till daylight. Cannonading commenced then again. Coffee & salt junk, boiled pork and crackers. I got up just after breakfast. Whit calls me lazy, Army loafer, Army worm, &c., &c. Heavy firing in morn but stopped before 9, when they commenced with light batteries and had it pretty heavy by spells along the centre. About 2 o'c Rebs commenced firing along the R. R. Heavy guns raked the track. We could hear the shells go past us and down the track. Cannonading stopped near us about 2 or 3; then we heard heavy cannons on the right again, same as yesterday, very heavy guns. Dinner: salt junk. Headache today. Borrowed 30 of Whit. Bought lemon .10, raisins .15; made some lemonade, also bought glass .05. Boy carrying it round.

At about 2 or 3 had to fall in line, bugle call, picket firing in front of us. Nothing, though. Stacked arms & left. Then ordered to get 3 days rations in haversacks & pack knapsacks. Recd. letter from home, 9 stamps & enclosed letter from Lizzie, also Sci. Am. & Home Journal.[72] Very warm day. Men saw balloon off in direction of Richmond, looked very small. Some think it is Reb's, but Whit thinks it is ours other side of Richmond.[73] Corpl. Robinson & Privts. Bird & Hutchins of this Co. been off sick, returned to camp today from Mass. Another order came to take one day's rations & prepare for picket, 24 hours in trenches. Men rolled up blankets and went out to relieve as usual before the battle. I did not go. Severe headache in P.M. All men who could not walk ordered back to Gen. hospital on R. R. From 3 to about 6 artillery in front of us was shelling the Rebs pretty briskly. Heavy firing at extreme right still at

[71] Among the enlisted men of the 1st to whom Perkins referred was Sgt. Henry J. Whitten of Company G. A Bostonian and an original member of the regiment, he served all three years and was discharged May 25, 1864. The "Adjt. General" was presumably the assistant adjutant general of Grover's brigade, Captain Joseph Hibbert of East Boston. Formerly the first lieutenant of Company C and acting adjutant of the 1st Massachusetts, he was promoted into the volunteer staff on May 12, 1862. *Mass. Soldiers*, 1, pp. 20, 46; *OR* 11, pt. 2, p. 125; Cudworth, p. 155.

[72] "Lizzie" was the diarist's teenage sister, Elizabeth B. Perkins. Both of the magazines were published in New York City. *Scientific American* evidently appealed to Perkins the engineer. What was called the *Home Journal* in the 1800's continues in the 20th Century under the title *Town and Country*. See the *Union List of Serials in Libraries. . .* (New York, N.Y., 1965), pp. 1876, 3823, 4246.

[73] The balloon near Richmond was indeed Confederate. It made its first ascent on June 27. Edward Porter Alexander, *Fighting for the Confederacy*, edited by Gary W. Gallagher (Chapel Hill, N.C., 1989), pp. 115-117.

intervals heard.[74] Coffee & crackers for supper & salt junk. Coffee was carried to men. Letter to Father in eve, 47 C. C. P. with memo from June 19 to 27. Picket firing in eve.[75]

Saturday, June 28, 1862: Heavy firing of picket last night. Up early. Breakfast: salt junk & coffee &c. & few baked beans from Burditt. Quiet morning. Cannonading about all forenoon to right, some in front of us. Picket firing some. Mass. 1st still in trenches at right of road. This A.M. all sick that remained and Q. M. stores and officers' baggage was sent back. They say there is a large Reb force in front of us here and they probably expect an engagement soon. Dinner: Salt junk, crackers & butter. Warm day. Heavy firing this A.M., seems to be nearer than it has been, perhaps at New Bridge.[76] Entirely quiet after dinner and rest of day very still indeed. All sorts of rumors in camp about burning stores at White House, Porter retreating &c., &c. None of which I have any confidence in.[77] Regt. came in at about 4 or 5 at usual time for returning. Warm day. Supper: rice and sugar & coffee &c. Men had their whiskey when they came in. Reading &c. this P.M. Turned in early with orders to sleep with boots on and be ready to move at moment's notice with knapsacks packed. Cooks sent off their kettles &c. and officers [sent away their] extra baggage & some of the Cos., I hear, destroyed Co. books.[78]

---

[74] More extensive artillery duels raged along the lines between the Williamsburg Road and the Chickahominy on Friday than on Thursday, and in late afternoon heavy infantry skirmishing flared at Garnett's Farm just south of that stream. But again on the 27th, most of the fighting which Perkins heard took place north of the river in the Battle of Gaines' Mill. After suffering repeated repulses, the Secessionists finally overran the Union position in the most decided Confederate victory of the entire Seven Days Battles.

[75] The three returning soldiers were Cpl. George D. Robinson of Boston and Pvts. Louis Bird and Frank Hutchins, both of Roxbury. All were original members of Company K. Hutchins was discharged for disability on November 3, 1862; the other two men served their full three years. *Mass. Soldiers*, 1, pp. 60, 62, 64.

[76] This firing resulted in the defeat of an incautious Confederate probe at Golding's Farm about two miles southeast of New Bridge.

[77] The rumors were all too true. Brig. Gen. Fitz John Porter's Federal forces north of the Chickahominy indeed retreated southward across that river overnight, June 27-28. Also on the 28th, McClellan broke up his base at White House on the Pamunkey River and began moving his whole army southward across the Peninsula in hopes of establishing a new base on the James River.

[78] After Holden was wounded on June 25, three sergeants remained with Company K. In "notes" of August 13, 1862, Perkins explained how two of them left their unit, under very different circumstances, on the night of June 28-29: "Sergt. Higgins had trouble in his feet. He stayed with the Company too long, did not want to stay on the sick list while the Company was out. He knew he could not march & had to be taken. The night of the 28 we knew we should move before morning & he started in eve for Savage Station where the rest of the sick went. . . . Sergt. J. Y. J. Clark, orderly at Fair Oaks, played off sick a good deal & men did not like him & when we left in

Sunday, June 29th, 1862: Up about 3 or 4 o'c. Packed up and left. Ate some baked beans, not quite done. Marched down Williamsburg Road apiece. Then sent back to the fortifications & stayed there while the Jerseys, whom we relieved, had time to pack up & leave.[79] We stayed in breastworks about 1/2 hour and then left very quietly. Were the last to leave the front line of defenses before Richmond. Marched down road about a mile, formed line of battle with other divisions to cover retreat, I suppose. We had an artillery fight here and infantry skirmish on other side of R. R., where they were also formed in lines.[80] This Regt. was moved round several times, supported 2 batteries and the shell and shot ranged pretty near part of the time.[81] Fooled around here about 2 hours, then commenced the retreat towards James River in several columns.[82] Marched until about 8 or 9 P.M., when we stopped for night. From here they say it is 4 or 5 miles to river. Everything that could not be carried in this march was destroyed: tents, commissary stores, &c., &c. As the march commenced, men began to throw away stuff: blankets, overcoats, haversacks, &c., &c. There were several men wounded by shells &c. at Savage Station (where we had the artillery fight), and they had to be left behind.[83]

---

the morning of 29th John Y. J. & Higgins left for Savage's Station night before. Clark, no doubt, could have marched with us, but he kept with Higgins & they were both taken prisoners."

[79] On Saturday afternoon, Carr's brigade had taken over Grover's and Sickles' assignment to picket Hooker's front. On Sunday morning, the First and Second Brigades returned to the front, so that the Third Brigade could break up its camp. The 1st Massachusetts garrisoned Battery 4 just north of the Williamsburg Road. Perkins does not mention the heavy fog which concealed the Federal disengagement that morning. *OR* 11, pt. 2, pp. 137, 151, 160; Cudworth, pp. 214-215.

[80] The Battle of Savage's Station was fought on June 29. Although Grover occupied the III Corps' right, immediately south of the railroad, neither he nor any other infantry of the corps saw much action, as the fighting raged north of the tracks. The First Brigade suffered only two men wounded, both from the 11th Massachusetts. *OR* 11, pt. 2, pp. 122-123.

[81] The 1st supported Battery K, 4th U.S. Artillery Regiment. Cudworth, p. 217.

[82] Heintzelman prematurely disengaged from the battlefield of June 29 and began moving his corps southward over White Oak Swamp toward the James. Rather than further clog the bottleneck where the main road crossed the swamp at White Oak Bridge, he attempted to pass the stream at three fords farther upstream. Using the most westerly, Jordan's Ford, could have entailed serious fighting, so one brigade crossed at the middle ford, Fisher's, and the other five brigades (including Grover and Carr) used various roads that converged on the most easterly ford, Brackett's. Perkins evidently took one of the routes to Brackett's Ford. Ibid., pp. 216-218; *OR* 11, pt. 2, pp. 22, 98-99, 110, 138, 161-162, 181-182, 185; Haynes, p. 106.

[83] Also left behind in McClellan's main hospitals at Savage's Station were approximately 2,500 wounded, sick, and injured men, who were too unwell to be evacuated and who fell into Confederate hands on the morning of June 30. Among these captured convalescents were 22 members of the 1st Massachusetts, including 10 men from Company K. That total includes Sergeants Clark and Higgins, who may have been captured in the hospital or along the routes of march. *OR* 11, pt. 2, p. 494; compiled service records of the 1st Massachusetts Infantry Regiment, RG 94, entry 519, NA.

Very warm day & I sweat very much; wore my blouse and coat, too. When we got about 9 miles from river, I stopped and took off shirt I had on (dark blue), cut it into strips and threw it away, also my second pair of socks in knapsack. Wiped my body with towel, put on clean shirt, put blouse in knapsack all wet, and trudged on again. Regt. now being ahead & I a straggler. Threw away also pepper in jar. Ate little salt junk for dinner with crackers. Felt awful tired towards last part of march and was among the stragglers a spell but soon got up with the Jerseys and kept along with them to camp in open field, at a place where they said it was 7 miles to river (on road).[84]

They said troops had been passing since 11 last night [on] this road and the other. Of the 1st Brig. only the 1st Regt. went this road. Found Whit when I got up and laid down along side of him and others, my feet near their heads by the knapsacks in rubber blanket & slept well until morning. Pickets fired in night, scared probably. No Rebs were here. 40,000 troops near here, they say. Chase stopped somewhere on road. Several of our boys got drunk on the whiskey they got among the stores left.[85]

As we passed along the R. R., saw piles & piles of stores burning. Any quantity of tents slit up and down. Everything left was destroyed. Heard explosions, probably blowing up stores. They say the Rebs were in our works 15 minutes after we left.

Monday, June 30, 1862:[86] Up at daylight. Whit cooked some coffee & I furnished sugar. He gave me some and salt junk & crackers & butter. Fine morning. Rested well, good sleep, feel rather "stiff" [?]. Great many men left along road yesterday, sunstruck, faint, & played out. Poor fellows. Started on

---

[84] Hooker's division spent the night on and near the Charles City Road—about a mile above that highway's junction with the Willis Church Road, according to Heintzelman. Grover specifies that his brigade bivouacked near St. Paul's Church. The editor of this diary has not been able to locate that church on wartime or modern maps. *OR* 11, pt. 2, pp. 110, 123, 131; Heintzelman, *Journal*, July 3, 1862, Heintzelman Papers, LC.

[85] When the Second Division broke camp on the Williamsburg Road, the chaplain of Perkins' regiment saw "molasses, vinegar, tea, flour, whiskey, cartridges, vegetables, mixed up in gutters by the roadside. . . ." More potable, according to the historian of the 2nd New Hampshire, were the offerings there of sutlers who "were keeping open shop, shouting to the men to help themselves to what they wanted, without money and without price. . . ." Cudworth, p. 215; Haynes, p. 104.

[86] June 30 marked the crisis of the Seven Days Battles. From north of White Oak Swamp, "Stonewall" Jackson threatened the Union rear; south of the swamp, five other Confederate columns struck eastward along the Charles City, Darbytown, Long Bridge, and River Roads to intercept McClellan's march southward. The heaviest fighting erupted around the key Charles City Crossroads. In the resulting Battle of Glendale, Hooker's division was the leftmost of five Federal divisions which faced westward to cover that intersection and the route of march along the Willis Church Road and a parallel but more easterly trail, both of which led toward the James River.

march about 9 or 10 o'c, marched about a mile and stopped in piece of woods near roadside in rear of line of battle. Warm day. Laid here behind our stacks about all day while wagon train passed. Cannonading in direction of Poplar Hill about all day, very heavy and rapid.[87] Also on left & musketry and soon got to be very heavy firing. At about 3 P.M. we were ordered up to support with New Hampshires. 1st took position in rear of 16th, who laid behind rail fence.[88] First [Perkins' regiment] acted reserve, kneeling, guns up & ready. Cowdin passing along line quite excited, saying every few minutes: "Hold your gun up, where's your bayonet, &c., &c." Hooker & Candler both dismounted also in rear of Regt.[89]

When the Rebs came up at the first fire they began to fall back, too severe for them. But our boys cheered them on & some went up in place of the skedaddlers, shamed them, and they went up again & held their ground.[90] Then 1st went through their ranks, charged across a field, across a ravine & brook in woods & out again and were going up a hill, when I saw troops filing along to left. Thought they were our men & most of us did & so did not fire but kept on. But they fired into us an awful fire. Scattered the Regt. in a moment. Great many killed & wounded.[91] Gen. Grover got us out of it as soon as possible. I

[87] Jackson's artillery on Poplar Hill dueled with Brig. Gen. William B. Franklin's cannons south of the stream, but Jackson did not attack with his infantry.

[88] Hooker's battle line ran First, Third, and Second Brigades from right to left. Within the First Brigade, the 16th and 26th held the front, right to left; the 1st supported the 16th, and the 2nd supported the 26th. The 11th Massachusetts was detached to the far left of the division and saw virtually no action. The Hampshiremen, too, were soon transferred to support Heintzelman's other division farther to the right, but that regiment returned in late afternoon. *OR* 11, pt. 2, pp. 111, 123, 131-132; Haynes, pp. 109-112.

[89] William L. Candler of Boston was first lieutenant of Company A of the 1st Massachusetts. Since June 8, however, he had been detailed to division headquarters as aide-de-camp to Hooker. He remained the general's aide through Chancellorsville. Commissioned into the volunteer staff on November 10, 1862, he was discharged from the regiment at the end of that year. He resigned from the army, May 12, 1863. *Mass. Soldiers*, 1, p. 4; 6, p. 758; Higginson, 2, p. 405; Cudworth, p. 199; compiled service record of William L. Candler, RG 94, entry 519, NA.

[90] Despite the many ambiguous pronouns in these two sentences, Perkins clearly refers to the Confederate attack against the Pennsylvania Reserve division beyond Hooker's right front. After enduring much more than the "first fire," that division did break. Some of its men fell back through Grover's line, and then the pursuing Southerners struck the 16th Massachusetts. Such dual shocks, together with the death of Colonel Wyman, caused the regiment to waver. It succeeded, however, in repulsing the Confederates. *OR* 11, pt. 2, pp. 111, 113-116, 123, 129.

[91] Most of the regiment's casualties occurred in this charge. The 1st's total loss in the battle was officially reported as 62 (four killed, 30 wounded and 28 missing). The regimental historian recounted the sub-totals to name five killed, 37 wounded (six of whom were captured), and 20 missing, still for a total of 62. More thorough postwar analysis of the records reduces the grand total to 58 but greatly increases the fatalities, since many of the missing had actually been killed. The final figures come to 19 dead, one missing and presumed dead, 23 wounded, eight others wounded and captured, and another seven captured. Again, Perkins' company had the dubious

fired several shots.[92] We retreated to rear of 15th Mass., who were at right of 16th.[93] Edge of woods in field. Here we remained some time, during which I went for my knapsack where we left them before going on.

After dark Regt. fell back to original position near road, formed line & turned in. Whit & I pretty well played out. Cowdin crazy while we laid in rear of 15th & carried back.[94] Maj. Chandler supposed killed.[95] Lieut. Carruth, slight buck shot in left side; Lieut. Sutherland, supposed killed; Bill Hall, shot dead when we went up to fence; Nelling & Jackson, wounded. 19 present at roll call O.K.[96] While charging across field & in woods saw great many Rebs shot

---

distinction of suffering the most severe casualties in Cowdin's command: four killed, two mortally wounded, three others wounded, three more wounded and captured, and another man captured: a total of thirteen. Ibid., p. 126; Cudworth, pp. 236-37; *Mass. Soldiers*, 1, pp. 2-66; compiled service records of the 1st Massachusetts Infantry Regiment, RG 94, entry 519, NA.

[92] Grover himself led the 1st's counterattack. Even after withdrawing the regiment from the unexpected fire against its left, he continued to believe that the shots were delivered from the Excelsior Brigade by mistake. Only when he returned to resolve the difficulty did he discover that the mistake was his. The attacking force really was Confederate, and it fired another volley at him, but he managed to escape. *OR*. 11, pt. 2, pp. 123-125; Cudworth, pp. 220-221.

[93] When fighting first broke out, the 69th Pennsylvania Infantry Regiment of Sedgwick's division was lent to Hooker and deployed on his extreme right. Late in the battle, the 15th Massachusetts (also from Sedgwick) relieved the 69th, which had spent its ammunition. The 15th thus served on the right of the 16th and so could shelter the withdrawing 1st, just as Perkins records. *OR* 11, pt. 2, pp. 89-90, 111.

[94] Robert Cowdin, a native of Jamaica, Vermont, and a resident of Boston in 1861, was the colonel of the 1st Massachusetts Militia Regiment when Civil War erupted. He took five companies of his unit into national service as the 1st Massachusetts Volunteers, added five other companies (including the Chadwick Light Infantry of Roxbury as Company K), and led the regiment until October 1, 1862, when he was promoted to brigadier general, ranking from September 26. He then commanded a brigade in the XXII Corps until March, 1863, when his commission expired for lack of Senate confirmation. He had no further wartime service. Death came on July 9, 1874. In writing about that officer's performance at Oak Grove on June 25, regimental historian Cudworth, in his usual effusive style, proclaimed that "Col. Cowdin exposed himself in utter disregard of personal hazard; waving his sword and cheering on his command all along the line; mounting stumps and logs, to see where the enemy were, notwithstanding that repeated rifle-shots, whizzing by his ears, told how prominent an object his tall form made him for the rebel sharpshooters." In contrast, the good chaplain is strangely silent about Cowdin's behavior on June 30. Grover's official report of Glendale extolled Wyman but merely lumped Cowdin and the other four regimental commanders together in the blanket statement that they "filled their positions unexceptionably and with credit to themselves." Warner, pp. 96-97; *Mass. Soldiers*, 1, p. 2; Cudworth, pp. 14-15, 206; *OR* 11, pt. 2, p. 124.

[95] As late as July 11, when Cowdin wrote his after-action report, he hoped that Chandler was a wounded prisoner of war. But just as Perkins apprehended, the major was killed on June 30. *OR* 11, pt. 2, pp. 125-126; *Mass. Soldiers*, 1, p. 2.

[96] Cowdin's hope that 1st Lt. William H. Sutherland of Boston survived as a wounded prisoner went unfulfilled. Sutherland, like Chandler, was killed at Glendale, as were Hall, and Pvt. Wesley Jackson of Boston. Private John W. Nelling of Boston would die on August 22, 1862, from wounds received on June 30. In this entry, Perkins does not mention the remaining fatalities in Company K, all privates from Roxbury: John Dolan, who was killed outright; William Clark, who was severely wounded and would die on July 21; and John Ross, who was thought missing but was actually

dead & dying. Some with our uniforms on.[97] Our artillery did fearful execution, grape & cannister & shell over our heads.[98]

Tuesday, July 1st, 1862: Slept well in tent with rubber over us, Whit & I. Up about 3 o'c. Artillery had been passing all night, they said, wagons, infantry, &c., probably from the right. We packed up and commenced to move slowly towards river. Arrived in big field about 6 or 7 o'c, stacked arms. Made some coffee & had salt junk &c. for B. After washed face & hands & legs, feel much better. Whole army seems to be in this field. Wagon trains in distance. Splendid position for defense, should think.[99] Splendid morning. Bands playing and men cheering. While making charge through woods & up hill saw great many dead & dying Rebs, wounded, &c.[100] In looking over K's list this morn, we find 5 killed (since Yorktown), 17 wounded, 19 sick, 24 present, 15 absent this morn, of which number probably 10 will turn up.[101]

---

dead. In his "notes" of August 13, 1862, however, the diarist wrote that, before the Peninsula Campaign, Ross "was next one to me when we had Sibley tents from Camp Banks [just upriver from Georgetown, D.C.] until we left Camp Union [at Bladensburg, Maryland]. We always slept [side by side] in the Second Mess. I liked some things about him very much. But some times we would quarrell in words. He was missing June 30th, supposed to have been killed." Those same notes convey a much higher regard for Jackson: a "tiptop fellow. We all liked him. He also was missing after the Battle of 30th June, supposed to have been killed." Besides Carruth, the wounded included Wheeler and Pvts. Lorenzo A. Payson, Thomas R. Mathews, Charles S. Leonard, and William J. Hudson, all of Roxbury. The last three soldiers fell into Confederate hands, as did Pvt. David V. Copeland, also of Roxbury. Jackson had enlisted on September 13, 1861; all the other men were original members of the regiment. Sutherland was the initial first lieutenant of Company K but had transferred to Company F on February 9 and served with Company D from May 27 until his death. *OR* 11, pt. 2, pp. 125-126; *Mass. Soldiers*, 1, pp. 60-66; compiled service record of William Sutherland, RG 94, entry 519, NA.

[97] During the Union counterattack, one reason why Grover and the 1st Massachusetts did not recognize their danger until too late was that the Southern soldiers who blasted his left were wearing blue uniforms. *OR* 11, pt. 2, pp. 123-125; Cudworth, pp. 220-221.

[98] Hooker had sent his own artillery battalion southward to Malvern Hill prior to the outbreak of fighting, June 30. Most of the III Corps artillery that was engaged at Glendale served on the center and right. The pieces that fired over the 1st Massachusetts probably belonged to the II Corps. Battery I, 1st U.S. Artillery Regiment, which occupied the left of Sedgwick's artillery battalion, may have been the particular outfit that served nearest to Cowdin's unit. *OR* 11, pt. 2, pp. 82-86, 100, 105-107, 119, 355, 360, 362.

[99] Perkins refers to Malvern Hill, where McClellan turned to make a stand against the pursuing Southerners.

[100] This sentence refers to the 1st Massachusetts' counterattack, June 30. The regiment was not engaged on July 1.

[101] The basis for Perkins' numbers is not clear. Studying the muster rolls indicates that from Company K's organization in May, 1861, through June, 1862, 119 men belonged to the unit. Prior to the Peninsula Campaign, one had died; nine had deserted; and 20 had been discharged. Before the Seven Days Battles, moreover, two officers were transferred to other companies, and two privates were detailed to higher headquarters (although the latter two men remained on the

Rested by stacks an hour or two, then fell in & went off to right. Formed line of battle facing woods. Artillery commenced firing rapidly over to another field in distance, where Rebel artillery was stationed and they had it pretty heavy for some time. Went into woods farther & formed again. Better place, shady. Artillery all forenoon very heavy. Some of the shells came pretty near but did no damage to this Brig. They say Regt. only had 180 muskets this morn.[102] Firing stopped this noon for an hour or so. In P.M. continued but not so heavy. And some infantry skirmishing. Most of artillery firing from our side. This A.M.gunboats fired few shots, jarred the ground very heavy. They say River is about two miles off.[103] Signaling going on today. Guess Johnny did not make

---

company roster). Subtracting these 34 men should leave 85, yet Perkins' numbers totaled only 80. The casualties, furthermore, proved worse than he reported. Seven were known dead by July 1; two of the missing had been killed; and three other casualties would die of their wounds during the summer. All 12 fatalities were incurred at Oak Grove or Glendale. Those battles also accounted for 14 of the 17 wounded (including three mortally wounded and three others wounded and missing); the remaining three wounded men had been shot at Williamsburg or near Yorktown. Only two men were absent sick; another 10 sick had been captured at or near the Savage's Station hospitals. One other prisoner of war, June 30, plus the AWOL Sgt. Wilkins raised the total number of missing to 17 (including the already mentioned two missing-and-dead and the three missing-and-wounded). Several of these categories obviously count the same person twice. It is unclear whether Perkins included the 10 captured convalescents among the "19 sick" or among the "15 missing." Those respective counts would leave either nine or 19 sick men accompanying the company. Also unclear is how many of the "15 missing" turned up. If that figure included the 10 men at Savage's Station, then no one else would have rejoined. But if the Savage's sick are numbered among the "19 sick," then eight stragglers could have rejoined. The second possibility is more likely since later on July 1, Perkins named two stragglers who did rejoin that day and stated that "others"also turned up then. By the time that the "June 30" muster rolls were prepared around July 7-8, 48 men were present—including Carruth, Finnerty, and Payson, who had recovered from their slight wounds. Those rolls do not differentiate between "present for duty" and "present sick." Muster rolls of Company K, 1st Massachusetts Infantry Regiment, May-June, 1862, RG94, entry 57, NA; Perkins, *Diary*, July 7-8, 1862, and "notes" for August 13, 1862, Perkins Papers, *CWTI* Collection, USAMHI; Cudworth, pp. 236-237; *Mass. Soldiers*, 1, pp. 60-66.

[102] By the time the rolls were prepared between July 1 and 12, six companies, the staff, and band reported 14 officers and 220 soldiers "present for duty." Those enlisted men represented 62 percent of the enlisted men for those eight commands who were "present." The remaining four companies (including K) did not differentiate between "present for duty" and "present sick" but simply gave the aggregate "present": four officers and 230 soldiers. Applying the proportion of 62 percent to the remaining companies would suggest, statistically, that 3 officers and 143 men of them were present for duty. Using such extrapolations would raise the total "present for duty" strength to 17 officers and 363 men (or 340 men without including the band). That total is twice as high as the count of 180 muskets for July 1 which Perkins heard. If his number is anywhere close to correct, it suggests that half the regiment's potential strength had straggled from the ranks during the retreat from the Williamsburg Road through Glendale to Malvern Hill—a measure of the ordeal which the march imposed on the soldiers. Perkins, *Diary*, July 7-9, 14, and 26, 1862, Perkins Papers, *CWTI* Collection, USAMHI; muster rolls of the 1st Massachusetts Infantry Regiment, May-June, 1862, RG 94, entry 57, NA.

[103] The naval vessels that fired in the morning were the *U.S.S. Aroostook* and the *U.S.S. Mahaska*. The flagship *U.S.S. Galena* added its fire in late afternoon. *NOR* 7, pp. 709, 712-713; *OR* 11, pt. 1, p. 224.

much by shelling this morn.[104] Crackers for dinner & in P.M. some of the men were sent for more, 4 apiece; Hinckley gave us few yesterday. Recd. 5 more rounds ammunition in P.M. patent. Pickets from Regt. Rebs moving to our right. Lieut. C. stayed with us most of day.[105] Parkinson, Ketler & others came in today.[106] Pleasant day, in shade most of time. Good water. Supper: crackers & water.

Wednesday, July 2nd, 1862: Last eve, pickets were relieved, one from each Co. by 2 from each Co. & we laid down for night, Whit & I together on his rubber & mine over both. 1/2 men on watch all time. Alarmed once about 8 o'c. Cavalry man said enemy were coming in force; turned out to be our own men. Men made breast work of rails &c. yesterday. Waked up about 3. Slept well. Whit up two hours before to watch. Trowbridge of Co. A died in fit as we waked up, left him unburied. When we left marched off on retreat in line parallel with river, I should think. Commenced to rain about sunrise. Crossed a creek and marched about all A.M. in mud & water.[107] Awful marching, got entirely wet through, worse than ever before, I believe. Was obliged to leave Regt. Could not keep with them. There were so many troops. Sometimes 3 columns marching along same road, 1 in centre & 1 each side. Wagon trains, artillery, &c., &c., all mixed up. On this retreat have had some chance to see the immense size of this Army. Last eve the artillery kept up firing until late, very rapid firing & heavy, must have done great execution. Crackers, salt junk & coffee for D [dinner].

---

[104] The III Corps occupied the sector just rightward of where the main battle raged, and Grover held the far right of the corps' line. Perkins thus was so far east that he was unaware that the Secessionists repeatedly assaulted the Federal left that afternoon and were bloodily repulsed every time. *OR* 11, pt. 2, pp. 102, 116.

[105] Since Carruth had suffered only a slight wound on Monday, he was evidently able to rejoin Company K by July 1. Cudworth, p. 237.

[106] Private William J. Ketler of Boston, an original member of the company, would be discharged for disability on October 6, 1862. Private Thomas Parkinson of Roxbury, who had enlisted in Company K on November 26, served until the regiment mustered out in May, 1864. *Mass. Soldiers*, 1, pp. 63-64.

[107] Official documents simply state that Pvt. William H. Trowbridge of Brookline died at Malvern Hill; Perkins explains how he perished. *Mass. Soldiers,* 1, p. 9. The III Corps actually crossed two streams. First came Turkey Island Creek, which flowed along the southern side of Malvern Hill, went under Turkey Bridge on the River Road, and emptied into the James River. About four and a half miles to the southeast, that road crossed Kimage's Creek, which flowed southward just west of Berkeley Plantation. Perkins probably refers to the more easterly stream, whose muddy flooded bottomlands made it the more memorable. *OR* 11, pt. 1, pp. 70, 121, and pt. 2, pp. 193-195, 217, 221, and pt. 3, pp. 292-293; Charles R. Johnson to his wife, July 4, 1862, from Harrison's Bend, Charles R. Johnson Papers, Harrisburg CWRT Coll., USAMHI; Luther S. Dickey, *History of the Eighty-fifth Regiment, Pennsylvania Volunteer Infantry, 1861-1865* (New York, 1915), p. 186.

When we arrived, cooks made the coffee for us. Wagons in camp. Whit & I went and got rails and made a shed roof, tents on top, branches of cedar on ground and blankets on them and formed quite good shelter. Very heavy rain. Camp in open field.[108] Any quantity of men, wagons by the acre, artillery &c. Rained most of P.M. Saw good many prisoners this morn. Not much tired & feel pretty well on getting to camp. Raw meat served out & cooked it ourselves. Roasted mine on stick. Randall gave me some tea & had some for supper. Whit got some oat meal & had some hasty pudding, quite a good supper on whole. Oiled my gun. Some cannonading in Eve. Turned in in woolen blanket & slept well.[109]

Thursday, July 3rd, 1862: Up before anybody else in Co. Clothes all of a smoke, so I went out in woods & got wood, 2 rails for cooks, about a mile & so dried myself pretty well. Made a fire and had coffee, tea & crackers for B[breakfast]. Does not rain this morning but rained hard all night. Awful muddy. After breakfast went with Whit to wash face & hands & towel (which I tore in halves the other day to make it smaller & threw in my box, blacking also) & handkerchief. Had to go about 1/2 mile to a brook or creek. Went back to camp & volunteered to go on detail of 2 from Co. K (with Frank Downs[110]) in team down to river to get commissary stores. Awfullest hard riding I ever had. Mud foot deep on average. Any quantity of shipping on river, Monitor, Galena &c.[111] Sty on eye coming but feel pretty well this morning.

Letter to parents, last night's mail. Wagons had to wait in mud some time before finding where they had to go for stores. While waiting, I went up to camp through mud 1/2 way to knees, never saw so much mud before. Fried some

---

[108] The large open fields east of Kimage's Creek extended south to the James River at Harrison's Landing, the wharf for Berkeley Plantation. Reaching there completed McClellan's transfer of his base from the Pamunkey River across the Peninsula to the James. According to Heintzelman, who spent the night near Hooker's camps, the Second Division bivouacked in the southeastern part of the clearings near the swamp on the right bank of Herring's Creek; this ground was part of Westover Plantation. Heintzelman, *Notes* and *Journal*, July 2, 1862; Heintzelman Papers, LC; *New York Times*, July 10, 1862; Massachusetts Adjutant General, *Annual Report. . .for . . .1862* (Boston, 1863), p. 85. Hereinafter cited as *Mass. AG*.

[109] Private Albert A. Randall of Boston enlisted May 24, 1861, and served all three years. *Mass. Soldiers*, 1, p. 64.

[110] Private Frank T. Downs of Boston belonged to Company K from May 24, 1861, until discharged for disability on October 18, 1862. Ibid., p. 61.

[111] Half of Commander John Rodgers's command within the North Atlantic Blockading Squadron was waiting in the James near Malvern Hill and Harrison's Landing when the Army of the Potomac completed crossing the Peninsula. The ironclad *U.S.S. Galena* was his flagship; among his eight other vessels in that vicinity was the most famous of all Civil War ironclads, the *U.S.S. Monitor*. *NOR* 7, pp. 531, 533-534, 539, 541-542.

meat and had some crackers. Carried some crackers to Frank Downs & G's & D's boys. Waited some time longer, then train went downriver about 2 or 3 miles, where the stores were landed.[112] Passed several splendid residences, acres of wagons and cattle. Driving cattle from steamer into river and they swam ashore. Comical sight. Loaded some hard bread and went back to camp. Saw on this trip some of the awfullest going. Saw teams go down & across ditches 3 feet deep & 3 feet wide at least. At camp about sunset. Regt. not there, had marched about mile or so & were going to camp there.[113] Things left behind. Wagon took their blankets up in eve. I sent Whit's rubber blanket. Supper: tea & more steak & crackers. And 1/2 dipper of coffee cooked myself. Turned in & slept well.

Friday, July 4th, 1862: Pleasant morning. 2 men came back from Regt. and say that Regt. moved ahead & back to same place again. Hooker got ahead too far and was shot at by the enemy. Report that an Indiana Regt. captured the battery of the enemy that fired shell at our camp yesterday morning.[114] Breakfast: tea and hard bread; stole some meal of Rich and made some hasty pudding; stole some beef steak which Whit left on his plate. Sun shining and I guess the mud will soon dry up. 32nd Mass. arrived at landing yesterday.[115] Cannonading this A.M. about 12 and men firing muskets to get old charges out, I suppose. Ought not to be allowed. I hate the sound of a gun.[116]

---

[112] On July 3, Federal supply officers began using Westover Landing, two miles east of Harrison's Landing. *OR* 11, pt. 1, p. 171.

[113] Both divisions of the III Corps slogged through the swamp and crossed Herring Creek to help occupy Evelington Heights on its left bank. Heintzelman *Notes* and *Diary* and *Journal*, July 3, 1862, Heintzelman Papers, LC; Charles R. Johnson to wife, July 4, 1862, from Harrison's Bend, Charles R. Johnson Papers, Harrisburg CWRT Coll., USAMHI; *Mass. AG*, p. 85.

[114] On July 3, "Jeb" Stuart's cavalry boldly occupied Evelington Heights around Westover Church and shelled McClellan's position with one battery. Before Secessionist infantry could reinforce the horsemen, a fresh Federal brigade (including the 14th Indiana Infantry Regiment), just arrived from northern Virginia, advanced across Herring Creek and secured the position by mid-afternoon (but did not capture the Confederate artillery). Other Yankee troops, including Heintzelman's corps, also moved out to the heights later that day. *OR* 11, pt. 2, pp. 246, 464, 519-520, 922, and pt. 3, p. 292; Heintzelman, *Journal*, July 3, 1862, Heintzelman Papers, LC.

[115] Although organized as a battalion in November, 1861, and as a regiment in May, 1862, the 32nd did not reach the front until July 3. It was assigned to the V Corps, with which it served for the rest of the war. Higginson, 1, p. 256.

[116] On July 3, Hooker ordered that "if any of your arms should require to be discharged, you have authority to do it at 11 o'clock today. To prevent accident, and to have them all discharged at the appointed hour Commanders of Regiments will give this matter their personal attention, after which no firing will be allowed in the Division." The threat from Evelington Heights that morning presumably caused the discharging to be postponed until Friday. Circular of July 3, 1862, Hooker's division, III Corps Papers, RG 393, pt. 2, entry 3801, p. 226, NA.

Bands playing good deal today.[117] Wagons carried knapsacks to the new camp. I left just before they did with some of the boys. About mile off whole brig. encamped in one line.[118] Fried some more beef steak and took my own plate (Mrs. P's.) (which have had ever since Camp Hooker),[119] crackers. Knapsacks came along after dinner & Whit & I pitched together alone. Pleasant day. Wrote letter to Parents. Sent memo up to today from June 25. Recd. mail after we got to camp. Letter from Father and one inclosed from James, with 9 stamps and ambrotype of James.[120] H. J. [Home Journal] & Sci. Am. Letter & Traveller from E. F. L. 1.00 in Father's letter. Sold stamps, sheet paper and env. for 10 cts. Morn .00. Burnt 2 fingers and thumb cooking steak. Camp in regular order in good place in open corn field. [illegible] Artillery shelling some in P.M. Bands playing about all P.M. Pleasant day. Supper: coffee &c. Paid Hollace Wrisley .25. Eve .95, H. N. 1.10. Letter to Father, 48 C. C. P. Letter to E. F. L. Eve bands playing & bugles blowing. Turned in, slept rather cool. Whit closed one end with his rubber & we laid on mine.

* * *

Volume IV-A of Charles C. Perkins' diary ends with the entry of July 4, 1862. The next volume resumes with July 5, and the diary continues

---

[117] McClellan explained that he "re-established the playing of bands, beating the calls, etc., by way of keeping the men in good spirits. . . ." McClellan, *Own Story*, p. 444.

[118] When the Confederate attack from Evelington Heights confirmed for McClellan his apprehension that his army might be trapped in the bottomlands right around Harrison's Landing, he extended his defense perimeter to include the heights and other more defensible ground. However, since there was not room for both of Heintzelman's divisions on the left bank of Herring Creek and since the most direct threat could potentially come straight east from Malvern Hill along the River Road, Hooker was moved back to the right bank of that stream to enable the IV Corps to close up on its left and hold the east bank of Kimage's Creek in force. As finally deployed on July 6, the III Corps held McClellan's center, with the IV Corps on its left, the VI Corps on its right, and the II and V Corps in reserve. By that Sunday, the 1st Massachusetts occupied the northward-facing sector immediately west of Herring Creek just below Rowland's Mill Pond. In the entry for July 4, Perkins describes preliminary repositioning in preparation for extricating Hooker from Evelington Heights and giving him his own sector running westward from the pond for about three-quarters of a mile. *OR* 11, pt. 3, pp. 300-303; Cudworth, pp. 240-241; Haynes, pp. 117-118; Perkins, *Diary*, July 5-6, 1862, *CWTI* Coll., USAMHI; Heintzelman, *Notes* and *Journal*, July 4-5, 1862, and letter from Seth Williams, July 5, 1862, Heintzelman Papers, LC; letter to Chauncey McKeever, July 5, 1862, Hooker's division, III Corps Papers, RG 393, pt. 2, entry 3801, p. 226, NA.

[119] Camp Hooker was situated at Budd's Ferry, Maryland, on the left bank of the Potomac downriver from Washington. His division wintered there from October, 1861, until the start of the Peninsula Campaign. Cudworth, pp. 96-135.

[120] Perkins' younger brother James was still a civilian in Salem. On September 2, 1862, he would enlist in Company A, 50th Massachusetts Infantry Regiment and serve a full nine-month tour until that unit mustered out on August 24, 1863. *Mass. Soldiers*, 4, p. 513.

for another eight volumes—through Second Manassas, Chantilly, Fredericksburg, Chancellorsville, Gettysburg, Manassas Gap, Kelly's Ford, Mine Run, the Wilderness, and Spotsylvania—until Perkins was safely en route back to Massachusetts, where the regiment mustered out of service on May 25, 1864. All 13 volumes of his diary are available for study at the U.S. Army Military History Institute at Carlisle Barracks, Pennsylvania.

THE GRAND CAMPAIGN:

A Journal of Operations in the Peninsula Campaign March 17 - August 26, 1862

Compiled by William J. Miller

On November 1, 1861, President Abraham Lincoln appointed Maj. Gen. George B. McClellan to command "the whole army" of the United States. Already the commander of the Army of the Potomac, the brilliant and ambitious 35-year-old McClellan would thenceforth be responsible for not just the actions of his own army, but the movements of all the Federal armies in all theaters of war. Lincoln privately expressed concern that his young general might find himself overtaxed by responsibility. McClellan confidently replied, "I can do it all."

Throughout the autumn and winter of 1861, as the Army of the Potomac gathered its strength and drilled in camps around Washington, pressure increased on McClellan to take some action in the eastern theater. Ignoring the growing outcry against his idleness, McClellan slowly and deliberately developed his plan for a campaign he believed would end the war.

Opposing McClellan in Virginia was the army of Gen. Joseph E. Johnston, one of the more intelligent, experienced and respected military men on the continent. A career soldier, the 54-year-old Johnston had played a major role in the Confederate victory at the Battle of Manassas the previous July. As his army wintered at Manassas and Centreville 30 miles from Washington, he counted among his responsibilities the safety of the capital of the Confederacy, Richmond, Virginia, which lay just 80 miles to the south. President Jefferson Davis learned early in the war that Johnston, for all his abilities, was proud and contentious. The two men worked together with difficulty.

Presidents, generals, soldiers and citizens in both North and South knew that spring would bring a major Federal offensive in Virginia. Some hoped and others worried that it might be the decisive campaign of the war.[1]

Early December, 1861: McClellan conceives the "Urbanna Plan" to capture Richmond. The plan calls for the movement of the Army of the Potomac from Washington, D.C., by water down the Chesapeake Bay to the river town of Urbanna, Virginia, on the Rappahannock River, 45 miles from Richmond. The movement to the Chesapeake must be made via Annapolis, Maryland, for the Potomac River below Washington is closed to Federal shipping by Confederate batteries. From Urbanna, the army can advance overland to Richmond. McClellan believes the plan's chief advantage is that it places his army between Richmond and the Confederate army commanded by Johnston at Manassas and Centreville. By interposing himself on Johnston's rear, he would threaten the Confederate lines of supply and communication and render the position at Manassas and Centreville untenable. If successful, McClellan would force Johnston to withdraw without having to fight a battle. Furthermore, because the movement to Urbanna is to be rapid, McClellan feels it should give the Federals an advantage in beating Johnston's army to Richmond. McClellan does not yet share his plan with President Lincoln or Edwin M. Stanton.[2]

January 31 (Fri.): Unaware of McClellan's plans, Lincoln orders the general to move on Johnston.

---

[1] This chronology was compiled largely from the *Official Records of the Union and Confederate Armies,* but other primary sources were used as well. Because of the general and skeletal nature of this daily record, I have not cited sources for all the quotations and events given here, but instead have listed general sources, most of them primary, to lead students to fuller descriptions of the events of the day. Weather notes come from Brig. Gen. Samuel P. Heintzelman's pocket diary in the Library of Congress (Samuel P. Heintzelman Papers, microfilm reel 1), unless they are attributed to McClellan, in which cases they come from his letters as printed in his memoirs, *McClellan's Own Story.*

[2] George B. McClellan, *McClellan's Own Story* (New York, 1887), pp. 202-203.

February 3 (Mon.): Fearful that the president's order will be final and cause him to abandon his plan to take Richmond, McClellan defends his Urbanna Plan in a letter to Secretary Stanton. Lincoln is apparently swayed by McClellan's arguments and does not attempt to enforce his January 31 order.[3]

February 19 (Wed.): General Johnston sits in on a cabinet meeting at the Confederate White House in Richmond. President Davis suggests the general withdraw from his advanced position at Manassas and move closer to Richmond, which seems likely to be the target of the Federal offensive in the spring. Johnston says the movement will hardly be possible before the roads dry, by which time the Federals will have begun their movement.[4]

March 7 (Fri.): General McClellan holds a council of war in Washington with 12 senior officers of the Army of the Potomac: Brig. Gens. Irvin McDowell, Edwin V. Sumner, Samuel P. Heintzelman, John G. Barnard, Andrew Porter, Fitz John Porter, William B. Franklin, Louis Blenker, William F. Smith, Erasmus D. Keyes, George A. McCall and Henry M. Naglee. McClellan presents to these officers his plan for the spring campaign aimed at capturing Richmond. McClellan asks the officers to vote on his plan and carry the results of their poll to President Lincoln. McDowell, Sumner, and Heintzelman, the senior officers present, vote against the plan, as does Barnard, the army's chief engineer. The other eight approve of McClellan's plan. The dozen men take their verdict down the block to the White House, where they meet with the president, Secretary of War Edwin M. Stanton and Assistant Secretary of the Navy Gustavus F. Fox. The president thanks the generals and asks them to return in the morning, when he will give them his decision.

March 8 (Sat.): Lincoln informs the gathered officers that he accepts McClellan's plan of campaign, with provisions. The Confederate

---

[3] McClellan, *Own Story,* pp. 228-236.

[4] Craig L. Symonds, *Joseph E. Johnston: A Civil War Biography* (New York, 1992), p. 145.

batteries on the Potomac must be removed before the army can depart, sufficient troops must be left behind to ensure that Washington will be secure in the army's absence; the movement must begin within 10 days, by March 18. The president, without consulting McClellan, also names five corps commanders: McDowell, Sumner, Heintzelman, Keyes, and Maj. Gen. Nathaniel P. Banks, whose corps will not accompany McClellan's expedition but will be used to protect Washington.[5]

In Hampton Roads, at the tip of the peninsula formed by the York and James Rivers, the ironclad *C.S.S. Virginia* (nee *U.S.S. Merrimack*) sinks one U.S. Navy vessel, forces the surrender of another and causes others to run aground. Observers report to Washington on the ease with which the ironclad dealt with the wooden-hulled ships. Stanton fears for the safety of the Atlantic Blockading Squadron, Washington, and New York. McClellan fears that the dominance of the ship may cause him to alter his plan of campaign.

Johnston begins the evacuation of Manassas with the intention of withdrawing down the Orange and Alexandria Railroad to positions on the Rappahannock River.[6]

March 9 (Sun.): The ironclad *U.S.S. Monitor* engages the *Virginia,* and the two ships fight to a draw, restoring some of the Federal administration's confidence. The Confederate evacuation of Manassas continues. As Johnston leaves northern Virginia, Confederate garrisons evacuate the batteries on the Potomac, opening the river to Federal shipping.[7]. Lincoln, McClellan and Stanton are together when word arrives that Johnston is evacuating Manassas.[8]

March 10 (Mon.): Wishing to exploit any opportunity presented by Johnston's withdrawal, McClellan moves the Army of the Potomac from

---

[5] McClellan, *McClellan's Own Story,* p. 222.

[6] Douglas Southall Freeman *R. E. Lee: A Biography,* 4 vols. (New York, 1934) vol. 2, p. 4.

[7] Mary Alice Wills *The Confederate Blockade of Washington, D.C. 1861-1862* (1975, rpt. Prince William County Historical Commission, 1992), pp. 156-62

[8] McClellan, *McClellan's Own Story,* p. 222.

its camps around Washington toward Manassas. The general establishes his headquarters at Fairfax Court House, Virginia.[9]

March 11 (Tues.): The Army of the Potomac finds the Confederate works at Centreville and Manassas abandoned. President Lincoln, reasoning that McClellan is now afield with his army and has plenty to occupy him in conducting the campaign, relieves him of his duties as general-in-chief of all U.S. armies. The president does not name a replacement. A messenger from the White House fails to gain an audience with McClellan, so the general learns of the change in his status through the newspapers.[10]

March 13 (Thurs.): McClellan holds another council of war, this time at army headquarters at Fairfax Court House. Since Johnston's withdrawal has made Urbanna unsuitable as a landing point, McClellan asks the four generals present, Sumner, Heintzelman, McDowell and Keyes, if they support his plan to move the army by water to Fort Monroe. The fort stands at the tip of the peninsula formed by the York and James Rivers east of Richmond. All four voice support of the plan.

March 14 (Fri.): McClellan orders quartermaster Brig. Gen. D. C. McCallum at Baltimore to load five locomotives and 80 railroad cars on ships and barges in preparation for shipment to the Peninsula. This order indicates the army commander's intention to use the Richmond and York River Railroad, the only railroad on the Peninsula.[11]

March 16 (Sun.): In a private letter to a friend on the eve of the campaign, McClellan bemoans the active efforts of his political enemies in Washington to discredit and hinder him, but he believes he has the

---

[9] Ibid., p. 224.

[10] Ibid., pp. 224-225.

[11] McClellan later ordered a sixth locomotive for use on the Peninsula. U.S. War Department, *The War of the Rebellion: The Official Records of the Union and Confederate Armies,* 128 vols. (Washington, D.C., 1890-1901), Series III, Vol. 5, p. 974. Hereinafter cited as *OR.* All other references are to series I unless otherwise noted.

confidence of the president. "The President is all right," he writes, "he is my strongest friend."[12]

THE PENINSULA CAMPAIGN BEGINS

March 17 (Mon.): Brig. Gen. Charles S. Hamilton's division (III Corps) embarks from Alexandria for Fort Monroe—the first element of the Army of the Potomac to move on Richmond in the campaign.

March 23 (Sun.): Maj. Gen. Thomas J. "Stonewall" Jackson attacks Federal troops at Kernstown, Virginia, in the Shenandoah Valley. Jackson is defeated, but the Federal commander in the Valley, Nathaniel P. Banks, realizes that the region is not secure and ceases sending troops from his command eastward to reinforce McClellan.

March 27 (Thurs.): President Davis orders General Johnston to reinforce the Army of the Peninsula. Brig. Gen. Fitz John Porter's division (III Corps) advances from Fort Monroe to Big Bethel.[13]

March 31 (Mon.): Concerned over his generals' failure to secure the Shenandoah Valley, Lincoln informs McClellan that Blenker's division, which was to have accompanied McClellan to Fort Monroe, has been ordered to the Valley.

April 1 (Tues.): McClellan protests the reassignment of Blenker's division and sets sail from Alexandria aboard the *Commodore* bound for Fort Monroe.[14]

---

[12] Stephen W. Sears, ed., *The Civil War Papers of George B. McClellan* (New York, 1989), p. 213.

[13] McClellan, *Own Story,* p. 256.

[14] Ibid., p. 254.

April 2 (Wed.): The *Commodore* drops anchor off the Old Point Comfort at the tip of the Peninsula. McClellan establishes headquarters of the Army of the Potomac in the vicinity of Fort Monroe.[15]

April 3 (Thurs.): Lincoln, realizing that McClellan did not leave behind all the troops he said he would to ensure the safety of Washington, detaches McDowell's I Corps from Army of the Potomac to cover Washington from the Fredericksburg area. Secretary of War Stanton suspends recruiting operations throughout the North.

April 4 (Fri.): The Army of the Potomac begins its march up the Peninsula toward Richmond, 65 miles away, and skirmishes with Confederates near Cockletown. Nathaniel Banks' V Corps is merged into the Department of the Shenandoah.[16]

THE SIEGE OF YORKTOWN BEGINS

April 5 (Sat.): The Army of the Potomac arrives before the Confederate fortifications at Yorktown and along the Warwick River. Brigadier General John B. Magruder, commanding the Confederate troops at Yorktown, creates an illusion of great strength by marching his 4,000 men continuously along his front where they may be seen by McClellan's arriving army. [17] After Lincoln informs McClellan that McDowell's division will be retained at Fredericksburg to help cover the capital, the general replies that "In my deliberate judgment the success of our cause will be imperilled by so greatly reducing my force when it is actually under the fire of the enemy and active operations have commenced."[18]

---

[15] Ibid., p. 254.

[16] *OR* 11, pt. 1, pp. 285, 298,299.

[17] The siege operations at Yorktown are addressed by 26 officers in reports listed in *OR* 11, pt. 1, pp. 1169-1170; See Robert U. Johnson and Clarence C. Buel, eds., *Battles and Leaders of the Civil War*, 4 vols. (New York, 1884-1889) in which writers discuss the events of the day in George B. McClellan, "The Peninsular Campaign," vol. 2, pp. 169-172; Warren Lee Goss, "Recollections of a Private," 2, pp. 188-194; Joseph E. Johnston, "Manassas to Seven Pines," 2, p. 203; Richard B. Irwin, "The Administration in the Peninsular Campaign," 2, pp. 436-437.

[18] McClellan, *McClellan's Own Story,* p.262.

April 6 (Sun.): *Rain.* Elements of Johnston's army arrive in Richmond from their Rappahannock positions and head east down the Peninsula toward Yorktown. Brigadier General Winfield S. Hancock, of Brig. Gen. W. F. Smith's Federal division, leads a reconnaissance of the Confederate fortifications along the Warwick and clashes with Southern defenders near Lee's Mill. Professor Thaddeus S. C. Lowe's balloon *Intrepid* takes its initial ascent on the Peninsula for McClellan's army to gather intelligence about the Confederate positions.

April 7 (Mon.): *Rain.* Johnston's troops begin occupying the Yorktown defenses.

April 8 (Tues.): *McClellan Reports, "Weather terrible; raining heavily last twenty-eight hours; roads and camps in awful condition."*

April 9 (Wed.): *McClellan Reports, "weather still execrable; country covered with water; roads terrible."* The Confederate Congress passes the Conscription Act. Lincoln wires to McClellan, "I beg to assure you that I have never written you or spoken to you in greater kindness of feeling than now, nor with a fuller purpose to sustain you, so far as, in my most anxious judgment, I consistently can. But you must act."[19]

April 10 (Thurs.): *Drizzle.* The Army of the Potomac enlarges its supply depot on Cheeseman's Creek, 8 miles from Yorktown.

April 11 (Fri.): After McClellan asks the war department for the I Corps divisions of Franklin and McCall for the purpose of taking the Confederate batteries at Gloucester Point on the north side of the York opposite Yorktown, the war department places Franklin's division subject to McClellan's orders.

---

[19] Ibid, pp. 276-278.

April 12 (Sat.): Johnston arrives in Richmond, where his area of command is extended to include the Departments of Norfolk and the Peninsula.

April 14 (Mon.): *Rain at Night at Yorktown.* President Jefferson Davis holds a council of war in the Confederate White House. The men present, Davis, Johnston, Gen. Robert E. Lee, Secretary of War George Randolph and Gens. Gustavus W. Smith and James Longstreet, consider the feasibility of holding the Yorktown line. Johnston thinks it unwise, impractical and even dangerous. Lee disagrees and thinks delaying McClellan there will buy the Confederacy time to gather strength. At 1 a.m. on the 15th, Davis finally decides that the army will hold the York-town line as long as possible.[20]

April 15 (Tues.): *Drizzle.*

April 16 (Wed.): *Weather "Beautiful."* Smith's division attacks Confederate positions at Dam Number 1 on the Warwick River.[21]

April 20-21 (Sun.-Mon.): *Rain and Drizzle. Temperature in the 50's.*

April 22 (Tues.): *Rain.* Franklin's division reinforces McClellan in front of Yorktown.

April 23 (Wed.): *Clear and Windy.*

April 26 (Sat.): *Rain.* McClellan names Brig. Gen. Fitz John Porter "director of the siege" of Yorktown.[22]

---

[20] Johnston, "Manassas to Seven Pines," 2, p. 203; Freeman, *Lee,* 2, pp.21-22.

[21] The engagement is addressed by 19 officers in reports listed in *OR* 11, pt. 1, p. 1121.

[22] McClellan, *Own Story,* p. 286.

April 27 (Sun.): Johnston informs Davis that he plans to evacuate Yorktown.[23]

April 28 (Mon.): Lee urges Johnston to hold on a little longer at Yorktown. Federals reconnoiter to Lee's Mill on the Warwick.[24]

April 29 (Tues.): Johnston informs the war department that he will evacuate Yorktown "as soon as can be done conveniently. . . ."[25]

April 30 (Wed.): *"Cloudy, damp, chilly in morning, turned to rain."* Federal Battery Number 1 opens on the Yorktown wharves and Gloucester to prevent resupply of the Confederate garrison.

May 1 (Thurs.): *Drizzle.*

May 3 (Sat.): Confederates screen their withdrawal from the York- town defenses by opening a bombardment after dark. Johnston begins pulling his troops out during the night.

THE SIEGE OF YORKTOWN ENDS
May 4 (Sun.): The Army of the Potomac occupies Yorktown. Skirmishers engage near Williamsburg.[26]

May 5 (Mon.): *Rain Begins About 2:30 a.m.*
BATTLE OF WILLIAMSBURG
Realizing he must turn in his retreat and confront the energetic Fed- eral pursuit, Johnston directs Longstreet to send troops to occupy pre- pared defenses east of Williamsburg. In a driving rain, Longstreet's brigades stop the attacks of Brig. Gen. Joseph Hooker's Federal division (III Corps) and later engage the division of Brig. Gen. Phil Kearny (also

---

[23] Freeman, *Lee*, 2, p. 41.

[24] Ibid.; *OR* 11, pt. 1, pp. 396-397.

[25] *OR* 11, pt. 3, p. 473.

[26] These skirmishes are addressed by 15 officers in reports listed in *OR* 11, pt. 1, p. 1167.

of the III Corps). Brig. Gen. Winfield S. Hancock's brigade (IV Corps) finds the Confederate left unguarded but is prevented from exploiting the advantage by Confederate reinforcements under Brig. Gen. Jubal A. Early.[27]

May 6 (Tues.): *Skies Clear About Midnight* Federal forces occupy Williamsburg. Johnston establishes temporary headquarters near Barhamsville. Through the night, Brig. Gen. William B. Franklin disembarks his I Corps division at Eltham's Landing at the mouth of the Pamunkey River north of Barhamsville. President Lincoln, Secretary of War Stanton and Secretary of the Treasury Salmon P. Chase arrive at Fort Monroe aboard the revenue cutter *Miami*.

May 7 (Wed.): *Clear and Sunny.*
ENGAGEMENT AT ELTHAM'S LANDING
Franklin establishes a base and perimeter at Eltham's Landing. Troops from Brig. Gen. W. H. C. Whiting's Division attack and drive in portions of Franklin's line before retiring. [28]

May 8 (Thurs.): *Clear and Sunny, Roads Drying.*
In the Valley District, Jackson halts his command on the height above McDowell, Virginia, and prepares to attack Federals in the valley below. The Federals attack first, but are repulsed and retreat during the night. Jackson pursues, continuing to be the aggressor.

On the Peninsula, Federals return from reconnaissance to Mulberry Point on the James River, and the U.S. Navy makes a demonstration at Sewell's Point.[29]

---

[27] The engagement is addressed by 76 officers in reports listed in *OR* 11, pt. 1, pp. 1166-1167; McClellan, "The Peninsular Campaign," p. 172; Goss, "Yorktown and Williamsburg," pp. 194-197; "The Opposing Forces at Williamsburg, Va." *B & L*, 2, p. 200; Johnston, "Manassas to Seven Pines," pp. 205-207; Gustavus W. Smith, "Two Days of Battle at Seven Pines," *B & L*, 2, p. 221; Daniel H. Hill, "McClellan's Change of Base and Malvern Hill," *B & L*, 2, p. 385; Irwin, "The Administration in the Peninsula Campaign," p. 437.

[28] The engagement is addressed by 12 officers in reports listed in *OR* 11, pt. 1, p. 1163.

[29] Ibid., pp. 24, 633, 634.

May 9 (Fri.): *Clear and Sunny.* Confederates begin evacuating Norfolk and destroying Gosport navy yard. Skirmishers clash at New Kent Court House. [30]

May 10 (Sat.): *Clear and Sunny, Windy in the Afternoon.* Confederate forces evacuate Norfolk south of the James River. Federal forces occupy Norfolk and Portsmouth.[31]

May 11 (Sun.): *Cool Wind in the Morning, Afternoon Rain.* The crew of the *C.S.S. Virginia,* left without a port from which to operate on the James since the fall of Norfolk, scuttle the ironclad, ending Confederate dominance of the river.

May 13 (Tues.): *Cool Morning, Pleasant Day.* Skirmishers engage at Baltimore Cross Roads, near New Kent Court-House.

May 14 (Wed.): *Rain.* The Virginia legislature in session in Richmond calls for the defense of the city to the last extremity.

May 15 (Thurs.): *Rain.*
ENGAGEMENT AT DREWRY'S BLUFF
Commander John Rogers, U.S.N., leads a gunboat squadron consisting of the *U.S.S. Monitor, Galena, Naugatuck, Aroostook* and *Port Royal* up the James toward Richmond. Confederate guns at Fort Darling on Drewry's Bluff below Richmond turn the Federals back.

May 16 (Fri.): *Clearing.* Johnston's forces withdraw to the south side of the Chickahominy River.[32]

May 17 (Sat.): *McClellan Reports, "clear and very hot."* McDowell's corps ordered to advance from Fredericksburg to the Pamunkey

---

[30] Ibid., p. 352.

[31] Ibid., pp. 634-635.

[32] Freeman, *Lee*, 2, pp. 59-60.

River as soon as he is joined by reinforcements enroute from the Shenandoah Valley. Expedition up the Pamunkey River.[33]

May 18 (Sun.): *Pleasant.* Brig. Gen. Fitz John Porter, U.S. Army, assumes command of the V Corps (reorganized). Maj. Gen. William B. Franklin, U.S. Army, assumes command of the VI Corps.

May 20 (Tues.): Federal forces cross the Chickahominy, the final major geographical barrier between them and Richmond.[34]

May 22 (Thurs.): *Rain, Night Very Warm.* Elements of the Army of the Potomac continue crossing the Chickahominy at Bottom's Bridge. McClellan maintains a portion of his army north of the Chickahominy, both to protect his supply line—the Richmond and York River Railroad—and to establish a link with McDowell's corps whenever it should advance from Fredericksburg. McClellan establishes army headquarters at Cold Harbor north of the Chickahominy. Johnston maintains headquarters on the Williamsburg Road two miles southeast of Richmond.

May 23 (Fri.): *Pleasant but Warm, Temperature in the 80's.*
McClellan is ill with dysentery in the evening and confined to his tent. Skirmishers engage at Ellerson's Mill, near Mechanicsville.[35] Jackson attacks Banks at Front Royal in the Shenandoah Valley.

May 24 (Sat.): *Rain All Day*
Jackson attacks Banks' retreating column at Middletown in the Shenandoah Valley. The Federal war department suspends McDowell's orders to move upon Richmond. On the Peninsula, skirmishers engage at New Bridge, Mechanicsville and Seven Pines.[36] Johnston meets with

---

[33] *OR* 11, pt. 1, pp. 637-638.

[34] Operations around Bottom's Bridge, May 20-23, are detailed in *OR* 11, pt. 1, pp. 25, 641-46, 648-49.

[35] *OR* 11, pt. 1, pp. 25, 31, 352-353, 652-654, 661, 663-664.

[36] Ibid., pp. 6, 25, 69, 668, 670, 673.

Davis in Richmond. Though the general is considering an offensive, he speaks vaguely and does not share any of his plans with the president.[37]

May 25 (Sun.): Jackson attacks and defeats Banks at Winchester. On the Peninsula, Federals mount an expedition toward the James from Bottom's Bridge.[38]

May 26 (Mon.): *Rain.* At Army of the Potomac headquarters near New Bridge, McClellan is still troubled by his "old Mexican complaint. . . ." but feels he is recovering.[39] Wishing to extend his lines northwestward to join with McDowell's I Corps, which was still expected to arrive from Fredericksburg, McClellan sends Brig. Gen. Fitz John Porter to eliminate a Confederate force at Hanover Court House on the Virginia Central Railroad north of the Confederate capital.[40]

May 27 (Tues.): *Clearing, Roads Becoming Passable.*
ENGAGEMENT AT HANOVER COURT HOUSE
Porter's command defeats Brig. Gen. Lawrence O'B. Branch's unsuspecting Confederate brigade at Hanover Court House.[41] Farther east, down the Peninsula, Federal supply trains begin running on the repaired Richmond and York River Railroad north of the Chickahominy River.

May 28 (Wed.): *McClellan Reports Rain.* Federal operations continue in vicinity of Hanover Court House. Northern cavalry burns high-

---

[37] Freeman, *Lee*, pp.60-61.

[38] *OR* 11, pt. 1, pp. 675-676.

[39] McClellan, *Own Story*, p. 396.

[40] *OR* 11, pt. 1, pp. 677-678.

[41] The engagement at Hanover Court House is addressed by 35 officers in reports listed in *OR* 11, pt. 1, p. 1109; See also additional reports on Hanover Court House in *OR* 11, pt. 2, pp. 242, 281; McClellan, "Peninsular Campaign," pp. 175-178; Johnston, "Manassas to Seven Pines," p. 211; Fitz John Porter, "Hanover Court House and Gaines's Mill," *B & L*, 2, pp. 319-323; William W. Averell, "With the Cavalry on the Peninsula," *B & L*, 2, p. 430.

way bridges and the Richmond, Fredericksburg and Potomac Railroad Bridge on the South Anna River.[42]

May 29 (Thurs.): *McClellan Reports Rain.* Federal troops destroy the Virginia Central Railroad Bridge on the South Anna River.[43] Federal pioneers complete Grapevine Bridge over the Chickahominy River. McClellan is ill with what he calls "my old Mexican enemy."[44]

May 30 (Fri.): *McClellan Reports Violent Rain Storm at Night.* Johnston plans to attack McClellan's forces south of the rain-swollen Chickahominy. His orders to subordinates are not explicit, and some of the commanders are unsure of their roles. Lee, suspecting that a battle was imminent, offers to serve as a volunteer on Johnston's staff.[45]

McClellan is still ill and confined to his bed. Elements of the armies skirmish near Fair Oaks.[46]

May 31 (Sat.): *Clearing.*
BATTLE OF SEVEN PINES (FAIR OAKS)
Johnston's plan of attack goes awry when his separated columns fail to converge. D. H. Hill's Division attacks at the Seven Pines crossroads and is later supported by Whiting's (Smith's) Division and a few troops from Longstreet's Division. Two Federal divisions of the IV Corps, Brig. Gen. Silas Casey's and Couch's divisions, suffer the blow of the Confederate attacks. Federal reinforcements, Kearny's division (III Corps) and Sedgwick's division (II Corps), blunt the Southern assaults. Johnston himself does not arrive on the field until late in the day and is severely wounded as the fighting approaches its end. Command of the Confederate army in the field devolves upon Maj. Gen. Gustavus W.

[42] *OR* 11, pt. 1, pp. 692-693; 11, pt. 2, pp. 242, 281.

[43] *OR* 11, pt. 2, pp. 242, 281.

[44] McClellan, *Own Story,* p. 397.

[45] Freeman, *Lee,* 2, pp. 66-67.

[46] McClellan, *Own Story,* p. 397; *OR* 11, pt. 1, pp. 754, 757-762, 913, 914, 916, 917, 942, 953; pt. 2, p. 646.

Smith. Later in the evening, President Davis informs Gen. Robert E. Lee that he will be appointed to command the army effective June 1. McClellan keeps to his sick bed in the morning, but rides toward the battlefield in the afternoon.[47]

June 1 (Sun.): The fighting at Seven Pines continues. The divisions of Kearny and Hooker (III Corps) and Brig. Gens. Israel B. Richardson and John Sedgwick (II Corps) are engaged with troops from Longstreet's, Hill's and Whiting's commands. The combat is broken off with little advantage gained by either side. Lee assumes field command of the Army of Northern Virginia.

June 2 (Mon.): *Heavy Thunderstorms at Night.* Lee meets with all of his division and brigade commanders to get acquainted with his lieutenants and to hear their views.[48] Federals mount an expedition to Wormley's Ferry on the Pamunkey River.[49]

June 3 (Tues.): *Temperature in mid-90s, Heavy Rain at Night.*
Wishing to make the best use of the terrain and his manpower, Lee orders his engineers to resurvey the defenses of Richmond. He hopes to make the defenses strong enough to be held by a relatively small force, freeing the larger portion of his army for field operations.[50] Federals begin an expedition to the James River to open communication with the Navy gunboat fleet. This movement continues through June 7.[51]

June 4 (Wed.): *McClellan Reports Rain.*

---

[47] The engagement is addressed by 119 officers in reports listed in *OR* 11, pt. 1, pp. 1098-1101; *OR* 11, pt. 2, pp. 506, 993, 994; McClellan, "Peninsular Campaign," p. 178; Johnston, "Manassas to Seven Pines," pp. 208-218; Smith, "Two Days of Battle," pp. 220-263; Irwin, "The Administration in the Peninsular Campaign," p. 437.

[48] Freeman, *Lee*, 2, p. 89.

[49] *OR* 11, pt. 1, p. 997.

[50] Freeman, *Lee*, 2, p. 82.

[51] *OR* 11, pt. 1, pp. 998-999.

June 5 (Thurs.): *McClellan Reports Rain.* Lee writes to Davis: "I think if it was possible to reinforce Jackson strongly, it would change the character of the war. This can only be done by the troops in Georgia, South Carolina, and North Carolina. Jackson could in that event cross Maryland into Pennsylvania. It would call all the enemy from our southern coast and liberate those states." Shifting his attention to the threat on his own front, Lee confides to Davis his opinion that, "McClellan will make this a battle of Posts. He will take position from position, under cover of his heavy guns, & we cannot get at him without storming his works, which with our new troops is extremely hazardous. . . It will require 100,000 men to resist the regular siege of Richmond, which perhaps would only prolong not save it—I am preparing a line that I can hold with part of our forces in front, while with the rest I will endeavor to make a diversion to bring McClellan out. He sticks under his batteries & is working day and night. . . . Our position requires you should know everything & you must excuse me for troubling you."[52]

June 6 (Fri.): *McClellan Reports Rain.* McClellan is again ill.

June 8 (Sun.): *Pleasant with Some Sun.*
The war department orders McDowell's corps to return from the Shenandoah Valley, whence it had gone in a vain effort to assist in subduing Jackson. Washington directs McDowell to operate in the direction of Richmond but cover Washington at the same time. In the Valley, a portion of Jackson's command defeats a Federal force at the Battle of Cross Keys.

June 9 (Mon.): Jackson defeats a Federal column at Port Republic, ending the Valley Campaign.

June 10 (Tues.): *Temperature in mid-50's, McClellan Reports Hard Rain.* Lee decides to reinforce Jackson in the hope that that general can

---

[52] Douglas Southall Freeman, ed., *Lee's Dispatches: Unpublished Letters of General Robert E. Lee, C.S.A., to Jefferson Davis and the War Department of the Confederate States of America 1862-1865* (New York, 1957), pp. 5-10.

"crush" the Federals in the Valley, thereby causing consternation in Washington and possibly the recall to the Federal capital of McDowell at Fredericksburg. Those tasks accomplished, Jackson's entire force could then join Lee before Richmond to attack McClellan.

June 11 (Wed.): *Clear.* Lee sends reinforcements to Jackson in the Valley District. The commanding general then discusses with Brig. Gen. J.E.B. Stuart, commander of the army's cavalry, the need for more information about the Federal right flank. McClellan's army remains divided by the Chickahominy.

June 12 (Thurs.): McClellan moves his headquarters to Dr. Trent's near Alexander's Bridge. Stuart begins reconnaissance Federal right.

June 12-13 (Thurs.-Fri.): McCall's division (I Corps) reinforces the Army of the Potomac.

June 13 (Sat.): Stuart's ride around Federal right continues, with skirmishes at Haws' Shop, Old Church, and Garlick's Landing.[53]

June 15 (Sun.): *Temperature in 90's.* Stuart returns from his reconnaissance, having ridden completely around the Army of the Potomac with the loss of one man. The cavalryman brings Lee important information on Federal troop positions and logistics and on the condition of roads, but Stuart's ride also points out to McClellan the vulnerability of the Federal right flank.

June 16 (Mon.): *Morning Temperature Around 60, McClellan Reports the Weather is "Splendid."* Lee directs Jackson to join him at Richmond with most of the Valley Army and stresses that, "To be efficacious, the movement must be secret."[54]

---

[53] The raid is addressed by 24 officers in reports listed in *OR* 11, pt. 1, p. 1154; W. T. Robins, "Stuart's Ride Around McClellan," B & L, 2, pp. 271-275.

[54] *OR* 12, pt. 3, p. 913.

June 17 (Tues.): *Clear and Sunny with a Cool Breeze.* Jackson's command moves from the Shenandoah Valley toward the Peninsula.

June 18 (Wed.): Skirmishers engage near Fair Oaks. McClellan orders several shiploads of supplies moved from White House Landing around the Peninsula and up the James to an undetermined point.[55]

June 20 (Fri.): *Pleasant Morning, Afternoon Warm.* Skirmishers clash near New Bridge.[56]

June 21 (Sat.): *"Warm and Dusty."* Jackson's army is at Gordonsville and moving toward Richmond.[57]

June 22 (Sun.): Jackson's command spends much of this Sabbath at rest at Fredericks Hall Station on the Virginia Central Railroad.[58]

June 23 (Mon.): *Afternoon Thundershower.* Lee holds a council of war at the Dabbs House, his headquarters northeast of Richmond. Present are Longstreet, D. H. Hill, A. P. Hill and Jackson, who has ridden more than 50 miles ahead of his troops. The generals discuss Lee's plan to attack McClellan and decide to begin executing it on June 26.[59]

June 24 (Tues.): Jackson rejoins his command at Beaver Dam Station on the Virginia Central Railroad.[60]

THE "SEVEN DAYS BATTLES" BEGIN

---

[55] *OR* 11, pt. 1, pp. 1060-1062; *OR* 11, pt. 2, 787; McClellan, "The Peninsular Campaign," p. 178.

[56] *OR* 11, pt. 1, pp. 1069-1070.

[57] Daniel Harvey Hill, "Lee's Attacks North of the Chickahominy," *B & L*, 2, pp. 348-350.

[58] Ibid., p. 349.

[59] Ibid., pp. 347-348.

[60] Ibid., p. 350.

June 25 (Wed.): *Rain in the Morning.* Hoping to move the front lines closer to Richmond, McClellan orders Heintzelman to carry the Confederate positions on the Williamsburg Road just west of the cross-roads of Seven Pines. Brig. Gen. Benjamin Huger's Confeder te Division holds the portion of the line to be assaulted. Hooker's and Kearny's divisions (III Corps) make the main assault; they are supported by troops of the IV Corps and the II Corps. McClellan's chief of staff, Brig. Gen. Randolph Marcy, recalls the attack after it begins in earnest, but the commanding general himself arrives on the scene and instructs Heintzel-man to press the assault. Huger's troops give ground, but regain it.[61]

Lee considers the possibility that his plan of attack has somehow been discovered by McClellan and that the Federal attack at Oak Grove was an attempt to preempt the Confederate offensive. After deliberating, Lee decides to proceed with the attack scheduled for the next day. In the night, Jackson informs Lee that due to "high water and mud" he is behind schedule and has only reached Ashland. Jackson writes that he intends to resume the march at 2:30 a.m.[62]

June 26 (Thurs.):

BATTLE OF MECHANICSVILLE

In the morning, Lee writes to Davis: "I fear from the operations of the enemy yesterday that our plan of operations has been discovered to them."[63]

The first engagement in Lee's effort to envelope and destroy the portion of McClellan's army north of the Chickahominy is marked by poorly coordinated Confederate movements and unsupported attacks. Jackson reaches his assigned position behind schedule and does not communicate sufficiently with the other Confederate commands awaiting the results of his movements. A. P. Hill, who was to coordinate his attack with the arrival of Jackson, impatiently attacks against extremely

---

[61] The engagement at Oak Grove is addressed by 40 officers in reports listed in *OR* 11, pt. 2, p. 1058; William B. Franklin, "Rear-Guard Fighting During the Change of Base," *B & L*, 2, p. 366n.

[62] Freeman, *Lee's Dispatches*, pp. 15-16.

[63] Ibid., pp. 15-16.

strong Federal positions held by McCall's division at Beaver Dam Creek, just east of Mechanicsville. These positions were to have been outflanked by Jackson, forcing the Federals to withdraw. Hill's Light Division attacks across the marshy Beaver Dam Creek. Brig. Gen. Roswell S. Ripley's brigade from D. H. Hill's Division joins the brigades from the Light Division and, like them, is repulsed with severe loss. Brig. Gen. Charles Griffin's brigade of Morell's division supports McCall's Pennsylvanians.[64]

Lincoln issues an order creating the Army of Virginia. The new army, to be commanded by Maj. Gen. John Pope, is to operate in central Virginia to relieve pressure on McClellan and, if possible, threaten Richmond from the north and west.

June 27 (Fri.):

Battle of Gaines' Mill

Engagement at Garnett's Farm (Golding's Farm)

Though they had held their position the day before, McCall's men at Beaver Dam Creek receive orders to withdraw at dawn to positions at Gaines' Mill, a few miles east. All of Lee's divisions, including those of Jackson's column, converge to assault Fitz John Porter's command in strong positions east of Gaines' Mill. The Federal divisions of Morrell, McCall, Brig. Gen. John Sykes (all V Corps) and Brig. Gen. Henry Slocum (VI Corps) withstand disjointed Confederate attacks until late in the day, when a concerted Southern assault breaches Porter's line and forces the Federals from the field.[65]

Brig. Gen. D. R. Jones' Confederate division probes the Federal positions south of the Chickahominy and strikes W.F. Smith's division (VI Corps) at Garnett's and Golding's Farms. Brig. Gen. Robert

---

[64] The engagement is addressed by 66 officers in reports listed in *OR* 11, pt. 2, p. 1052; Porter, "Hanover Court House and Gaines's Mill," pp. 325-331; Hill, "Lee's Attacks," 351-353, 361; James Longstreet, "The Seven Days' Including Frayser's Farm," *B & L*, 2, pp. 397-398.

[65] The battle at Gaines' Mill is addressed by 158 officers in reports listed in *OR* 11, pt. 2, pp.1020-21; McClellan, "Peninsular Campaign," pp. 181-182; Porter, "Hanover Court House and Gaines's Mill," pp. 331-343; Philip St. George Cooke, "The Charge of Cooke's Cavalry at Gaines's Mill," pp. 344-346; Hill, "Lee's Attacks," pp. 356-362; Evander M. Law, "On the Confederate Right at Gaines's Mill," pp. 363-365; Longstreet, "The Seven Days," p. 398; Fitz John Porter, "The Battle of Malvern Hill," p. 406.

Toombs, with his own brigade and that of Col. G.T. Anderson, presses the attack on his own initiative. Smith's men repulse the Confederate attacks.[66] This is the bloodiest of the even Days.

June 28 (Sat.):
Engagement at Golding's Farm

Abandoning his works at Gaines' Mill before dawn, McClellan begins his retreat toward the James with the intention of establishing a new base of operations on that river. He prepares to relinquish his hold on what had been his supply line—the Richmond & York River Railroad—and crosses his entire army to the south side of the Chickahominy.

The combatants aligned at Garnett's and Golding's Farms again clash in a small sharp engagement.

When Confederates see dust clouds south of the Chickahominy, Lee decides McClellan is retreating from Richmond. He quickly throws his cavalry under Stuart down the Chickahominy to watch the bridges. If McClellan heads down the Peninsula toward Yorktown and Fort Monroe, he must cross those bridges. By evening, Lee decides McClellan is heading for the James rather than Fort Monroe.

Federal troops hastily abandon the supply base at White House Landing on the Pamunkey, burning virtually everything that cannot be removed.[67]

June 29 (Sun.): *Torrential Rain at Night.*
ENGAGEMENT AT ALLEN'S FARM (PEACH ORCHARD)
BATTLE OF SAVAGE'S STATION

Having surmised McClellan's intentions and probable routes of retreat, Lee issues new orders to the commanders of his columns. The Confederate goal is now to pursue and intercept the Federals before they reach the James.

---

[66] The engagement at Garnett's and Golding's Farms is addressed by 43 officers in reports listed in *OR*, series I, vol. 11, pt. 2, p. 1021; Franklin, "Rear-Guard Fighting," pp. 366-69.

[67] The evacuation of White House Landing is addressed by eight officers in reports listed in *OR* 11, pt. 2, p. 1094.

Colonel G.T. Anderson's brigade advances in pursuit of the withdrawing Federals and engages elements of Sumner's II Corps at Allen's Farm west of Savage's Station.[68] Sumner eventually withdraws and joins Heint elman and Franklin with their corps at Savage's Station on the Richmond and York River Railroad. Magruder has orders from Lee to press the pursuit and expects Jackson to cross the Chickahominy and join him in the assault on Savage's Station. Jackson remains north of the river as Magruder advances and attacks tentatively.

Before the Confederate attack comes, Heintzelman withdraws without informing Sumner and joins the general movement of McClellan's army southward toward the James. The Federals that remain on the field at Savage's Station withstand Magruder's attacks and withdraw during the night.[69]

Seeing an opportunity to intercept, envelope and destroy McClellan's army before it reaches the James, Lee orders his pursuing columns to press the Federals at the White Oak Swamp crossings and directs his intercepting columns—Longstreet and Hill—to converge on the crossroads of Glendale.

June 30 (Mon.): *Weather Hot*

BATTLE OF GLENDALE (FRAYSER'S FARM)

Lee's plan to envelope McClellan at Glendale goes awry when his pursuing columns, Jackson's and Huger's, fail to exert sufficient pressure on Federal rear guards. Th Federals are therefore able to devote most of their attention to Lee's intercepting columns, those of Longstreet (including A. P. Hill) and Brig. Gen. Theophilus Holmes. Though McClellan leaves the field before the battle begins and appoints no one to command in his stead, Sumner, Heintzelman and Franklin patch together a rear-guard defense that holds off the converging Confederate columns. Huger is stopped on the Charles City Road and Jackson at

[68] The engagement at Allen's Farm is addressed by 42 officers in reports listed in *OR* 11, pt. 2, p. 1060.

[69] The engagement at Savage's Station is addressed by 46 officers in reports listed in *OR* 11, pt. 2, p. 1070; McClellan, "Peninsular Campaign," p. 182; Franklin, "Rear-Guard Fighting," pp. 371-375; See also *OR* 11, pt. 2, pp. 50-51.

White Oak Bridge, and both engage only in artillery duels. Holmes' attack is broken up by Federal artillery before it begins. Late in the day, Longstreet and Hill repeatedly hurl frontal attacks at Federal positions.

On this pivotal and bloody day, the Federals lose ground and guns but accomplish the objective of protecting the retreat of the army. Lee's final and best opportunity to destroy much of McClellan's army passes. The Unionists abandon the field after dark and move southward toward the James.[70]

July 1 (Tues.):
MALVERN HILL —THE "SEVEN DAYS BATTLES" END

McClellan's artillery and infantry in strong positions on Malvern Hill repulse Lee's uncoordinated assaults. The day is marked by much valor in futile attacks.[71]

July 2 (Wed.): *Hard Rain at Night.* McClellan's army continues its retreat to Harrison's Landing on the James.[72]

July 3-4 (Thurs.-Fri.): Skirmishes near Herring Creek, or Harrison's Landing.[73]

July 4 (Fri.): Skirmishers clash at Westover.[74] After examining McClellan's position at Harrison's Landing, Lee writes to Davis: "As far as I can see, there is no way to attack him to advantage; nor do I wish to expose the men to the destructive missiles of his gunboats. . . ."[75]

---

[70] The engagement is addressed by 101 officers in reports listed in *OR* 11, pt. 2, p. 1023; Franklin, "Rear-Guard Fighting," pp. 377-381; Hill, "McClellan's Change of Base," pp. 388-390, 395; Longstreet, "The Seven Days," pp. 396-397, 399-405.

[71] The engagement is addressed by 190 officers in reports listed in *OR* 11, pt. 2, pp. 1048-1049; McClellan, "Peninsular Campaign," pp. 183-186; Hill, "McClellan's Change of Base," pp. 390-395; Porter, "Malvern Hill," pp. 408-426.

[72] Averell, "With the Cavalry on the Peninsula," pp. 432-434.

[73] *OR* 11, pt. 2, pp. 921-922, 520, 531.

[74] Ibid., pp. 605, 617, 620.

[75] Freeman, *Lee's Dispatches*, pp. 25-27.

July 5-6 (Sat.-Sun.): Confederate artillery shells Federal shipping in the James River.[76]

July 8 (Tues.): President Lincoln arrives at Harrison's Landing to consult with McClellan and assess the condition of the army. After Confederate artillery again bombards McClellan's positions ashore and his transports in the James, Lee determines no real damage can be done to the Army of the Potomac and withdraws his army "higher up the river, in order to meet the enemy should he again advance on Richmond."[77]

July 9 (Wed.): Lincoln confers with the corps commanders about the security of the army and the advisability of withdrawing from the Peninsula. All the officers state that the army is secure and a majority (3-2) opine that the army should remain where it is for the time being. Lincoln prepares to return to Washington, generally pleased with the condition and morale of the army.[78]

At some point during the president's visit, McClellan presents Lincoln a long letter dated July 7. This epistle comes to be known as the "Harrison's Landing (or Harrison's Bar) Letter." In it, McClellan declares, among other things, that Lincoln must be a stronger, more effective leader in conducting the war according to the highest Christian principles. Lincoln reads the letter in the general's presence, then simply thanks the officer and puts the letter in his pocket.[79] Federals reconnoiter on the Long Bridge Road.[80]

July 10 (Thurs.): Federals reconnoiter from Harrison's Landing toward White Oak Swamp, where skirmishers exchange fire.

---

[76] *OR* 11, pt. 2, pp. 924-925.

[77] Freeman, *Lee's Dispatches*, pp. 28-32.

[78] For a description of the condition of the Army of the Potomac at Harrison's Landing, see George L. Kilmer, "The Army of the Potomac at Harrison's Landing," *B & L*, 2, pp. 427-428.

[79] McClellan, *Own Story*, pp. 487-488.

[80] *OR* 11, pt. 2, pp. 929-930.

July 11 (Fri.): Lincoln appoints Maj. Gen. Henry W. Halleck general-in-chief. Federals reconnoiter from Harrison's Landing past Charles City Court House.[81]

July 13 (Sun.): Lee orders Jackson to Louisa and Gordonsville on the Virginia Central Railroad to counter the threat posed by Pope's advance into the Piedmont of Central Virginia.

July 22 (Tues.): Skirmishers clash at Westover.[82]

July 23 (Wed.): Halleck arrives in Washington from the western theater and assumes command of the armies of the United States.

July 25 (Fri.): Halleck arrives at Harrison's Landing to confer with McClellan. McClellan declares his intention to cross to the south side of the James and attack Petersburg, Virginia, a transportation hub 30 miles south of Richmond. After capturing Petersburg, thus severing the capital's link with the rest of the Confederacy, McClellan feels he could assault Richmond from the south. Halleck points out the danger and impracticability of the plan. McClellan then states that with 30,000 reinforcements he could advance directly on Richmond from Harrison's Landing with "a good chance of success." McClellan represents his own strength as about 90,000 men and tells Halleck that his intelligence gatherers have confirmed that Lee has 200,000 men at Richmond. Halleck states that no more than 20,000 new men are available to send to the Peninsula, and if McClellan cannot take Richmond with that number, (110,000 total) then the army must be withdrawn to northern Virginia, whence it could unite with Pope's Army of Virginia. Halleck suggests that McClellan discuss the alternatives with his generals. McClellan meets privately with his lieutenants.[83]

---

[81] Ibid., pp. 930-931.

[82] Ibid., p. 932.

[83] *OR* 11, pt. 3, pp. 337-338.

July 26 (Sat.): McClellan informs   alleck that he will attack Richmond with the 20,000 reinforcements but does not seem sanguine of victory, saying merely that the attack has "a chance" of success and he is "willing to try it." Halleck returns to Washington.[84]

July 27 (Sun.): Halleck arrives in Washington to find a request dated July 26 from McClellan for between 35,000 and 55,000 reinforcements in addition to the 20,000 agreed upon at Harrison's Landing. Out of patience and convinced McClellan will not fight, Lincoln directs Halleck to order the Army of the Potomac to abandon the Peninsula.[85]

Although he does not know of the imminent Federal withdrawal from Harrison's Landing, Lee orders A. P. Hill's Division to join Jackson at Gordonsville in preparation for a movement against Pope.

July 29 (Tues.): Federals reconnoiter from Harrison's Landing to St. Mary's Church.[86]

July 30 (Wed.): The U.S. war department orders McClellan to remove his sick. Federals reconnoiter from Harrison's Landing to Jones' Ford on the Chickahominy.

July 31 - August 1 (Thurs.-Fri.): Confederates attack Federal camps and shipping between Shirley plantation and Harrison's Landing.[87]

August 2-8 (Sat.-Sat.): Federals re-occupy Malvern Hill.[88]

August 3 (Sun.): Federals reconnoiter on the south side of the James, and skirmishers exchange fire at Sycamore Church. In the eve-

---

[84] Ibid.

[85] Ibid., pp. 333-334.

[86] *OR* 11, pt. 2, p. 934.

[87] Ibid., pp. 934-943.

[88] Kilmer, "Harrison's Landing," p. 428.

ning, Halleck issues orders for McClellan to withdraw his forces from the Peninsula and move to Aquia Creek near Fredericksburg.[89]

August 4 (Mon.): McClellan receives his withdrawal orders and protests to Halleck, writing: "Your telegram of last evening is received. I must confess that it has caused me the greatest pain I ever experienced, for I am convinced that the order to withdraw this army to Aquia Creek will prove disastrous to our cause. I fear it will be a fatal blow."[90] Halleck's orders stand. Federals reconnoiter to Sycamore Church.[91]

August 5 (Tues.): Federals continue reconnaissance to Sycamore Church. Skirmishers meet at White Oak Bridge and Malvern Hill.[92]

August 6 (Wed.): Skirmishers exchange fire at Malvern Hill.

August 9 (Sat.):
BATTLE OF CEDAR MOUNTAIN
In Culpeper County, Jackson repulses a portion of Pope's army in an indecisive battle.

August 13 (Wed.): Though increased Federal activity indicates that a movement is afoot, Lee is still unsure about McClellan's intentions. Nevertheless, threatened with the growing menace of Pope in central Virginia, Lee orders Longstreet to join Jackson.[93]

August 14-15 (Thurs.-Fri.): Now certain that McClellan is withdrawing, Lee makes plans to join Jackson and Longstreet at Gordons-

---

[89] *OR* 11, pt. 1, p. 76; pt. 2, p. 946, 948; Averell, "With the Cavalry on the Peninsula," p. 433; McClellan, *Own Story*, pp. 495-496.

[90] McClellan, *Own Story*, p. 496.

[91] *OR* 11, pt. 2, pp. 948-949.

[92] Ibid., pp. 954-955.

[93] *OR* 11, pt. 3, pp. 675-678; Freeman, *Lee,* 2, pp. 272-274.

ville. The Federal III and V Corps move from Harrison's Landing for Aquia Creek.[94]

August 15 (Fri.): Lee meets with his generals in council of war at Gordonsville.[95]

August 14-19 (Thurs.-Tues.): Cavalry covers the withdrawal of the Army of the Potomac from Harrison's Landing to Williamsburg.[96]

August 20 (Wed.): The V Corps embarks at Newport News.

August 21(Thurs.): The III Corps sails from Yorktown.

August 23 (Sat.): The VI Corps embarks at Fort Monroe.

August 25 (Mon.): Jackson begins a long, rapid march around Pope's flank and into his rear. The movement culminates i the destruction of Pope's supply base at Manassas.

August 26 (Tues.): The II Corps leaves Fort Monroe.

[94] *OR* 11, pt. 2, p. 964.

[95] Freeman, *Lee,* 2, p. 279.

[96] *OR* 11, pt. 2, p. 967.

Index compiled by Michael L. DeVivo, San Jose, California

INDEX

Other Civil War titles available from
Savas Woodbury Publishers

The Campaign for Atlanta & Sherman's March to the Sea, vols. 1-2, edited by Theodore P. Savas and David A. Woodbury. Fifteen essays in a landmark series covering a broad range of topics on the pivotal 1864 campaigns. Three fold-out maps in text and two over-size campaign maps folded into front pocket. 6x9, hardcover, photos, index. 496pp ISBN 1-882810-26-0 Price: $42.50 plus $3.00 s&h.

". . .a refreshing must for those who dare to reassess these epic campaigns, the leaders, and the challenges posed in the Empire State of the Confederacy more than 130 years ago."
— Blue & Gray Magazine

Leadership and Command in the American Civil War, edited by Steven E. Woodworth. A collection of five penetrating essays exploring myriad leadership issues during the epic events of 1861-1865. Topics include J. E. Johnston in Virginia, Bragg & Longstreet in the West, Sumner at Antietam, Pickett after Gettysburg, and Jefferson Davis & his generals in the East. 6x9, hardcover, index, 243pp. ISBN 1-882810-00-7. Price: $29.95 plus $3.00 s&h.

Abraham Lincoln, Contemporary: An American Legacy, edited by Frank J. Williams and William D. Pederson. Papers delivered at the 1993 Louisiana State University Lincoln Symposium by some of the nations leading Lincoln scholars. 6x9, hardcover, d.j., photos, index, 236pp. Price: $29.95 plus $3.00 s&h.

Last Stand in the Carolinas: the Battle of Bentonville, March 19-21, 1865, by Mark Bradley. A definitive examination of the military events that culminated in the bloody fighting at Bentonville, North Carolina, between the veteran campaigners of William T. Sherman and Gen. Joseph E. Johnston's motley Confederate army. 6x9, hardcover, d.j., photos, maps, index, 458pp. Price: $29.95 plus $3.00 s&h.

". . .Bradley has researched and written a *tour de force*. . . .there has long been a need for a quality history focusing on the Battle of Bentonville." —Edwin C. Bearss, former Chief Historian of the National Park Service

The Red River Campaign, edited by Theodore P. Savas and David A. Woodbury. This special, stand-alone issue of *Civil War Regiments* journal contains three in-depth essays on aspects of the critical, but overlooked 1864 campaign in Louisiana. Introduction by Edwin C. Bearss, Assistant to the Director, Military Sites, National Park Service. 6x9, softcover, photos, maps, index, 157pp. Price: $12.00 ppd.